People and Place

THE WEST COAST OF NEW ZEALAND'S
SOUTH ISLAND IN HISTORY
AND LITERATURE

People and Place

THE WEST COAST OF NEW ZEALAND'S SOUTH ISLAND IN HISTORY AND LITERATURE

LEN RICHARDSON

PRESS

Published by ANU Press
The Australian National University
Acton ACT 2601, Australia
Email: anupress@anu.edu.au

Available to download for free at press.anu.edu.au

ISBN (print): 9781760463441
ISBN (online): 9781760463458

WorldCat (print): 1152557014
WorldCat (online): 1152557367

DOI: 10.22459/PP.2020

The ANU.Lives Series in Biography is an initiative of the National Centre of Biography at The Australian National University, ncb.anu.edu.au.

Cover design and layout by ANU Press

Cover photograph: Looking down the Grey Valley from the north bank above the site of the Brunner Mine, once the industrial hub of the Grey district (photo by Len Richardson).

CONTENTS

ACKNOWLEDGEMENTS

Some 60 years ago, in the introduction to his path-breaking *West Coast Gold Rushes*, Philip Ross May wondered whether one could acknowledge a debt to a place and its people. In different ways, May, Patrick O'Farrell and Bill Pearson, the three writers whose work inspired this book, accepted that, as the question applied to their particular 'West Coasts', it most certainly could. The attempt to understand how each of them came to see the West Coast, and tracing the enduring influence of their writing, has enriched and sharpened my own sense of what the relationship between people and place has been over the last 150 years. Reading again the work of the subsequent generation of writers who have stood, as it were, on their shoulders has strengthened my conviction that the West Coast has continued to nurture historians and writers deeply conscious of this distinctive relationship. Long may it do so.

The greatest debt is to my wife, Beverley, whose particular 'West Coast' was shaped by life in Blackball and Ahaura and owes much to her maternal grandparents, Ann and Bill Bromilow, who arrived from Wigan in the first decade of the twentieth century and feature in the photo of the Blackball Socialist group in Chapter 6. Christopher, Jeffrey and Philippa May made available a photo of their father at Captains Flat, New South Wales, taken by Jeffrey in 1969 when the family was living in Canberra. Gerard O'Farrell kindly allowed the reproduction of a photo of his father while Patrick was working on his doctoral thesis at The Australian National University in the 1950s. My indebtedness to all those who have sought in their writing to understand the Coast is acknowledged throughout the text.

I have benefited over the years from discussing the West Coast and its history with a great number of people, especially Tom Brooking, Chris Connolly, Graeme Dunstall, Patrick Evans, Stuart Macintyre, Jim McAloon, Doug Munro, Paul Millar, Philippa Mein Smith, Melanie Nolan, Erik Olssen, the late Elizabeth Plumridge, Luke Trainor and Brian

Wood. I have been talking about the Coast with Des Wood since we were at primary school in Greymouth just as Pat O'Farrell made his way over the 'Hill' to begin his university studies.

The mysteries of the modern publication process have been made much less painful by my daughter Shelley, who understands these things. 'I am grateful to Emily Tinker and the publishing team at ANU Press and also its eight anonymous readers who provided helpful suggestions for improving the manuscript. Geoff Hunt has been an extremely patient, cheerful and perceptive editor and is beginning to experience life at the northern extension of the South Island's West Coast discussed in this book.

Len Richardson

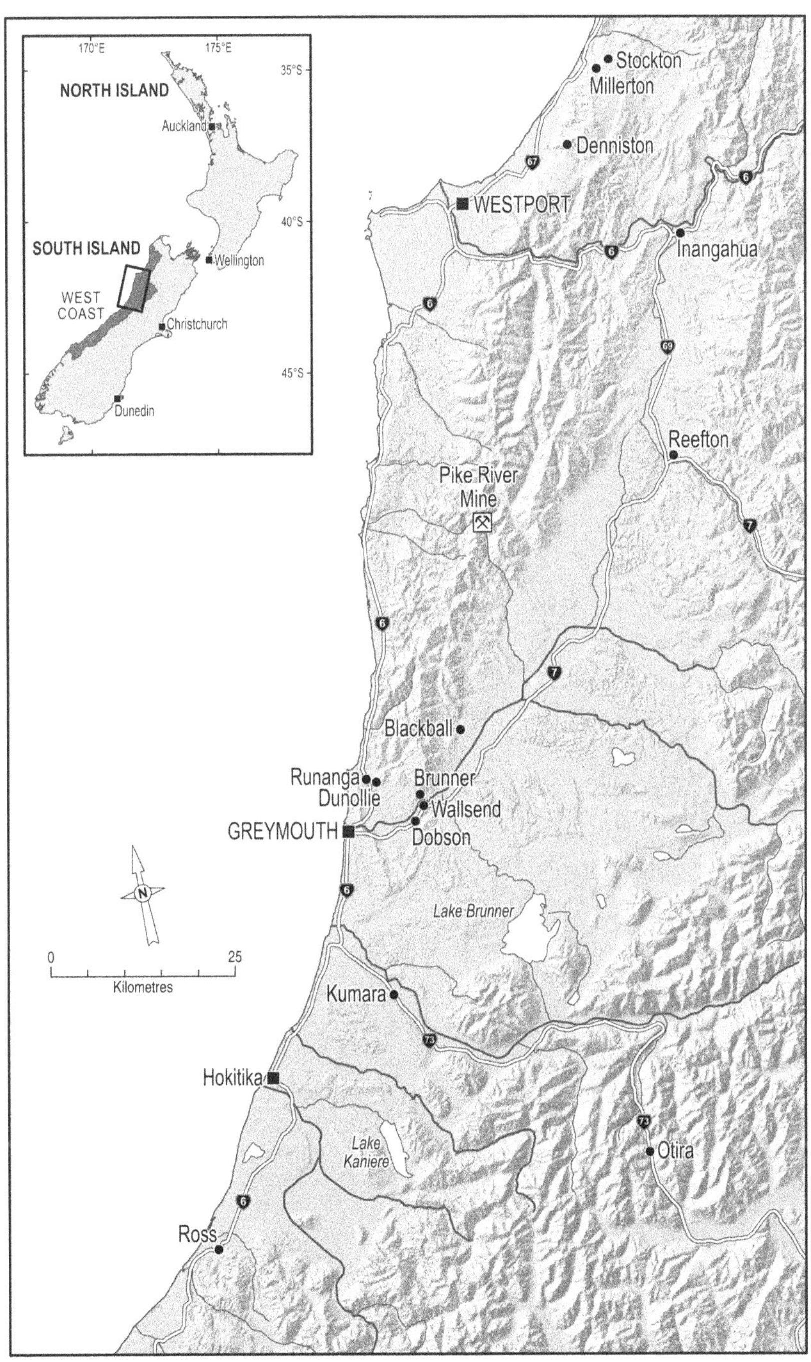

Map: The West Coast, South Island, New Zealand.

Source: The author.

1

INTRODUCTION

The interaction between people and place is the basic ingredient of human history. The historians who interpret this complex and ever-changing relationship are inevitably bit players in the processes they seek to unravel. In settler societies the terms of the relationship are re-negotiated and the heightened awareness of the new and the different reshapes expectations and communal attitudes. Shunted off from the handful of disparate settlements that owed their existence to mid-nineteenth-century British colonial expansion, the west coast of New Zealand's South Island stands at the edge of this experience. Its European history can be briefly put: home to Māori attracted by the presence of pounamu (greenstone), it remained little known until the discovery of gold produced a veritable human invasion that compressed and distorted the process of settlement and left in its wake a region in search of a future. In the century that followed, neither coal nor timber was able to overcome the twin tyrannies of remoteness and harshness. Historians who traversed this tale of brief, brilliant flowering giving way to a pervasive uncertainty born of reliance upon wasting natural assets inevitably cast their narratives within this framework—a framework that would seem introspective and limiting.

Yet, neither the tale itself nor the historians who tell it may be described adequately in such crudely environmentally determined terms. This discussion of a small slice of New Zealand's history examines how three writers—two historians and a novelist/social commentator—have interpreted the place of their birth and provided a foundation for a distinctive regional historical identity. Philip May, Patrick O'Farrell and Bill Pearson emerged as a talented trio of university-trained writers in the 1960s. They were products of an age when imperial ways of thinking about our past were giving way to more explicitly nationalist ones.

These stirrings were visible in the upsurge of provincial celebration that marked the passing of the first 100 years of European settlement. Within the historical profession the standard bearer of the new mood was Keith Sinclair's *A History of New Zealand* (1959), a nationalist account that emphasised the radical and innovatory and stressed New Zealand's Pacific environment.[1] It became the defining, if not uncontested, perspective for a generation of historians. Indeed, within a year, Bill Oliver produced an elegant counterpoint, *The Story of New Zealand* (1960).[2] As its author has subsequently written, it was 'determinedly provincial'[3] and presented the national experience as a conservative one played out within boundaries set by the 'foundational inheritance'.[4]

Thus, at the very moment that a national history was being made its shape was being challenged by historians whose essential point was that the regional building blocks that would allow safe generalisation remained to be written.[5] To a degree, the point became submerged in a contemporaneous debate about the emphases within the national story. Dressed in the garb of a provincial rivalry that saw the radical/nationalist position attributed to an Auckland school and the conservative/imperial associated with Canterbury, it was a characterisation that rested in part upon recognisable regional difference. In the 1940s and 1950s, the planned South Island colonies of Canterbury and Otago had led the way in celebrating and recording their respective histories.

As different as May, O'Farrell and Pearson's 'West Coasts' are, each derives something of its perspective from these currents of historical opinion. Their very choice of subject was a product of a new national consciousness. The published versions of their research came too late to influence the rival national histories of Sinclair and Oliver, but, as the product of a mid-nineteenth-century gold rush, the European settlement of the West Coast finds a place in the national story. It does so as a by-product of an ephemeral event whose consequences were judged of relatively little significance to the nationalist, radical theme. The region

1 Keith Sinclair, *A History of New Zealand*, Auckland, Penguin, 1959.

2 W.H. Oliver, *The Story of New Zealand*, London, Faber and Faber, 1960.

3 W.H. Oliver, *Looking for the Phoenix*, Wellington, Bridget Williams Books, 2002, p. 97.

4 Oliver, *Looking for the Phoenix*, p. 97.

5 Elaborated in 1957 in a seminal article by W.J. (Jim) Gardner, 'Grass Roots and Dredge Tailings: Reflections on Local History', *Landfall 43*, vol. 11, no. 3, September 1957, pp. 221–33; and reprinted in W.J. Gardner, *Where They Lived: Studies in Local, Regional and Social History*, Christchurch, Regional Press, 1999, pp. 3–7; the theme is developed by W.H. Oliver in his influential 1969 Hocken Lecture, *Towards a New History?*, Hocken Library, University of Otago, 1971.

makes a reappearance as the home of militant industrial labour in the early twentieth century. Unlike the diggers of the 1860s, the coalminers, as socialist vanguard, assume a more obvious role in a political narrative that emphasises a radical nationalist impulse with its roots in late nineteenth-century liberalism and its culmination in the democratic socialism of the first Labour Government (1935–49).

In the quest for the synthesising generalities of a national story this might seem adequate representation of a remote and thinly populated region. In part this involves little more than acknowledging what one historian has called the 'homogenising impulse'[6] held to be implicit in the notion of all national histories. The 'West Coasts' of May, O'Farrell and Pearson take their place alongside this emergent national story, at times confirming it, sometimes in exaggerated fashion, and at others offering a distinctiveness that suggests other frameworks that might be more compatible with the evolution of the region. Nowhere is this ambiguity more obvious than in the making of the region's European settlement. Born of a gold rush that derived the great bulk of its people from the goldfields of the Pacific borderlands, the West Coast was cast in a different mould to the Wakefieldian planned settlements that preceded it. Such was its isolation that the region long remained a land apart. At times, it looked not eastwards to its political parent, the Canterbury province, but west to Melbourne and the goldfields of Victoria. It was from here that it derived capital as well as people and it was to Melbourne that the West Coast gold rushes yielded their profits. The movement of people to and fro across the Tasman Sea created a society that in its foundation years was truly Australasian. It was long to remain the region's defining characteristic and its persistence is observed by O'Farrell and Pearson as they trace the fortunes of the coalmining communities of the late nineteenth and early twentieth centuries.

The 'Australasianness' of West Coast beginnings, with its emphasis upon the Pacific world rather than upon old-world and British links, sits comfortably with the emergent nationalist account. The Australasian connection did not, however, at least in its goldfields phase, extend to a common radical disposition. Phil May's goldmining communities did not a Peter Lalor or a Eureka Stockade produce. Innovative as the diggers were in their quest for gold, theirs was the democracy of the enfranchised

6 Desley Deacon, Penny Russell and Angela Woolacott, eds, *Transnational Ties: Australian Lives in the World*, Canberra, ANU E Press, 2008, p. xiv, make the point in discussing the making of an Australian national history.

small property owner. Pat O'Farrell's coalminers, led by a strong Victorian socialist vanguard, were, however, to play a crucial role in the radicalising burst of the early twentieth century that forms a crucial component of the radical/nationalist interpretation. And Bill Pearson's concerns encompass the erosion of this radical impulse as the coalfield communities began to mimic the goldtowns and head into terminal decline. In these ways the history of the West Coast that emerges in the 1960s from the work of May, O'Farrell and Pearson can be placed within the dominant historiographical impulses.

In the strength and persistence of its Australasian dimension, West Coast history displays, in exaggerated form, a strand of the more general antipodean experience. As a land apart, building connections where it could, the West Coast story unfolded in ways that were broadly consistent with settler societies everywhere. In its foundation phase when all seemed different and the need for common bonds was more urgent, difference mattered less. The negotiation of difference was part of the pioneering process. It was as obvious in dress, accent and religious observance as it was in mining techniques and attitudes to authority. Behind these visible and public differences lay patterns of connectedness that spilled beyond the boundaries of any one nation state. Whatever the homogenising tendencies implicit in the new national history, it could not be said that the New Zealand variety of the species was blind to the variety of regional and individual experiences that shaped its national story. Unsurprisingly, initial critiques of what came to be called the radical nationalist tradition were more concerned with labelling it as an 'Auckland' interpretation than with attempting to suggest that the New Zealand story needed to be cast in an imperial mould.

In defining their 'West Coasts', Phil May, Pat O'Farrell and Bill Pearson stand at even greater distance from the imperial connection. That they do so is not so much a matter of calculation as a question of time and place. As a trio of writers, their regional historiographical antecedents amounted to little more than a few celebratory works surveying the region's first 50 years. Written in the 1920s, they were optimistic and imperial in tone. By the 1950s and 1960s the optimism and the sense of a past linked inextricably with the fortunes of Empire had given way to less sanguine assessments suggesting a future no less problematic than the past. As different as their 'West Coasts' were, each is shaped by a sense of a land set apart. They were 'West Coasts' whose integration into the wider national fabric was at best partial, yet whose experiences nonetheless reflected, if often in exaggerated form, a distinctively New Zealand experience that paradoxically derived some of its character from the persistence of its links with Australia and the borderlands of the Pacific.

It should then come as no surprise that Australia should play a significant role in shaping the academic interests of all three writers. Each made his way to The Australian National University (ANU), an institution whose origins were rooted in the same post–World War II sense of reconstruction that invigorated the writing of New Zealand history. Its very name stood, as W.K. Hancock wrote, 'like a defiant flag, [announcing] we are marching forward, we measure ourselves against the world!'[7] O'Farrell was the first of the trio to make his way to the new university taking shape in Canberra. After completing his MA at the University of Canterbury in 1954, he was awarded a PhD scholarship in history in the Research School of Social Sciences. His study of the West Coast labour movement had emphasised the role played by an influx of radical Australian coalminers in the ideological ferment that produced the New Zealand Labour Party in 1916. It was a theme that led to a biography of Harry Holland; a Queanbeyan-born, militant socialist, prolific pamphleteer and pacifist, MP for a West Coast mining electorate and leader of the New Zealand Labour Party, 1919–33.[8]

Bill Pearson's road to Canberra was less direct. Slightly older than O'Farrell and May, he had embarked on a PhD in London in the late 1940s and his 'West Coast phase' was largely the work of an 'expat' writing from Hampstead Heath. In 1967, however, just three years after the eventual publication of *Coal Flat*,[9] he was putting the finishing touches to *Henry Lawson Among Maoris*[10] while holding a senior research fellowship in the Department of Pacific History and studying imaginative literature in English on the Pacific islands. This was the beginning of a new strand in his literary development. And while it would be too long a shot to see the West Coast as contributing significantly to this, it is consistent with an interest in the environment that had shaped his early thoughts on New Zealand society. That it was ANU that provided this opportunity reflected the peculiar openness of this post–World War II university to its Australasian and Pacific environment.[11]

7 W.K. Hancock, *Country and Calling*, London, Faber and Faber, 1954, p. 236.

8 P.J. O'Farrell, *Harry Holland: Militant Socialist*, Canberra, Australian National University Press, 1964.

9 Bill Pearson, *Coal Flat*, Auckland & Hamilton, Paul's Book Arcade, 1963.

10 W.H. Pearson, *Henry Lawson Among Maoris*, Canberra, Australian National University Press, 1968.

11 Helen Irving and Stuart Macintyre, eds, *No Ordinary Act: Essays on Federation and the Constitution by J.A. La Nauze*, Carlton, Victoria, Melbourne University Press, 2001.

Pearson was to be joined at ANU, in 1969, by Phil May. After the publication of *West Coast Gold Rushes* in 1962 he had begun developing further his thoughts about the interconnectedness of the goldfields bordering the Pacific. This led in 1967 to a year's study leave in California and, in 1969, he took up a two-year appointment as a senior research fellow in history at the ANU Research School of Social Sciences. The fellowship was part of a program designed to allow academics time away from teaching duties to complete major projects. At the time, the History Department was headed by John La Nauze (1911–1989), whose two major works—a biography of Alfred Deakin and the *Making of the Australian Constitution*—made him unquestionably the leading historian of Australian Federation.[12] He had succeeded Keith Hancock and, as Stuart Macintyre has written, brought a 'less directive' attitude to the position and 'likened his department to a potting shed where individuals propagated their various cuttings'.[13] La Nauze had been born in the Western Australian goldfields town of Boulder and it may not have been entirely coincidental that goldfield studies bloomed brightly in his department in the late 1960s. Whether by accident or design, Phil May took his place in the potting shed alongside Weston Bate, then nurturing his study of Ballarat published in 1978 as *Lucky City: The First Generation at Ballarat 1851–1901*.[14] ANU was itself the product of the post–World War II upsurge of interest in Australian history and culture. Its establishment and the fillip it gave to Australian history was a matter of some envy amongst New Zealand historians. In practice it proved to be something approaching an Australasian university, actively seeking and encouraging New Zealand historians. And, as the individual case studies that make up this collection show, the West Coast, standing proud against the Tasman Sea, had strong and lasting links with Australia (and especially Melbourne and Victoria).

That was certainly how it seemed to me in 1969 as I contemplated following in the footsteps of May, O'Farrell and Pearson. As an undergraduate, I was taught by Phil May and it was with him, on the eve of his departure for California, that I first discussed taking up the story of West Coast labour from where O'Farrell left off—at the

12 J.A. La Nauze, *Alfred Deakin*, Carlton, Victoria, Melbourne University Press, 1965; J.A. La Nauze, *The Making of the Australian Constitution*, Carlton, Victoria, Melbourne University Press, 1972.

13 Irving and Macintyre, *No Ordinary Act*.

14 Weston Bate, *Lucky City: The First Generation at Ballarat 1851–1901*, Carlton, Victoria, Melbourne University Press, 1978.

outset of World War I—as my MA thesis topic. With Jim Gardner and David McIntyre, May taught an Honours paper in comparative history (Australian, Canadian, United States and New Zealand history) precisely at the time he was formulating his projected study of the goldfields of the Pacific borderlands. Jim Gardner, who had been teaching undergraduate courses in Australian history, was fresh from study leave in Adelaide where he had pursued, among other things, the Australasian genesis of the idea of industrial conciliation and arbitration.[15] It was Jim Gardner, Canterbury's most celebrated historian and supervisor of the West Coast theses of Phil May and Pat O'Farrell, who became my supervisor in 1966. In 1969–70, as a temporary assistant lecturer, I was to teach one of Phil May's undergraduate courses while he spent two years at ANU. When I arrived in Canberra in January 1971 to take up a PhD scholarship and once more follow in the footsteps of Pat O'Farrell, Phil May was preparing to return to the University of Canterbury. There he would launch an Honours paper on the goldfields of the Pacific borderlands that he was to teach until his tragic death, at 47 years of age, in 1977.

I had returned from ANU in 1974 to join Jim Gardner in teaching what we called 'Australasian History' at first- and second-year levels. La Nauze seized the chance to prick the surrender of Kiwi sensitivities implicit in the convenient label: was it not, he asked, like the New Zealand cricket side accepting a place in the Sheffield Shield competition?[16] There was of course more than convenience involved in the label. It recognised that the published body of New Zealand history emanating from the universities lagged at least a decade behind its Australian counterpart. In very large part, this reflected the strength of the imperial connection: Britain was the destination of choice for postgraduate study. It is a point nowhere more plainly acknowledged than in W.H. Oliver's confession that, when he sat down to write his *Story of New Zealand* in the late 1950s, great was his ignorance of his country's history. Like many of his contemporaries, he had 'studiously avoided' New Zealand history and made his way to Balliol College, Oxford, and the English history that he believed 'snobbishly', as he later recalled, was 'in the mainstream of historical scholarship'.[17] Plainly, the possibilities offered by ANU presented a way of redressing the

15 W.J. Gardner, *Prelude to Arbitration in 3 Movements: Ulster, South Australia, New Zealand 1890–1894*, Christchurch, W.J. Gardner, 2009.

16 C. Connolly and L. Richardson, 'Kiwi and Kangaroo: Teaching Australian History to New Zealanders', *Australian Historical Association Bulletin*, no. 15, June 1978, pp. 7–10.

17 Oliver, *Looking for the Phoenix*, p. 96.

slower development of New Zealand's academic historical community. As a relatively new institution intent upon fostering greater awareness of its antipodean environment, it offered a congenial intellectual environment for New Zealanders embarking upon postgraduate study. At ANU they might tackle subjects that were, if not specifically related to aspects of New Zealand history, focused upon parts of the Australian story touching upon themes that were part of a common Australasian experience. Nor was the academic trans-Tasman traffic a one-way affair. When Jim Gardner retired at the end of the 1976 academic year, his successor was Chris Connolly, a product of the University of New England, who had completed his PhD in La Nauze's 'potting shed' at ANU.[18] In this sense, Pat O'Farrell, Bill Pearson and Phil May were the frontrunners of a trend that was to maintain its momentum into the 1970s and 1980s, and beyond.

While the purely West Coast dimension of the ANU connection faded over time, continuities that reflect a common historical pedigree are evident in the flow of postgraduate students who made their way from Canterbury to Canberra. In the 1970s, the sense of place and of regionality found expression in a study of the labour movement in Wollongong and an examination of pastoralism in the Hunter Valley.[19] Each had been preceded by a regional New Zealand study. In the 1980s, ANU was as attractive to a cluster of Canterbury postgraduates who were at the forefront of women's history. For them, as for their predecessors, the attraction of ANU was to be found in the extent to which Australia provided a more developed historiography than was then available in the New Zealand environment. Their interests were diverse. Libby Plumridge studied New Zealand expat women artists and how, as women and artists, they negotiated the circumstances of colonialism and gender. Philippa Mein Smith moved from work on pregnancy and childbirth in New Zealand 1920–35 (extended and published in 1986 as *Maternity in Dispute*[20]) to study infant welfare in Australia from 1900 until the end of World War II. Melanie Nolan's Canterbury MA thesis was a study of the workers' representative on the arbitration court (from which was to emerge a path-breaking work in

18 Other Australians to make their way to the Canterbury University History Department and teach Australian or Pacific history were Luke Trainor, Ian Campbell, Peter Hempenstall and Jane Buckingham.

19 Len Richardson, 'The Labour Movement in Wollongong, New South Wales, 1928–39', PhD thesis, ANU, 1974; Stevan Eldred-Grigg, 'The Pastoral Families of the Hunter Valley, 1880–1914', PhD thesis, ANU, 1978.

20 Philippa Mein Smith, *Maternity in Dispute, New Zealand 1920–1939*, Wellington, Historical Branch, Department of Internal Affairs, New Zealand, 1986.

collective biography as well as the publication of the Jack McCullough diaries[21]) and led her into Australian labour history and a doctoral thesis on Victorian women workers.[22] Yet, as different as these paths are, they share a common framework that is very much the product of their distinctively Australian and New Zealand perspectives.

In their academic careers, Melanie Nolan and Philippa Mein Smith further exemplify the trans-Tasman connection lying at the heart of the West Coast past that May, O'Farrell and Pearson endeavoured to capture in their writing. While professor of history at the University of Canterbury, Philippa Mein Smith headed the New Zealand, Australia Research Centre and co-authored *A History of Australia, New Zealand and the Pacific*,[23] and Melanie Nolan, as Professor of History, Director of the National Centre for Biography and General Editor of the *Australian Dictionary of Biography*, has continued to expand the trans-Tasman dimension to the histories of Australia and New Zealand.[24]

If the trans-Tasman dimension of the West Coast experience has a long and fruitful life, other elements of the region's past have proved equally productive. An examination of the writing of West Coast historians since the 1960s suggests the flowering of an increasingly distinctive regional voice that extends the interpretations of the foundational histories.

21 Melanie Nolan, ed., *War & Class: The Diary of Jack McCullough*, Wellington, Dunmore Publishing, 2009; Melanie Nolan, *Kin: A Collective Biography of a New Zealand Working-Class Family*, Christchurch, Canterbury University Press, 2005.

22 Elizabeth Plumridge, 'The Negotiation of Circumstance: New Zealand Women Artists, c.1890–1914', PhD thesis, ANU, 1985; Melanie Nolan, 'Uniformity and Diversity: A Case Study of Female Shop and Office Workers in Victoria, 1880 to 1939', PhD thesis, ANU, 1989; Philippa Mein Smith, 'Reformers, Mothers and Babies: Aspects of Infant Survival Australia 1890–1945', PhD thesis, ANU, 1990 (revised and published as *Mothers and King Baby: Infant Survival and Welfare in an Imperial World, 1880–1950*, London, Macmillan, 1997).

23 Donald Denoon and Philippa Mein Smith with Marivic Wyndham, *A History of Australia, New Zealand and the Pacific*, Oxford, Blackwell Publishers Ltd, 2000; Philippa Mein Smith, *A Concise History of New Zealand*, Cambridge, UK, Cambridge University Press, 2005; Philippa Mein Smith, Peter Hempenstall, Shaun Goldfinch, with Stuart McMillan and Rosemary Baird, *Remaking the Tasman World*, Christchurch, Canterbury University Press, 2008.

24 The following works by Melanie Nolan in whole or in part pursue Australasian and West Coast themes: 'Personalising Class Conflict across the Tasman: The New Zealand Great Strike and Trans-Tasman Biography', *Journal of New Zealand Studies*, no. 18, December 2014, pp. 118–36; '"The View from Over the Hill": Developing a Balanced View of Blackball '08 from a Wider Range of Perspectives', *Journal of New Zealand Studies*, no. 8, April 2009, pp. 1–27. Recent PhD theses completed in history at ANU that pursue Australasian themes: Karen Fox, 'Representing Difference: Celebrated Māori and Aboriginal Women and the Print Media, 1950–2000', 2009; Catherine Bishop, 'Commerce Was a Woman: Women in Colonial Sydney and Wellington', 2012; Shelley Richardson, 'Family Experiments: Professional Middle-Class Families in Australia and New Zealand c. 1880–1920', 2013; Nicola Francis, '"My Own Sort of Heaven", Rosalie Gascoigne's Stellar Rise to Artistic Acclaim', 2015.

In doing so, it explores how subsequent historians have responded to the changing face of twentieth-century capitalism as it reshaped the pattern of existence within the region. As a region whose economy was built around two dominant extractive industries—coalmining and sawmilling—the post-industrial age raised fundamental questions about the future. As it did in industrial wastelands throughout the Western world, the 'retreat' of industrial capitalism created a social as well as an economic vacuum. The adjustments called for by changes in the economic structure struck at the very heart of a regional identity that drew heavily upon a deeply embedded past and respected the vagaries of an enduring and forbidding environment. These understandings of time and place were important components in the framing of a body of writing that is as distinctive as the foundational literature from which it grows.

The dislocation undergone by industrial communities in the post-industrial age that has recently been thrust to the forefront of British and American politics is the Grey Valley experience writ large. What gave the Grey Valley response to change its special character, and set it apart from the American rust belt and the north of England, was the conjunction of industrial decline and the rise of environmentalism. Influenced by the wilderness aesthetic and focused upon the preservation of the natural environment, the conservation movement envisaged the West Coast's native forests as a heritage estate and potential national park. The debate that followed, in New Zealand as elsewhere, was often conducted in a moral landscape and in the language of extremes. An Australian historian has recently characterised this ideological battleground as being framed within a simple dichotomy: 'between the unused landscape and the misused one, the pristine landscape and the exploited and degraded one'.[25] On the West Coast, this divide could not be and was not simply, or even mainly, an ideological one. It posed fundamental questions about regional identity and understandings of local environments. The responses to the arrival of the environmentalists were shaped in part by the economic interests of the sawmilling industry and those who depended upon it. Just as assuredly, Grey Valley reaction to the rise of conservationism was rooted in a 'sense of belonging' and its companion, history.

25 Tom Griffiths, *The Art of Time Travel: Historians and Their Craft*, Carlton, Victoria, Black Inc., 2016, p. 60.

Environmentalists often patronised the past. Their polemic, according to one critic, could 'flatten the past into an undifferentiated and hateful caricature, beyond redemption, where ordinary men and women have no control over their lives'.[26] The insensitivity to regional understandings of local environments that frequently characterised early conservation campaigns was as evident in the Grey Valley as elsewhere. Even more apparent, as is made clear in recent Grey Valley historical writing, is the ease with which disdain for the past could lead to compromises that limited the future. As but a small episode within the wider debate about humanity's engagement with the natural environment, the issue of how best to preserve large tracts of its pristine natural bush represents a critical juncture in the region's history. The 1986 Accord between the Labour Government, industry and environmental organisations, which effectively set out the terms of the West Coast's future, offered a compromise that sanctioned a degree of selective logging of native timber while proclaiming the greater part of West Coast bush a national park. Few expected the compromise to survive. Fewer still were surprised when the Helen Clark–led Labour Government simply imposed a ban on the milling of native timber. It was a step that invigorated a latent 'narrative of betrayal'[27] that had taken root as successive governments stepped away from subsidies and regional development schemes that offered some protection against the economic stagnation threatening to engulf the Grey Valley.

It was a narrative of betrayal already gathering momentum amid the wind-down of the coal industry. The process became inextricably interwoven with history and politics. In the days when coal was king, the Grey Valley coaltowns were in the vanguard of the drive for industrial and political changes that laid the foundation for the nation's variant of democratic socialism. The rupture between ethos and doctrine that followed the election of the fourth Labour Government thus struck at the very heart of the region's identity. The rolling back of the state and deregulation of the economy and industrial relations that followed left the future of the region and its people more compromised than ever. These new uncertainties, aided by electoral redistribution and the introduction of a mixed-member proportional (MMP) system in the 1996 general election, transformed the political environment that had for more than 70 years shaped a Labour heartland. In 1991, for the first time since 1918,

26 Griffiths, *The Art of Time Travel*, p. 88.
27 The theme is explored in Paul Maunder, *Coal and the Coast: A Reflection on the Pike River Disaster*, Christchurch, Canterbury University Press, 2012.

Grey Valley workers found themselves represented by a non-Labour MP. Labour recovered the seat three years later but the old predictability was gone; in 2008 voters under the new MMP system delivered a second National Party representative.

This changing economic and political environment gave rise to a new and distinctive form of regional radicalism. A much fractured collection of interest groups that reached backwards to the pit socialism flourishing when the coalfields were in their pomp, the new voice of protest grew in volume as the twin pillars of the local economy—coal and timber—succumbed before the combined onslaught of two unlikely accomplices: neoliberalism and environmentalism. At the time, the embryonic regional protest was dismissed by the political elites as politically regressive or, as Helen Clark described its more extreme fraction, a feral and inbred response to change. This elitist contempt for populist resistance added fuel to the 'betrayal strain' within regional resistance and shaped the political approach to the reorganisation of the coal industry. Here, the unthinking disciples of the nineteenth-century doctrines of unregulated capitalism, decked out in the new and dangerous garb of neoliberalism, dismantled the complex and interlocking body of mining and labour legislation upon which the safe operation of the pits depended. The ideology that drove the political and economic transformation and its quest for managerial efficiency placed communities and their understandings of their relationship with their working environments at the mercy of the market.

Regions or communities exposed to the dictates of the market received scant respect from political elites in thrall to the nostrums of neoliberalism. Claims to 'exceptionalism' were dismissed as special pleading or simply ignored. The cavalier shovelling aside of the past and its lessons was especially blind to the understandings of place and the sense of 'belonging' that came with generational continuity and occupational cohesion. The recent history of the Grey Valley, if not the West Coast in its entirety, has seen a clash of cultures. An older and withering regional industrial community has confronted an emergent, national political elite bent upon remaking the nation's economy. Steeped in the traditions and customs bestowed by history and sensitive to the precariousness of their relationship with the land, they were working communities accustomed to making haste slowly and in their workplaces valued experience over theory. The certainties that drove the agents of the new corporate age and their quest for change seemed to mining communities to presage a return to what an earlier generation of miners had dubbed the 'tyranny of the manager'. The essential first step in banishing the authority of the old order was the destruction of the industrial legislation built over generations by mining communities that democratised the enforcement of safety procedures.

Above all else, the New Zealand Labour Party elite of the 1980s and 1990s privileged change. To Grey Valley mining towns, the Lange Government's fulsome endorsement of the market economy struck a deadly blow to the party's rationale. The party that had built the welfare state now led the nation, in the words of Eric Hobsbawm, to become one of the 'most inegalitarian' of the 'developed market economies'.[28] Labour was in the process of rejecting its own history and indeed the very idea of a labour movement. By denying a past in which the lived experience of working communities had been the basis for a progressive democracy, the 'Rogernomics' regime with its rigid adherence to the market economy put paid to values that had sustained the Labour Party since its formation in 1916.[29] Opposition to change was cast as being rooted in nostalgia, obstructionist or misguided. Once the lifeblood of a fluid, open and participatory democracy, the labour movement had simply become a burdensome addendum to the bureaucratic party machine highjacked by an inner cabal. In thrall to the new neoliberal doctrines, as revealed to them by Treasury ideologues, the fourth Labour Government effectively set itself adrift from its traditional base.

This then is the context in which the second generation of West Coast historical writing takes root. It is a context in which past and future remain starkly present. At times they rub up against each other in ways that create a friction reminiscent of that present in Pat O'Farrell's response to Phil May's *The West Coast Gold Rushes.*[30] He detected in May's history an over-identification with the place and the people of the golden age. The historian as he saw it, could not present the past on its own terms and was obliged to adopt the role of social critic. The validity, or otherwise, of this critique is discussed later. Here, it is sufficient to observe that Bill Pearson rather than any other author discussed in this book adopts the stance of social critic. Even so, if there is a shift in the emphases of recent

28 Eric Hobsbawm, *Age of Extremes: The Short Twentieth Century 1914–1991*, London, Abacus, 1995, p. 407.

29 The name 'Rogernomics' derives from the Christian name of Roger Owen Douglas, Minister of Finance in the David Lange–led Labour Government, 1984–1990.

30 P.J. O'Farrell, 'Review: P. R. May, *The West Coast Gold Rushes*. Christchurch, Pegasus Press, Second Revised Edition, 1967', *New Zealand Journal of History*, vol. 3, no. 1, April 1969, pp. 89–90.

Grey Valley writing it is one that takes its particular form from within an environment in which the past was being deconstructed and the future reshaped in new directions. The Grey Valley found itself confronted by a most unlikely ideological combination—they were caught between the unbending disciples of the market economy and their counterparts within late twentieth-century environmentalism.

2

REGION AND NATION

Phil May, Pat O'Farrell and Bill Pearson were products of the interwar years. They were far from prosperous times and as the chill winds of economic depression settled over the Coast, like the infamous 'Barber' snaking down the Grey Valley, the inherent weaknesses of the local economy were laid even barer. The gold rushes of the 1860s had populated a wilderness. An event rather than an industry, they encapsulated what was to become the region's lasting dilemma. Briefly and brilliantly, gold conquered the remoteness of the place. But the moving tide of diggers moved on and so too did the investment that might have enabled those who remained to tame its rugged, dangerous terrain. In hindsight the gold rushes had simply come too soon; there was nothing in either the local or the national economy in the 1860s that could carry the West Coast into the future. Refrigeration, which was to provide a new dynamic for a floundering colonial economy, was still several decades away. Despite its role in providing a viable national export economy, on the West Coast its primary impact was to stimulate the exploitation of another wasting mineral asset—coal. The two decades of economic stagnation that separated gold and coal as the mainspring of the local economy ensured that it was outside capital that reaped the benefit in the days when coal was king. Indeed, by the 1920s and 1930s, the coalmining communities of the Grey Valley had already begun to mimic, more slowly if just as terminally, the process of exploitation and decay that had marked the earlier goldtowns.

The shadow of the past thus looms large in the 'West Coasts' the three writers individually and collectively created in the 1950s and 1960s. The stories they weave explore the interaction between people and place where these two fundamentals of human experience rub together in ways that challenge both the human spirit and ingenuity. They share a concern with communities whose very existence is determined by a diminishing mineral asset. As much as the gold and coal mining communities that peopled the West Coast brought with them quite different attitudes, forms of organisation and expectations, they shared a common need to come to grips with an environment little softened by the trappings of civilisation. Each had travelled light to their new home; nor did they expect that the West Coast would be their last move in the journey of life. They were, in this sense, transients and the considerations that eventually persuaded them to stay or move on were inevitably tied to the minerals that alone could sustain them in an otherwise inhospitable environment. The camp-like settlements in which they clustered were overwhelmingly male and youthful in their composition, improvised and primitive in nature and a testimony to a pragmatic reluctance to commit to a place with no past and an uncertain future. How something more permanent was built in this environment and the implications of this struggle for the individuals and communities who made up the 'West Coast' is the central concern of all three writers. Taken together, their writings about the Coast set a framework that has proved to be an enduring and a creative one.

Philip Ross May's *West Coast Gold Rushes* (1962) devotes its first 100 pages to recounting how 'one long solitude, with a forbidding sky, frequent tempests, and impenetrable forests' frustrated and sometimes defeated navigators, explorers, prospectors and adventurers. Only gold possessed the ability to populate such a place. The lure of instant riches allowed the West Coast to squeeze, as May puts it, the 'normal process of colonization' into just 'three hectic years'.[1] May's thick description of this accelerated history emphasises the distinctiveness of the West Coast experience and an awareness of the common ingredients that bound together the nineteenth-century gold rushes of the Pacific borderlands. His sympathies are with the 'digger' confronting what must surely have been the most threatening landscape encountered by those whose gold trail stretched from California to Ballarat and Bendigo before grappling with the incessant rain and impenetrable bush that was the West Coast. Nowhere is this more evident than in his evocation of their spirit in his final paragraph:

1 Philip Ross May, *The West Coast Gold Rushes*, Christchurch, Pegasus, 1962, p. 13; O'Farrell, 'Review: P.R. May, *The West Coast Gold Rushes*', p. 90.

> The diggers have not gone.
>
> Motor up the Waimea Valley some frosty night in June. Take your stand on the slopes of Scandinavian Hill. You'll find Jimmy the Slogger and Liverpool Bill, Gentleman George and Yankee Dan, all hard at work. The gullies echo to the ringing shovels, and the picks go flashing in the moonlight.[2]

This stirring end to *The West Coast Gold Rushes* is itself a response to an environment that had all but reclaimed the creeks and gullies that had once been rushed by the diggers. It is the historian's Eureka—an affirmation that by diligent prospecting the researcher could bring people and place of times past once more to the surface so that the present might rub shoulders with the past. *The West Coast Gold Rushes* was universally hailed as a notable piece of historical research and a landmark in the writing of New Zealand regional history.

The appearance of a second edition in 1968, however, drew a questioning of both the historical perspective that underpinned it and, by implication, the interpretation of West Coast history it presented. The critique came from Patrick O'Farrell, a fellow West Coaster and, like May, a product of the University of Canterbury's History Department. The essence of O'Farrell's criticism was that as much as *The West Coast Gold Rushes* was 'a prodigy of dedicated, scrupulously careful, exhaustive and extremely well-organised historical research',[3] it was, nonetheless, infused with a 'curious air of isolation'. As an event, the rushes unfolded, in O'Farrell's view, very much on their own terms, as part of a 'picaresque narrative local history' in which the author is present as chronicler or guide but rarely as 'social critic' or 'interpreter of the past to the present'. By taking his stand on Scandinavian Hill with 'Jimmy the Slogger and Liverpool Bill, Gentleman George and Yankee Dan', May had recovered the 'three hectic years' that were the West Coast gold rushes and produced, as O'Farrell writes, a 'slice of the past preserved in antiquarian's aspic'.[4]

O'Farrell leaves us in no doubt as to the interpretation he would place upon this 'scrap of New Zealand history'.[5] Where May found vigour, ingenuity and significant achievement, he suggests 'historical tragedy, the

2 May, *West Coast Gold Rushes*, p. 503.
3 O'Farrell, 'Review: P.R. May, *The West Coast Gold Rushes*', p. 89.
4 O'Farrell, 'Review: P.R. May, *The West Coast Gold Rushes*', pp. 89–90.
5 May, *West Coast Gold Rushes*, p. 14.

more bitter for its essential triviality, the more dismal for its enactment in drizzle, cloud and rain'.[6] Where May expressed the hope that 'those who cannot forget the sound of the rain on a tin roof, the smell of the bush, and the sight of the Alps' would enjoy his book, O'Farrell 'missed the sour smell of decay which is also of the bush, the cheerless rotting damp, and the rust on the tin roof … the erosion of minds and hearts, the bitter lines etched deep in the faces as well as land'.[7] His West Coast is very different from that evoked by May; its people and its places scarred by past and present struggles to build community in an environment as unyielding as it was unforgiving. O'Farrell's assessment plainly turns as much upon the interaction of people and place as it does upon a particular conception of the historian's role.

May's first excursion into the history of the West Coast reflects the colour and frenzied movement of a short span of years that catapulted the region into the pages of New Zealand's European history. The focus of O'Farrell's review and his future West Coast writing was upon the 40 years that followed. Gold had populated a wilderness, but in the years that followed there was no obvious sustaining economic activity capable of surmounting the realities of time and place. Too remote, too rugged and too wet, the West Coast was a land hard won. Communication along the narrow coastal strip bordering the Tasman Sea long remained at the mercy of the elements. The inland route across the Southern Alps to the more ordered Wakefieldian settlement of Canterbury stretched nerves and patience. Fifty years were to pass before a tunnel more than 5 miles in length was cut through the Southern Alps to provide a rail link with the more prosperous eastern settlements. And the continued reliance upon the sea for access to markets and produce placed all development at the mercy of the notorious harbour mouths of the Grey and Buller rivers. Coal offered the best hope for the long-term future. It required, however, a level of capital investment beyond the resources of the post–gold rush community and something of an act of faith by prospective coal barons. Not the least of the problems was finding skilled labour. Attracting canny colliers to risky, colonial ventures set in environments raw beyond their comprehension depended, as always, upon push factors propelling them to leave their present situation to embrace a future in places unknown.

6 O'Farrell, 'Review: P.R. May, *The West Coast Gold Rushes*', p. 90.

7 May, *West Coast Gold Rushes*, p. 19; O'Farrell, 'Review: P.R. May, *The West Coast Gold Rushes*', p. 90.

It was to this predicament that O'Farrell turned his attention as historian. He was drawn to what he came to see as a contest between people and place as post–gold rush West Coast sought to forge a future. His MA thesis, 'The Workers and Grey District Politics, 1865–1913', completed in the History Department of what was then Canterbury College in 1955, was, like May's thesis that preceded it, a pioneering work. In the first place, it was written at a time when it was a commonplace to regard the New Zealand experience as not quite the stuff of which history was made. Able students were directed towards the histories of those societies where the historian's footprint was already more visible and where scholarly debate allowed newcomers to the profession to display the trappings of scholarship and engage with 'big' ideas. Commonly, and perhaps inevitably in the 1950s (although the tendency may have been more pronounced in the Canterbury experience), students were directed towards things English. In those days, before the Celtic fringe reasserted itself, England was not so much a geographical entity as a synonym for Britain. To allow students to embark upon an exploration of the New Zealand past, and the past of a failed province at that, was thus, at least within the more rarified confines of colonial academia, questionable if not dangerous. It was neither sufficiently replete with scholarly markers nor concerned with matters of historical moment to warrant the attention of the emergent historian.[8]

That May and O'Farrell should embark upon research projects that spurned the preferred academic pathways of their time owes a very great deal to the particular ways in which, as both a place and a past, the region shaped their historical thinking. Their decisions also reflect the changing nature of the colonial world. As historians who first made their mark in the decades after World War II, they stood on the cusp of a significant shift in the way New Zealanders saw themselves. In 1940 when historians reviewed the centenary of what was a settler colony bound by treaty to the Māori, they did so within a framework defined very largely by, what F.L. Wood called, the 'silken bonds of Empire'.[9] World War II loosened these bonds and created an environment in which the New Zealand past could be seen through lenses that were more overtly nationalist and less cringingly colonial. The talisman of this shift was Keith Sinclair's *History of New Zealand* (1959), a determinedly nationalistic account whose 'nervy,

8 Oliver, *Looking for the Phoenix*; Keith Sinclair, *Halfway Round the Harbour: An Autobiography*, Auckland, Penguin, 1993.

9 F.L. Wood, *New Zealand in the World*, Wellington, Department of Internal Affairs, 1940, p. 94.

energetic and staccato'[10] prose stressed the radical and the innovatory and a shared Pacific environment. Something of this new mood is evident in the way Pearson, May and O'Farrell look at their respective 'West Coasts'. Looking as much to Australia as to other parts of New Zealand for its capital and people, the West Coast seemed the ultimate frontier. Innovation was necessary for survival. In short, the West Coast past challenged the less exciting and more prevalent view that saw New Zealand's story as 'conservative, traditional and shaped by its foundational inheritance'.[11] As pioneering West Coast historians, May and O'Farrell wrote before what came to be seen as rival interpretations of our past had been consolidated into Keith Sinclair's *History of New Zealand* and Bill Oliver's *Story of New Zealand*.[12]

Alongside these academic concerns, New Zealand history had since the 1940s developed a more public face. The passage of 100 years moved communities everywhere to reflect upon achievement and prospect. To a degree a South Island phenomenon, it was a mood nowhere better captured than in the monumental histories produced by the Wakefieldian settlements of Otago and Canterbury.[13] As W.J. Gardner, fresh from writing his path-breaking *The Amuri: A County History* (1956), observed in a seminal *Landfall* article, centennials 'made these histories possible' but also 'made it impossible for them to be definitive'.[14] Reflecting upon his article more than 40 years later, he observed: 'there were probably some raised eyebrows, even shock as readers came upon my article. Local history as then perceived by the literati, lay outside any pale of serious study'.[15] Of necessity, the genre rested upon an 'army of enthusiasts' whose lack of context easily allowed the 'antiquarian' to triumph over the analytical. At a time when popular national histories were emerging, it seemed more

10 Oliver, *Looking for the Phoenix*, p. 97.

11 Oliver, *Looking for the Phoenix*, p. 97.

12 Keith Sinclair, *A History of New Zealand*, Harmondsworth, Penguin Books, 1959; Oliver, *The Story of New Zealand*.

13 A.H. McLintock, *The History of Otago: The Origins and Growth of a Wakefieldian Class Settlement*, Dunedin, Otago Centennial Historical Publications, 1949; James Hight and C.R. Straubel, general eds, *A History of Canterbury, Vol. 1: To 1854*, Christchurch, Whitcombe & Tombs/Canterbury Centennial Historical Association and Literary Committee, 1957; W.J. Gardner, ed., *A History of Canterbury, Volume II: General History, 1854–76 and Cultural Aspects, 1850–1950*, Christchurch, Whitcombe & Tombs/Canterbury Centennial Historical and Literary Committee, 1971; W.H. Scotter, *A History of Canterbury, Vol. III: 1876–1950*, Christchurch, Whitcombe & Tombs/Canterbury Centennial History and Literary Committee, 1965.

14 Gardner, 'Grass Roots and Dredge Tailings: Reflections on Local History', *Landfall 43*, vol. 11, no. 3, September 1957, p. 227.

15 Gardner, 'Grass Roots and Dredge Tailings: Reflections on Local History', *Where They Lived*, p. 9.

important than ever that the generalisations in which these histories were couched should be grounded in the experience of the 'ordinary lives of ordinary people'. As Gardner saw it, local history was 'a wonderful antidote to schematic history' and a testing ground for the meaning of the shorthand labels of the generalisers who, by the stroke of a pen, turned individual pastoralists into 'oligarchs' or collectively into members of a 'squattocracy' and wealthy city folk into 'bourgeois radicals'.[16]

Outside the South Island's Wakefieldian settlements of Canterbury and Otago, the histories of the regional building blocks of the national experience remained largely unwritten. To a degree, the West Coast had fared better than most. The contours of the region's written history as they were available to Pearson, May and O'Farrell had altered very little from those identified in A.J. Harrop's *The Romance of Westland: The Story of New Zealand's Golden Coast* (1923).[17] At its hub was gold. A tale of 'adventure rather than avarice' and of 'magnificent fortunes won and lost' by 'vigorous men', who provided the basis of the 'permanent settlement of an 'isolated, bush-covered Westland'. Previously visited only by whalers, ever in danger of being 'cast away on the desolate shore' and 'fearful of the fierce [Māori] inhabitants',[18] the explorers who paved the way for the gold seekers thus become, by Harrop's account, 'the first martyrs to the cause of Westland—men who died while endeavouring to make a road to the west open to all'.[19]

The celebration of the exploits and hardships of pioneers is, of course, a familiar enough feature of colonial history. In the West Coast variant, the timing of its creation—during the years immediately after the 1914–18 war—sees it couched in explicitly imperialist terms:

> The examples of self-sacrifice and heroism in which the story of Westland abounds must play no mean part in moulding the future of the race. The fathers of Westland knew how to face death bravely, and the sons of Westland have since proved that the race has not degenerated—the spirit that taught men how to face the floods of Westland was very active in the men who fought in Gallipoli and in France.[20]

16 Gardner, 'Grass Roots and Dredge Tailings', *Where They Lived*, p. 5.
17 A.J. Harrop, *The Romance of Westland: The Story of New Zealand's Golden Coast*, Christchurch, Whitcombe & Tombs, 1923.
18 Harrop, *Romance of Westland*, pp. 167–68.
19 Harrop, *Romance of Westland*, p. 168.
20 Harrop, *Romance of Westland*, p. 170.

Thus was the struggle to establish a viable future, in an environment almost universally seen as inhospitable, linked to the progress of Empire.

The historical framework available to May and O'Farrell in the 1950s was primarily an optimistic one. It was an optimism that coloured predictions of the region's economic prospects. However much political rivalries and parochialisms may have hindered progress in the past, the opening of the Otira tunnel in 1923 was seen as marking the dawn of a new prosperity. 'In 50 years time', wrote Harrop, Westland could be 'as busy and populous as her neighbour [Canterbury] is today'.[21] Harrop was vague about precisely what the economic driving force of the new prosperity would be. Like most commentators, he assumed that coal would continue to be king in the postwar world and that it would remain the central pillar of the local economy. Timber milling, farming and tourism would, he believed, become increasingly important. What was needed above all else was enterprise: 'Enterprise first opened up Westland for the white man, and it is enterprise which Westland requires today'.[22]

Thirty years later, as the Coast prepared to celebrate its golden century, some of the optimism had evaporated. The coal industry was now in retreat. New and less labour-intensive technologies had eroded the bargaining power of the coalminers and ultimately spelt the end for the communities that had grown around the pits that had given them life. Already the coaltowns had begun to resemble the decayed goldtowns that had flourished and withered before them. The industrial and political radicalism that had flourished as these communities had sought to confront the realities of time and place had been largely played out. As the mining communities withered so did their mouthpiece, the *Grey River Argus*, once proudly defiant as Labour's pioneer daily, begin the slide that would see it finally expire as the 1960s came to an end.[23] The completion of the Haast Pass promised to increase the flow of tourists—always an element in the West Coast's appeal.

As a cluster of young writers, May, O'Farrell and Pearson were products of this period of shrinking horizons. Philip Ross May (1930–1977) proudly proclaimed himself a native of Ross, the 'Ballarat of Westland', where his

---

21 Harrop, *Romance of Westland*, p. 169.

22 Harrop, *Romance of Westland*, p. 169.

23 In 1966 the Grey River Argus Company was taken over by the Buller Westland Publishing Company. The paper was relaunched in February 1966 as the *Argus Leader*. Gone was its traditional claim to be New Zealand's pioneer Labour daily. In November 1966 the *Leader* closed its doors.

father for nearly 25 years managed a timber mill and served several terms as mayor. Born in Hokitika, he was educated at Ross Primary School. Like Pearson, he was a student at Greymouth Technical High School before going 'over the Hill' to Canterbury College in the late 1940s. In 1954 he was awarded an MA with first class honours in history after completing a thesis, 'The West Canterbury Gold Rush to 1865: The Analysis of a Gold Rush of the Mid-Nineteenth Century' (1953). After a time as a high school teacher in Christchurch, he joined the history staff of the University of Canterbury and was able to complete the transformation of his thesis into the path-breaking *West Coast Gold Rushes* (1962).

Thus it was that May's arrival on the historical scene coincided with the centennial moment. In late 1959 the Westland Centennial Council published its official centennial souvenir and proclaimed 1960 as centennial year. Its objectives, as spelt out by the then mayor of Greymouth, F.W. Baillie, were 'to present a summary of the thrilling and romantic history of our beautiful province and to recall the indomitable spirit of our pioneer forbears'.[24] Gold loomed large in the official history and was emblazoned in its title, *Westland's Golden Century*. Choosing the historic moment had exercised the mind of the committee. They were conscious that Westland's historical pedigree lacked the 'planned and organised' stamp of the Wakefieldian settlements of which they were offshoots. And they were equally aware that it was the rushes of 1864 and 1865 that marked the birth of the West Coast they knew. They chose as their founding document 'the completion of the purchase of Westland from the Maoris, in 1860'.[25]

The year 1960 was a time of celebration up and down the Coast, and it was as part of this community and public remembrance that May (and, as we shall see, O'Farrell) emerges as historian. He contributed three short articles to *Westland's Golden Century*: 'Exploration and Purchase', 'The First Gold Discoveries' and 'The Year of the Rush'.[26] They were followed two years later by the monumental *West Coast Gold Rushes*. Its 588 pages offered a detailed picture of the West Coast's foundation years, with nearly 100 pages devoted to the exploration and mapping of the region before the rushes of 1864–65. It was an immediate success; the 2,000 copies printed

24 Rupert A. Kay, ed., *Westland's Golden Century 1860–1960: An Official Souvenir of Westland's Centenary*, Greymouth, Westland Centennial Council, 1959, 'Foreword'.

25 Kay, *Westland's Golden Century 1869–1960*, 'Foreword'.

26 Kay, *Westland's Golden Century 1860–1960*, pp. 13–19, 21–26, 27–32.

sold within three months and it was selected by the New Zealand Literary Fund advisory board as one of the 10 New Zealand books to be displayed at the International Book Design Exhibition in London in 1963. And, when Hokitika came to mark its own centenary in 1965, May 'added some new material' to 'relevant sections' of the *West Coast Gold Rushes* and produced a 48-page booklet, *Hokitika: Goldfields Capital* (1964).[27] In short, by the mid-1960s the name Philip Ross May was synonymous with the West Coast. As one reviewer put it, 'no other area of the country has had such a well-balanced and exhaustive treatment of the foundation years of settlement'.[28]

Patrick James O'Farrell (1933–2003), unlike both May and Pearson, was a first-generation New Zealander. His Irish Catholic parents had migrated to New Zealand separately from Borrisokane, Tipperary, Ireland, before World War I. They married in New Zealand and settled in Greymouth where Patrick was born and where his father worked as a tailor. Educated by the Sisters of Mercy and the Marist Brothers, O'Farrell joined the exodus of the young over the Hill and studied history at Canterbury University College. In 1955 he completed an MA thesis 'The Workers and Grey District Politics, 1865–1913', which traced the fortunes of the labouring classes in the aftermath of the gold rushes. At its centre were the coalminers of the Grey Valley and their organised industrial and political responses to the particular circumstances in which they lived and worked. Like May, O'Farrell had been drawn into the celebratory enterprise that was *Westland's Golden Century*, contributing an article, 'Politics in Westland'.[29] By then, he had already become the first of what was eventually a cluster of Canterbury history graduates to take up a PhD scholarship at The Australian National University, newly established in Canberra. Thus O'Farrell, unlike May, did not immediately or directly develop his West Coast research for publication.

Less obviously, his doctoral thesis, a political biography of the Australian-born Harry Holland who led the New Zealand Labour Party from its foundation until his death in 1933, unfolds against a West Coast backdrop. Arriving in New Zealand in 1912, Holland quickly thrust himself to the forefront of radical politics. When fellow Australian 'Paddy'

27 Philip Ross May, *Hokitika: Goldfields Capital*, Christchurch, Pegasus, Hokitika Centennial Committee, 1964.
28 Murray McCaskill, 'Review: *The West Coast Gold Rushes* by P.R. May', *Historical Studies: Australia and New Zealand*, vol. 11, no. 41, November 1963, p. 141.
29 Kay, *Westland's Golden Century 1860–1960*, pp. 42–48.

Webb, MP for Grey, was imprisoned in 1918 for refusing military call-up, Holland successfully contested the by-election that followed. Boundary changes that preceded the 1919 general election saw the West Coast coalfields Labour strongholds moved into the Buller electorate based on Westport. And it was the northern coalfields town rather than Greymouth or Hokitika that Holland called 'Home' during his parliamentary years. Later revised and published as *Harry Holland: Militant Socialist* (1964),[30] O'Farrell's thesis drew him inevitably to dwell further upon the nature of the West Coast community, its place in the national history and especially its role in the emergence of organised labour.

The amalgam of industrial unionism, labourism, socialism and communism that swirled around pit-top debate was the dominant strand of West Coast labour politics in the early 1920s. Holland was comfortable moving within it; more comfortable than he was in the wider New Zealand political environment. It was in his dealings with Grey Valley unionists that Holland came to recognise and accommodate the important role played by the working-class Irish Catholic community within organised labour. It was this dimension of the West Coast experience that engaged O'Farrell's attention. The proportion of Irish-born in New Zealand had never been high and had declined from 46,037 (6.5 per cent) in 1896 to 37,380 (3.5 per cent) in 1916. It was an unevenly spread population and considerably more thickly deposited on the West Coast. Even before the birth of the New Zealand Labour Party, in July 1916, something approaching an alliance had developed between the labour movement and Irish nationalists. In 1913, when Paddy Webb won the Grey seat for the Social Democratic Party—a forerunner of the New Zealand Labour Party—the conservative press had proclaimed his victory a triumph for an unholy alliance of the 'Reds and the Greens'. Holland championed the Irish cause. In 1916 he wrote a series of articles on the historical foundations of Ireland's Easter Rebellion. Whether or not they shared his militant socialism, a significant section of the West Coast's Irish Catholic community recognised and endorsed Holland as a voice of protest.

At precisely this juncture, O'Farrell's parents, Paddy and Mai, set up their home in Puketahi Street at the heart of Greymouth's Catholic community. Here the young Patrick O'Farrell observed at close quarters the making of Greymouth's Catholic/Labour politics. It was a formative experience evoked

30 O'Farrell, *Harry Holland: Militant Socialist*; Patrick James O'Farrell, 'H.E. Holland and the Labour Movement in Australia and New Zealand: With Special Emphasis on the Activity of Militant Socialists', PhD thesis, ANU, 1960.

brilliantly some 50 years later in *Vanished Kingdoms* (1990).[31] A masterly personal excursion, it shows how the O'Farrell family saga illuminates the interaction between people and place that was the West Coast experience in the first half of the twentieth century. Its pages reveal Irish loyalties strongly held. To 'symbolise his commitment to the ideals of 1916', his father changed the family surname from Farrell to O'Farrell. This apart, Ireland and things Irish did not dominate family life. If there was an ideological commitment in the Puketahi Street household Pat O'Farrell grew up in, it was 'a very practical involvement in the New Zealand Labour Party'. And it is from this that he traces the unfolding of his historical interests. 'The Workers and Grey District Politics' led naturally enough to examining the socialist impulses that produced the New Zealand Labour Party, exploring the impact of the Russian Revolution upon Australasian labour movements and the biography of Harry Holland.

As Westland celebrated its centennial in the early 1960s, O'Farrell was teaching Russian history at the University of New South Wales. His research in this area was limited by rudimentary Russian language skills. By chance, however, he came across a British White Paper examining allegations that there had been negotiations between Sinn Fein and the Bolsheviks under Lenin.[32] The discovery led in 1965 to a period of study leave in Ireland (where he taught primarily Russian history), a decision greeted dismissively in Australian academic circles where Ireland was seen as 'a historical backwater, where nothing ever happened'.[33] As O'Farrell wrote in 1999, the time in Dublin took him, however, into Irish history and 'radically changed' his life.[34] Before travelling to Ireland, he had begun work on the history of the Catholic Church in Australia, and in the process of immersing himself in the Catholic Archives had sampled, in the correspondence of Irish bishops and priests, 'a treasure trove of private and very illuminating historical conversations between Ireland and Australia'.[35] His return to the University of New South Wales in 1967, where he began teaching a course on Anglo-Irish relations, marks the beginning of the Irish Catholic phase of his academic career.

31 P.J. O'Farrell, *Vanished Kingdoms: Irish in Australia and New Zealand. A Personal Excursion*, Sydney, University of New South Wales Press, 1990.

32 P.J. O'Farrell, *The Irish Echo* (Australia), 7–20 October 1999, p. 14.

33 P.J. O'Farrell, *The Irish Echo* (Australia), 21 October–3 November 1999, p. 12; also: Brad Patterson, ed., *The Irish in New Zealand: Historical Contexts and Perspectives*, Wellington, Stout Research Centre for New Zealand Studies, Victoria University of Wellington, 2002, p. 3.

34 O'Farrell, *The Irish Echo*, 7–20 October 1999, p. 14.

35 O'Farrell, *The Irish Echo*, 21 October–3 November 1999, p. 12.

The most obvious product of this shift of emphasis was the publication of *The Catholic Church in Australia: A Short History* (1968) and *Ireland's English Question: Anglo-Irish Relations 1534–1970* (1971).[36] The link between the two books is obvious and direct. Less obvious, but just as significant, was the revisiting of the West Coast in the review of the second edition of Phil May's *West Coast Gold Rushes* that came in the midst of this transition in O'Farrell's historical preoccupations. The optimism that infused his earlier treatment of the Grey district labour movement, especially evident in the treatment of the arrival of the Red Feds (the radical New Zealand Federation of Labour), gives way to an emphasis upon the relationship between a harsh and unyielding environment and the individuals who struggled to make the best of the circumstances they had been dealt. In traversing the turbulent slice of the past—1887 to 1923—that lay at the heart of his first foray into Irish history, O'Farrell was grappling with the issues that in Borrisokane, Ireland, and in Greymouth shaped, in different ways, the lives of his parents and their generation. They were years of reform and rebellion: the Anglican Church had been disestablished in 1869; Land Acts notwithstanding, peasant unrest remained endemic; Home Rule become a religious crusade and, after the 1911 Parliament Act, a possibility; revolt came closer as Ulster dug in its heels, partition gained popularity in Britain and a revolutionary vanguard emerged determined to free Ireland.

Over the next 20 years, in which he produced four books, O'Farrell's historical concerns were Ireland and Australia rather than New Zealand and the Grey Valley. After a further academic year in Dublin, 1972–73, there followed, in quick succession, *England and Ireland since 1800* (1975) and *The Catholic Church and Community in Australia* (1977), a revised version of the earlier *Short History*[37] that doubled the length of the original work. A hospital operation that, as O'Farrell put it, 'went wrong, leaving me without speech, my writing hand and severely reduced mobility' slowed down the production line. The creative surge that followed subsequently in the 1980s and early 1990s was remarkable. In many respects, *Vanished Kingdoms*, with its skilful interweaving of the threads of Catholic, Irish and West Coast experience, is O'Farrell at his most brilliant. It is in this

36 P.J. O'Farrell, *The Catholic Church in Australia: A Short History: 1788–1967*, Melbourne, Nelson (Australia), 1968; P.J. O'Farrell, *Ireland's English Question: Anglo-Irish Relations 1534–1970*, London, Batsford, 1971.

37 Patrick O'Farrell, *England and Ireland since 1800*, London, Oxford University Press, 1975; Patrick O'Farrell, *The Catholic Church and Community in Australia: A History*, revised edn, West Melbourne, Nelson (Australia), 1977.

exploration of how old-world themes were worked out in new-world settings that O'Farrell captures that convergence of people and place that shaped the West Coast experience.

The son of a railway clerk, Bill Pearson (1922–2002) was born in Greymouth just as the O'Farrells had settled in the town. He was educated at the Grey Main Primary School and the Greymouth Technical High School before going 'over the Hill' to Canterbury University College in 1939. He subsequently trained as a teacher in Dunedin and was for five months a probationary assistant teacher at the Blackball Primary School. He served in Egypt during World War II and on return to New Zealand graduated MA in English from Canterbury University College in 1948 before embarking on a PhD at the University of London. After completing his doctorate in 1952, he taught for a period in London schools and then returned to New Zealand to take up a lectureship in English in 1954 at Auckland University College. It was while in London that he began work on what became *Coal Flat*. At this time also he wrote his celebrated essay 'Fretful Sleepers', a critical assessment of the New Zealand character.[38] The relationship between the two has been much commented upon and for present purposes they will be considered as forming a part of Pearson's West Coast phase.

Pearson was a product of the 'bit in-between' the two world wars. Whereas O'Farrell can be firmly placed in Greymouth's Irish Catholic community, Pearson grew up in a more austere Scots Presbyterian household. His father was a member of the local Masonic Lodge and stood apart from the 'boozy' West Coast that was to attract admiration and condemnation in roughly equal measure. Where O'Farrell senior was active in the fledgling Labour Party and a director of the town's pioneer labour daily, the *Grey River Argus*, Pearson senior preferred to take a conservative Christchurch daily and to keep his politics to himself. What the two families shared was a lowly position on the Grey Valley hierarchy of physical endeavour that prized male manual work and placed all other occupations in relation to coalminers and timber workers. In this sense, both Bill Pearson and Patrick O'Farrell stood 'alongside' the slice of life that was to dominate their West Coast writing.

38 Pearson, *Coal Flat*; Bill Pearson, 'Fretful Sleepers: A Sketch of New Zealand Behaviour and Its Implications for the Artist', *Landfall 23*, vol. 6, no. 3, September 1952, pp. 201–30; reprinted with corrections in Charles Brasch, ed., *Landfall Country: Work from Landfall, 1947–61*, Christchurch, Caxton Press, 1960, and in Bill Pearson, *Fretful Sleepers and Other Essays*, Auckland, Heinemann Educational Books, 1974, pp. 1–36.

The mining communities were, even on the West Coast, communities apart. Set at some distance from the larger towns of Greymouth and Westport, the mining towns only slowly disintegrated as road and rail transport made it possible for miners to live in the more congenial environments of the port towns. O'Farrell and Pearson lived in times when it was still common to hear Grey Valley critics of the miners refer to the 'foreign twangs' and equally foreign ideas that prevailed in the mining towns. As first-generation New Zealanders they were both especially aware of the differences of accent and nationality that could be used to place the miners outside what it suited their critics from within to define as the mainstream of the West Coast community. Yet, in many respects, the Grey Valley labour movement that the miners spearheaded was one of the strongest bonds bridging the town and mining communities. It was also the point at which the convergence between the numerically strongest groups of 'outsiders'—the miners and the Irish Catholics—occurred. O'Farrell saw this alliance between the 'Reds' and the 'Greens' from close to the power centre of lay Catholicism; Pearson from the Protestant end of town. Each was attracted by the community, unionist and socialist solidarities mining towns affirmed. Both were conscious of generations of ideologues who had turned to the coalfields in the hope that the miners would be the revolutionary vanguard of their dreams and equally aware of the realities of time and place that had frustrated them.

The five months Pearson spent in Blackball as a probationary assistant teacher had enabled him to observe a mining community at closer range than on the fleeting opportunities he had experienced while living in Greymouth. It left a 'lasting impression'. The thought of writing about it was something that continued to preoccupy him after he enlisted in 1941 and, as he was later to recall, was first conceived when he was with the J-Force in Japan in 1946 at the end of the Pacific War. To that point, he had envisaged a story about 'a young idealist crushed by a materialist community'. In the long gestation that preceded *Coal Flat*'s publication in 1963, the relative weighting given to the individual and the collective shifted as Pearson 'found the young man less interesting than the community'. By the late 1940s, this preference for the collective rather than the individual led him to toy with adopting elements of the emerging discipline of sociology or, as he put it, 'those studies that see all the parts in relation to the whole, taking in geography, history, economic and social relations'.[39] It was a style he had admired in Lewis Mumford's books on technology and cities. He became aware of a New Zealand study, H.C.D. Somerset's *Littledene* (1938), said to employ, to some degree, this sociological framework in a pioneering study of the community based on the rural Canterbury town of Oxford. Pearson appears to have first read *Littledene* in 1949 during a short time spent teaching at Oxford, but recalled some 40 years later that 'it wasn't the sort of study of a small town that I had in mind'.[40] One suspects that he was already moving towards the novel as the chosen vehicle for the social realism to which he was attracted.

It was to be more than a decade before this thinking resulted in the publication of what was to be Pearson's only novel, *Coal Flat* (1963). After returning from the war, in 1946, he had joined the throng of returned servicemen who filled university lecture theatres and completed an MA in English at Canterbury College (1947–48). The following year he took up a PhD scholarship at King's College, London, and completed his thesis on the nineteenth-century English Catholic poets in 1952. It is hard to conceive of anything more removed from the idea of a novel set at Blackball, nestled as it was beneath the Paparoa Range on an elevated plateau above the Grey River, than the Hampstead Heath environment in which Pearson returned to the project. The idea of using a West Coast mining community to explore a range of attitudes and assumptions held to be widespread in New Zealand society was brought back into closer focus by the playing out of New Zealand's own Cold War drama—the 1951 waterfront dispute. Viewed from London, the Emergency Powers promulgated by the Sidney Holland–led National Party smacked even more starkly of incipient fascism than they did from Blackball. That Holland was able to assume such an authoritarian approach was possible, in Pearson's view, 'because the ground is already prepared in these conditions: a docile sleepy electorate, veneration of war heroes, willingness to persecute those who don't conform, gullibility in the face of headlines and radio peptalks'.[41] Precisely what elements of individual and community behaviour evident in the functioning of a West Coast coalfield town of the late 1940s provided Pearson with the link between

39 Bill Pearson, 'Beginnings and Endings', *Sport* 5, Spring 1990, pp. 15, 21.

40 H.C.D. Somerset, *Littledene: Patterns of Change* (1938), 3rd edn, Wellington, New Zealand Council for Educational Research, 1974; Pearson, 'Beginnings and Endings', p. 15. See also Paul Millar, *No Fretful Sleeper: A Life of Bill Pearson*, Auckland, Auckland University Press, 2010, p. 163.

41 Pearson, *Fretful Sleepers and Other Essays*, pp. 3–4.

'Fretful Sleepers' and *Coal Flat* will be explored in Chapter 5. But, as we have already observed, it had become clear to him by this stage that his interest was increasingly less engaged by the inner struggles of the idealistic young man at the centre of his story and more concerned with the community in which he moved. How much this owed to the peculiarities of place and how much it reflected the wider preoccupations of life in the 1950s is likewise central to an understanding of how *Coal Flat* came to play a critical role in the wider perception of the West Coast as a place apart. Whatever the source of Pearson's interpretation, readers of *Coal Flat* would have found little of May's optimism and more of O'Farrell's concern for the harshness and grimness that surrounded the efforts of both individuals and communities. For some, the final words of the novel seemed 'bleak and laconic', if not fatalistic, and indicative of a surrender to the contingencies of time and place.

Pearson rejected such a reading of *Coal Flat* as being based on an ignorance of just how good a West Coast summer could be and certainly at odds with his intention. He had been attracted by the artistic symmetry involved in leaving his story very much as he had entered it—an idea he later attributed to Arthur Koestler's novel *Arrival and Departure.*[42] Thus, when readers meet *Coal Flat* it is on 'a sunny February morning throbbing with cicadas'; they leave on a 'sunny November morning' where 'already the air was singing with grass cicadas'.[43] Life goes on much as it always had, seemingly untouched by the crises that had enveloped the lives of the individuals at the centre of the novel. Its central character, whose estrangement from that community provided the dynamic of the narrative, comes to accept much of what Pearson calls the 'hopes and beliefs'[44] of the majority. Exploring precisely what this compromise tells us about the West Coast environment in which it was negotiated, as distinct from the literary artifice employed by the author, takes us to the essence of the relationship between people and place.

42 Arthur Koestler's novel *Arrival and Departure* was published in 1943 and was the third novel in a trilogy that explores the conflict between morality and expediency. See also Pearson, 'Beginnings and Endings', p. 21.

43 Pearson, *Coal Flat*, pp. 6 and 418.

44 Pearson, 'Beginnings and Endings', p. 21.

3

PHILIP ROSS MAY

Making a Goldfield: Populating a Wilderness

In the foreword to *The West Coast Gold Rushes* Phil May ponders 'whether one can acknowledge a debt to a place' and admits that 'it is not easy to get the Coast out of one's bones'.[1] The creeks and gullies that surrounded the Ross township in which he grew up carried the names and associations of the rush of 'sixty-five' and conjured up images of an event that brought people and place together with a suddenness that was as bewildering and unpredictable as it was chaotic and colourful. As historian, May sought to find meaning in the apparent randomness and, by taking his stand as it were alongside the diggers, presented a 'scrap of New Zealand history in its own terms'.[2] As a phenomenon in their own right, the West Coast gold rushes took their place in that sequence of mid-nineteenth-century events that rippled through the Pacific borderlands from California to eastern Australia before reaching New Zealand. Those who opened up the West Coast goldfields were thus veterans who 'moved with the speed and assurance of a well-trained army',[3] taking with them the merchants, storekeepers, publicans, wardens, bank agents, entertainers, rogues and prostitutes who made up a goldfield's community.

1 May, *West Coast Gold Rushes*, pp. 18–19.

2 May, *West Coast Gold Rushes*, p. 14.

3 May, *West Coast Gold Rushes*, p. 107.

Figure 1: Philip Ross May in 1970 washing a 'colour' near Captains Flat, an old New South Wales mining town.

Source: Courtesy May family.

The combination of isolation and rugged terrain limited human habitation. Traditional accounts suggest that Māori had discovered the alpine passes to the West Coast in the seventeenth century and had begun to value the place as a source of greenstone. Such accounts also suggest that by the nineteenth century the land between Hokitika and Greymouth, the hub of May's 'West Coast', was under the control of Tuhuru, a principal chief of the Ngāti Waewae hapu of Ngāi Tahu. The heart of the Māori community was the Arahura River and its catchment, the principal source of pounamu. In the 1830s this control was weakened when the Ngāti Rārua, Ngāti Tama and possibly representatives of other northern tribes defeated the Poutini Ngāi Tahu in battle. After a brief occupation (1832–37), during which the Poutini Ngāi Tahu remained in residence, the victors withdrew but continued to assert authority over the entire west coast. Poutini Ngāi Tahu did not recognise this claim to the south of Kahurangi Point, and by the 1840s were occupying and cultivating land on the banks of the Kawatiri (Buller) River.

On the eve of the gold rushes, the 'West Coast' was still defined by the pattern of Māori occupation and use. 'Tiny'[4] in number—probably no more than 100—with the heaviest concentration between the Grey and Arahura rivers, theirs was a presence dictated, as was that of the Europeans who followed, by a precious mineral. It was greenstone that explains the substantial community of five storehouses and six substantial houses at Taramakau and the three houses that lent a sense of permanence to the Māori presence at Arahura. The camps along the alpine pathways to the east were staging posts in the passage of greenstone to the Ngāi Tahu community at Kaiapoi. Elsewhere, along the coast and on inland river flats were numerous settlements occupied seasonally for fishing, eeling and gardening. There was a settlement on the northern bank of the Kawatiri (Buller) River, a garden on the southern bank, and camps and gardens at Tauranga, Totara and Waimangaroa and in the Inangahua Valley at Oweka. The subsistence activities that sustained the quest for greenstone had flourished in isolation. Reflecting upon the position of West Coast Māori, as he had found them in 1846, Heaphy described a people without pigs, few European crops, virtually no iron implements and dressed in the traditional flax mat.[5] Such observations point to a people apart and, as Atholl Anderson puts it, among the last Māori communities in the colony to adopt a 'largely European mode'[6] of economic organisation.

4 Harry Evison, *The Ngai Tahu Deeds*, Christchurch, Canterbury University Press, 2006, p. 388.

5 Atholl Anderson, Judith Binney and Aroha Harris, *Tangata Whenua: A History*, Wellington, Bridget Williams Books, 2015, p. 166.

6 Anderson, Binney and Harris, *Tangata Whenua*, p. 166.

It was gold rather than settler pressure for land that refocused attention—both European and Māori—upon defining and asserting presences on the West Coast. There was less urgency on the European side to engage in the formal processes of colonisation inaugurated by the Treaty of Waitangi—a treaty process in which West Coast Māori had not been directly involved. Colonial administrators had regarded implementing the provisions of the Treaty of Waitangi on the West Coast as simply a minor detail of its South Island purchase. In the 1848 Kemp Purchase, 'a careless and unsatisfactory' transaction from which Poutini Ngāi Tahu received 'no significant sum of money',[7] the Crown was said to have acquired all land between Arahura and the Buller River. The following year, an agent of the Crown, W.D.B. Mantell, attempted to pay £110 to relatives of Poutini Ngāi Tahu. Little of the attempted payment found its way across the Alps and there was no effort to lay out any reserves, as required by the Treaty of Waitangi. The Poutini Ngāi Tahu had every right to think that any agreement to sell their lands was null and void.

Throughout the 1850s the colonial government negotiated payments to Māori (Ngāti Toa, Ngāti Tama, Ngāti Awa, Rangitāne) with historic claims to greenstone in the Māwhera district—between Hokitika and Greymouth. Negotiation with the Poutini Ngāi Tahu continued to be regarded as a loose end that needed some time to be tidied. European commentators, however, noted a change in the attitude amongst the Poutini Ngāi Tahu. Whereas in 1846 Thomas Brunner had noted an open hospitality, observers now identified the sharpness of the trader: 'they required payment for everything, not in pounds, shillings, and pence, which latter coins they entirely ignored, but in pounds only'.[8] Europeans digging for gold were said to be viewed coolly by Māori grown uneasy about the slowness of the Crown to settle the land question. May observes this greater sensitivity and shows how gold hastened European purchase of the 'West Coast'. By the terms of what became known as the Arahura Deed (1860) Poutini Ngāi Tahu ceded their land to the crown for £300 in cash. Some 6,724 acres were to be assigned as individual allotments; a further 3,500 acres were set aside as Reserves and preserved Māori control of the Arahura River bed—the hub of the traditional greenstone supply.

7 May, *West Coast Gold Rushes*, p. 50.

8 Julius von Haast, *Report of a Topographical and Geological Exploration of the Western Districts of the Nelson Province, New Zealand*, Nelson, Nelson Provincial Government, 1861, p. 29.

The rush of newcomers in 1865 inevitably swamped the tiny Māori population. But in the period immediately following the settlement, Māori involvement remained significant. Māori were active in discovering and reporting the presence of gold deposits. It was Māori who in 1861 discovered gold on the Buller River and subsequently at Waimangaroa, and on the Lyell River.[9] Ihai Tainui's discoveries in the Hohonu district in 1862 drew attention to the Taramakau. A year later a group of Māori joined with Europeans working gold in the Hohonu.[10] Later discoveries in the Grey Valley and in the watershed of the Arnold were appropriately named Maori Gully (No. 1) and Maori Gully (No. 2). Māori were particularly prominent in the Totara and in the working of the old Buller diggings as the main body of the gold seekers moved on to richer pickings.[11] Along the entire length of the goldfields, if predominantly in the area between Greymouth and Hokitika, 'big parties of Maoris, men, women and children'[12] found a natural place alongside the cooperatively organised parties that characterised the early phase of the West Coast rushes. 'Never prominent on the big fields in their settled phase', May notes that 'the rumour that a Maori party was starting out to prospect could set half a mining camp striking tents and rolling swags'.[13] Such was the level of Māori involvement that, among diggers with experience of the Australian goldfields, it engendered, or so newspaper commentators claimed, an attitude that 'contrasted with the diggers' poor opinion of the Australian 'blacks'.[14] Nevertheless, as the trickle of newcomers became a 'rush', the settlement that preceded invasion was to irritate diggers impatient to exploit the moment.

Like the gold seekers themselves, Phil May as pioneering historian had to give meaning to the term 'West Coast'. The term itself was a product of the unfolding of the European presence. Prior to the establishment of the Wakefieldian settlements of Nelson, Canterbury and Otago, the term 'West Coast' was used to describe a 300-mile strip of country stretching from Kahurangi Point in the north to beyond Jackson Bay in the south. When the settler administrations drew their boundary lines, the title 'West Canterbury' was attached to land south of the confluence of the Grey

9 May, *West Coast Gold Rushes*, pp. 71–73.
10 May, *West Coast Gold Rushes*, p. 89.
11 May, *West Coast Gold Rushes*, p. 311.
12 May, *West Coast Gold Rushes*, p. 311.
13 May, *West Coast Gold Rushes*, p. 311.
14 May, *West Coast Gold Rushes*, p. 311, quoting *Nelson Examiner*, 20 January 1866.

and Arnold rivers and 'West Nelson' to all land to the north. The term 'West-land', came to be used as an alternative to 'West Canterbury'. In the aftermath of the gold rushes it was adopted to describe the County of Westland (1868) and, from 1873 to 1876, the Province of Westland. May endorsed the contemporary definitions; the 'West Coast' of his title extends from Kahurangi Point in the north to beyond Jackson Bay in the south. There can be no doubt that the epicentre of his history is Hokitika and its hinterland; within a radius of 17 miles lay three of the biggest West Coast diggings—Waimea, Kaniere and Ross.

Māori presence notwithstanding, to the diggers the West Coast was an empty land. To historians, what set the West Coast variant of the gold rush apart was the coming together of experienced, acquisitive newcomers and a wilderness. The forty-niners in California were preceded by cattle ranches and mission stations, the eastern Australian rushes of New South Wales and Victoria took place in a gigantic sheep walk, and in New Zealand the squatters had already explored and occupied the gold-bearing country inland from Dunedin. Pioneers as well as miners, the diggers thus became, in European terms, the region's founding fathers. Their arrival initiated settlement and compressed into a few frenzied years the foundation of a region whose development was otherwise destined to be dictated by the more measured exploitation of coal and timber. Only gold could attract the capital needed to overcome an environment whose treacherous harbours, frequently swollen rivers and broken terrain had frustrated explorers and confined investment to the planned colonies of the east and the pastoral and agricultural potential of their hinterlands. Indeed, as May makes abundantly clear, the pioneering phase of West Coast history needs to be seen as part of a 'rushing' phenomenon that marked the search for gold across the Pacific borderlands in the middle of the nineteenth century. Within this framework the West Coast rushes developed as part of an Australasian mining frontier in which it became an economic dependency of Victoria.

As a mining frontier land and as an extension of the Australian goldfields, the West Coast developed in ways that gave it a number of distinctive features. Despite coming at the end of the gold rush chain, the West Coast's founding population remained surprisingly youthful. Nearly 80 per cent of those who rushed to Hokitika and Greymouth were aged between 21 and 40, at a time when less than half the colonial population fell into that age group. Put another way, in 1867 the West Coast contained 12 per cent of New Zealand's European population but 25 per cent of the men between 21 and 40 years of age. The preponderance of men and the continued unrestrained flow of gold seekers seemed briefly to threaten the neat calculations that underpinned the settlement plans of provincial leaders in the east. But, as in so much of West Coast history, the Southern Alps determined that the contamination of the planned east by the unrestrained and unrestrainable diggers faded as quickly as the hopes of disappointed gold seekers. And it remained a fact of life on the diggings that men long outnumbered women. Even in 1867 there were fewer than 3,500 on the entire West Coast.[15]

Behind the fears of gender-imbalance expressed by east Canterbury political leaders lay questions of potential disorder and disruption. The spectre of an unruly gold-rush horde peopled by undesirables was quickly dismissed by May. In social background the goldmining communities of the West Coast differed in significant ways from the relatively homogeneous planned colonies of Canterbury and Nelson. Like their parent communities, they were mostly British-born (80 per cent), and noticeably more cosmopolitan: with 14 per cent from continental Europe and 3.7 per cent from America, when the proportion of foreign born in Canterbury and Nelson totalled barely 4–5 per cent. There was also a 'big Irish minority':[16] 26 per cent as opposed to 13 per cent for the colony, 4.1 per cent for Nelson and 10.9 per cent for Canterbury.[17] Of these differences, it was the Irish element that was to play the more significant part in the unfolding of West Coast history. As they applied to gold rush society, however, these defining differences—more cosmopolitan and more Irish—were of greater concern to sections of the Canterbury establishment than they were to the diggers. As May puts it, the bulk of the Canterbury settlers had more in common with the typical digger than with the 'cultured middle-class families' who set the social tone and provided the political leadership of the province. Conversely, by the time the typical digger had made his way along the goldfield chain of the Pacific borderlands, he had 'undergone a process of' natural 'selection more rigorous than any English emigration agent might' have applied.[18]

15 May, *West Coast Gold Rushes*, pp. 282–83.
16 May, *West Coast Gold Rushes*, p. 286.
17 May, *West Coast Gold Rushes*, p. 284.
18 May, *West Coast Gold Rushes*, pp. 284–85.

The typical digger might have been a seasoned hand but would the label settler or colonist fit as well? May detected 'few signs of attachment to the place'[19] among the early diggers. The richest claim was always a 'homeward-bounder'.[20] The utilitarian approach to the land and its resources that marked their activities modified only slowly. The rawness of the terrain through which they moved coupled with an almost frenetic mobility that allowed little of permanence to take root produced squalor. Kaniere was 'a mere bog, the houses surrounded with pools of foetid water'.[21] On stormy nights the primitive campsites of tents and whares were a cacophony of 'flapping canvas and corrugated iron'.[22] Overrun by rats, bombarded by bush flies, mosquitoes and sandflies, the camps were incubators of sickness and disease. More than San Francisco and what May calls the 'the trinity of colonial capitals'[23]—Sydney, Melbourne and Dunedin—the emerging river ports of Greymouth, Westport and Hokitika were thrown together in the midst of what must have seemed like a 'peculiar human tsunami'.[24] Greymouth preceded Hokitika in sequence but took some time to shrug off the appearance of 'a big transit camp through which men drank their way into the Grey Valley'.[25] It was upon Hokitika that the title 'goldfields capital' was bestowed. Yet even here a sense of permanency developed slowly. One early visitor thought the town likely to be washed out to sea.[26] Another commentator described a town where:

> The Commissioner lives in a tent, the wardens are accommodated ditto; prisoners are locked into a couple of twelve feet square wooden boxes; the court-house is a flimsy weather-boarded affair, about the size of a small cottage; hotels are of cabbage trees, calico, unseasoned boards and corrugated iron, tricked out with desperately big signs and loud bars; houses, tents, hovels and V-huts of so unsubstantial a character as to baffle description. Many of them seem to be nothing but masses of rags and old iron, the sort of rubbish that is usually found in a marine store.[27]

19 May, *West Coast Gold Rushes*, p. 294.
20 May, *West Coast Gold Rushes*, p. 286.
21 May, *West Coast Gold Rushes*, p. 289.
22 May, *West Coast Gold Rushes,* p. 289.
23 May, *Hokitika: Goldfields Capital*, p. 11.
24 James Belich, *Making Peoples: A History of the New Zealanders from Polynesian Settlement to the End of the Nineteenth Century*, Auckland, Penguin Press, 1996, p. 346.
25 May, *West Coast Gold Rushes*, p. 354.
26 May, *Hokitika: Goldfields Capital*, p. 29.
27 May, *Hokitika: Goldfields Capital*, p. 29.

Among the calico, canvas and corrugated iron, the survival instincts of the merchants and shopkeepers found communal expression in the formation of an Improvement Committee. This incipient sense of community came to be matched on the diggings by a cooperation born of agitation about claim, sluice and water rights. And, as we shall see, these separate forms of combination came to constitute the critical divide in goldfields politics.

Life on the diggings was predicated upon luck. The West Coast environment put a premium on experience and versatility; the seasoned had more luck than the adventurer. It was the precise nature of this seasoning that interested May. The West Coast goldfields had much in common with the other alluvial fields of the mid-nineteenth century. Each goldfield possessed distinctive features that taxed the ingenuity of the practical miner and it was only when experience and circumstance gelled that gold was more efficiently and quickly won. More diggers from California on the Waimea, May suggests, might have led to an earlier recognition that the field met the preconditions for the adoption of hydraulic mining—abundant rainfall, a very general distribution of gold and the prevalence of terrace country. Recovering the beach leads and buried beach leads of the West Coast[28] can also be traced to Californian diggers. Hartley and Reilly had passed on the method of saving river beach gold to men on the Clutha River and this experience came westwards with Otago miners and was adapted to suit local circumstances. On the West Coast deep-lead mining was unique to Ross, but the Victorians were well-steeped in its intricacies.

The experience of individual diggers was the single most important ingredient in the development of the West Coast goldfields. Westland's founding fathers were, as May was later to write, not so much New Zealand colonists as 'a variety of the *genus* Pacific Man whose habitat is no particular country but the goldfields'.[29] If their individual experiences frequently determined the where and when of gold recovery, their collective prehistory, as it was understood by contemporaries, did much to shape the framework in which it was played out. And, in the unfolding tale of the Pacific borderlands gold rushes, the New Zealand fields benefited from bringing up the tail. Nowhere was this more fundamental

28 May, *West Coast Gold Rushes*, pp. 250–51.

29 Philip Ross May, 'Gold Rushes of the Pacific Borderlands: A Comparative Survey', in Len Richardson and W. David McIntyre, eds, *Provincial Perspectives: Essays in Honour of W.J. Gardner*, Christchurch, University of Canterbury/Whitcoulls, 1980, p. 100.

than in the construction of the legal and political framework against which the New Zealand rushes took place. This accident of chronology does much to explain why violence and disorder were less in evidence on the West Coast and Otago goldfields than in California. In 1848, when California became American and gold was discovered, the territory was under tenuous military control, the legal provisions governing precious metal exploitation were weak, and the goldfields remote from a federal authority absorbed with the pressing issue of slavery. Australia's goldfield communities largely stood on the shoulders of the Californian experience but developed a comparatively less troubled mining frontier. May describes the legislative framework in which the Australian gold rushes occurred as 'musty'. It was the presence, he suggested, of a more homogeneous and overwhelmingly British army of diggers familiar with, if not always amenable to, British law, that shaped events in Australia. Drawing heavily upon the Australian experience, New Zealand's goldfields legislation (*Gold Duty Act 1858* and *Gold Fields Act 1858*) preceded the discovery of gold and, with subsequent modifications (1860–67), provided a less contentious legislative framework.[30]

If the West Coast's founding fathers were (in comparison with the bulk of New Zealand's colonists) seasoned colonists, there remained some ambiguity about the label. Their very occupation was synonymous with transience and impermanence. Whether they became settlers or disappeared into the history books as sojourners was determined in one way or another by what they made of their circumstances. As we have already seen, attachment to place developed firstly as an offshoot of commercial and mercantile calculation. Among the diggers the sense of a West Coast goldfield community was moulded by the exigencies of time and place. To newcomers it seemed 'queer country for a gold rush'.[31] Everywhere the thick bush complicated assessment of the gold-bearing potential of the place: would a few creek-finds a gold rush make? Many did not ponder the question long and in any given week departures might outnumber arrivals. The rush to the Waimea, in March 1865, transformed expectations as 3,500 miners crammed into a maze of creeks and side gullies. By July there were 3,000 on the flats and terraces of the Kaniere district. And 100 wood and iron businesses serviced a more technologically diverse goldfield with tunnels into the sides of terraces and

30 May, *West Coast Gold Rushes*, p. 256.
31 May, *West Coast Gold Rushes*, p. 153.

shafts 20 feet into the low-lying paddocks. Together with the rush to the Totara (Ross), where cradling, shallow-sinking and deep-lead mining all prevailed, these southern rushes were to establish Hokitika as a goldfields capital. Between 1864 and 1867, it was the great West Coast entrepôt for the entire goldfields from Ōkārito to Westport.

Grey Valley developments were more gradual and less spectacular. The initial discoveries had suggested that Greymouth would become the predominant entry port. It struggled, as we have noted, to become anything more than a staging post on the road to Hokitika. The shallow creek workings that developed along the lateral tributaries of the Grey River did not produce significant goldtowns but gave rise to separate camps—such as Blackball, Moonlight, Red Jacks, No Town and Twelve Mile Creek—of typically between 100 and 500 miners and reliant upon Greymouth as their service centre. The exploitation of beach-sand gold at South Beach and Cobden redressed the balance, but it was not until the advent of 'King Coal' in the first two decades of the twentieth century that the economic and political centre of gravity shifted north.[32] In comparison with the southern port, Greymouth struggled to throw off the image of impermanence.[33]

A more hazardous river port than Hokitika, Greymouth developed a substantial coastal and Australian trade: its custom's revenue was the sixth largest in the colony; its imports ranked seventh in value; and more vessels called there than at Lyttelton.[34] To its geographical disadvantage was added the complication of land tenure. Greymouth was not one town, but two. Boundary Street marked the divide between the 'Maori Township' and the 'Government Township', the one occupied on Māori lease, the other on business licence (and after 1866 on freehold as well). It was a divide that was to shape the early development of the town and, by discouraging commitment to the place by storekeepers and merchants, lent a greater impermanence to the townscape. To add to the hesitations caused by land tenure was the complication of a provincial boundary that took the Grey River as its marker and produced a brief jostling for dominance as the Nelson Provincial Government sought to develop Cobden as a port.

32 T.E.Y. Seddon, *The Seddons: An Autobiography*, Auckland, Collins, 1968, pp. 185–86.
33 May, *West Coast Gold Rushes*, p. 354.
34 May, *West Coast Gold Rushes*, p. 353.

In less than three years, Hokitika had shrugged off the appearance of a calico and canvas settlement and become a significant colonial town. With a population of 4,688 in 1867, it was New Zealand's sixth largest. May chronicles the transformation and demonstrates that the power of gold and the ingenuity of the gold seekers brought instant civilisation to a scarcely encouraging setting. With a 'capricious river at the front door, the stormy sea at the back, and a forested swamp at the side', Hokitika's natural boundaries were formidable and suggested 'a strong probability of the whole fabric going some day out to sea'.[35] Incessant rain could quickly convert the town into 'an unmitigated swamp'. So flimsy were many of the buildings that storms frequently tore sheets of corrugated iron from their side walls, stripped the more substantial wooden facades from frontages and drove them into the mud. The tents and shanties of new arrivals stood alongside 'pigsties, slaughterhouses, and stables' that produced an 'indescribably disgusting stench',[36] which 'wafted over the whole of Hokitika'.[37]

The speed and flimsiness of instant Hokitika was in part a product of the tenuous leasehold that business licences bestowed on the owners of the original town allotments. In 1866, however, the Canterbury Government withdrew Hokitika from the Gold Fields Act and licence holders were able to convert their leases to freehold; as they did so, the townscape gradually took on a more substantial look. Shanties became hotels and stores, the bigger ones adorned with verandahs and plate glass windows. Nearer the river a residential quarter emerged with 'pleasant villas and pretty flower gardens'. And, as May noted, with obvious pleasure, by 1866 Hokitika was dismissing Christchurch as 'that delectable cluster of nondescript buildings'.[38] In such irony did the germ of civic pride or sense of place begin to take root.

Important as Hokitika and Greymouth were as markers of civilisation and as the visible sign of an emergent West Coast, it is 'the miners' in the camps and settlements of the goldfields who take centre stage. By placing the miners firmly against the particularities of the West Coast goldfields, May creates a distinctively Antipodean digger. In doing so, he worked an important shift in the way historians thought about the gold rushes.

35 May, *Hokitika: Goldfields Capital*, pp. 28–29.
36 May, *Hokitika: Goldfields Capital*, p. 31.
37 May, *Hokitika: Goldfields Capital*, p. 31.
38 May, *Hokitika: Goldfields Capital*, p. 35.

In 1940 W.P. Morrell had produced *The Gold Rushes*, an ambitious survey that traced the quest for gold from ancient times to those of Spanish America, through Siberia to California, to British Columbia and the Rocky Mountain states, to Ballarat and Bendigo, across the Tasman to New Zealand and back to Western Australia and South Africa before heading to Alaska and the Klondike. His context was a European one:

> it was upon the gold-seekers that there descended most of the spirit of the Conquistadores and the Elizabethans—not their zest for the unknown, their carelessness of consequence. They were as typical of the nineteenth century as those other adventurers of the sixteenth, though they plundered Mother nature rather than their fellow-men.[39]

Yet whereas 'only a few hundred could conquer with Cortes and Pizarro or sail with Drake', tens of thousands of men took part in the nineteenth-century rushes and made them 'adventures of the common man'.[40] As Morrell saw it, the best of them were transformed by the experience and became 'a new type of self-reliant character' who created a 'new free, careless social life'.[41]

May's picture of the gold seekers is a more subtle one. Similar in social background to the greater majority of colonists in the planned settlements of Nelson, Otago and Canterbury, the West Coast gold seekers, by virtue of the experiences gleaned along the goldfields of the Pacific borderlands, were seasoned hands rather than new chums. They brought with them the rudiments of practical geology and mining lore and, as practical men, sought to apply their experience to a goldfield that presented its own peculiar set of problems. Their reading of the land they passed over drew upon the peculiar mix of experience they could call upon. The first wave of diggers who trudged along the beaches between Hokitika and Greymouth would, May reminds us, have been unaware of Californian beach-workings. Any 'forty-niners' among them would have moved out from California long before sea-beach claims there had proved payable. But, by August 1865, when a lump of gold and mercury amalgam weighing more than a hundredweight and yielding more than 100 pounds was discovered, forty-niners were thicker on the ground. Taking their lead from the 'Californians', the diggers familiarised themselves quickly with

39 W.P. Morrell, *The Gold Rushes*, 2nd edn, London, Black, 1968, p. 415.

40 Morrell, *Gold Rushes*, p. 415.

41 Morrell, *Gold Rushes*, p. 415.

the methods of fine-gold saving using mercury.[42] A new form of cradle using copper plates covered with mercury film, introduced by 'an old Brazilian and Californian miner',[43] soon became the preferred option.

Similarly, May's discussion of the introduction of hydraulic sluicing (directing a jet of water under pressure against a terrace face) further illustrates the constant interplay between the practical diggers' collective Pacific borderland experience and their new mining environment. In *The West Coast Gold Rushes*, May suggests that the origin of hydraulic mining lay in California (a suggestion he was later to develop in a monograph, *Origins of Hydraulic Mining in California* (1970)).[44] The West Coast's much-terraced landscape, high rainfall and dense bush that yielded the timber for boxing and fluming needed for sluicing provided an ideal environment for hydraulic mining. Its widespread adoption came slowly. Only as defined leads were exhausted and the miners confronted great blocks of relatively poor auriferous country did the advantages of hydraulicking become obvious. As in the case of beach-sand deposits, the miners pooled their cumulative experiences. Diggers, familiar only with the water-scarce goldfields of Victoria, followed the leads of those with experience of the water-rich Californian and Otago goldfields.

May's closely textured narrative follows the miners as they adjust and adapt techniques and procedures to fit the realities of the West Coast mining environment. Water dominated all else. Its abundance made hydraulic mining possible but also created insuperable drainage problems. Storm channels, underground adits, giant waterwheels and a range of pumping devices necessarily became a distinctive feature of West Coast goldmining. Ground-sluicing, whose significance, May shrewdly observes, had been underrated by gold rush historians because it was a technique that lacked any distinctive piece of equipment, became the universal mode of working the inland diggings. The plentiful supply of timber meant that steam engines were soon a common sight driving pumps and circular saws, and the larger communities began to take on a heightened industrial appearance;[45] the more complex and diverse pattern of mining marked the end of the diggings as a small man's frontier.[46]

42 May, *West Coast Gold Rushes*, pp. 176–77.

43 May, *West Coast Gold Rushes*, p. 177.

44 Philip Ross May, *Origins of Hydraulic Mining in California*, Oakland, California, The Holmes Book Company, 1970.

45 May, *West Coast Gold Rushes*, p. 200.

46 May, *Origins of Hydraulic Mining in California*, p. 29.

The story of how a rush became an industry presented in *The West Coast Gold Rushes* is further developed in *Gold Town*,[47] May's history of Ross. Here, extensive terraces deeply trenched by gullies demanded greater capital investment and spoke of a future in which individual diggers pooled their resources and, increasingly, waged men became a feature of the goldfields. The transformation is best observed as attention turned to the deep leads of Ross. Aptly christened the 'Ballarat of Westland', it was here that the most imposing mining complex emerged, as progressively more sophisticated methods were needed to lift water and gravel from the deeper shafts. May chronicles the transformation with enthusiasm. Beyond 45 feet hand-windlasses were ineffective and horse whims (a wooden drum, mounted near the mouth of a shaft, with a horse harnessed beneath walking in a circle and revolving the drum) were soon in evidence. To open up the even deeper leads, a 20-horsepower steam engine was driving a 17-hundredweight flywheel on a 42-foot poppet-head of heavy unhewn spars above a 125-foot shaft divided into three compartments—two for winding and one for pumping. Each 24-hour day the Scandinavian Company brought 400–500 loads to the surface and employed some 50 wage labourers. Half a dozen similar industrial plants followed and they gave the district a greater permanence than was the norm for an alluvial field. May sketches the scene at Jones's Flat: 'at the mouth of the gully, hand-windlasses; beyond them, thirty-three whimshafts and an occasional whip of waterwheel claim; beyond these, the poppet-heads of the companies dwarfing the stores and shanties'.[48] Such was the face of Ross, the product of a combination of capital and labour unique on the West Coast goldfields.

Behind this transformation lay a hardheaded practicality, a single-minded concentration upon the immediate environment and the quest for gold. If these preoccupations appeared at first so narrowly conceived as to be devoid of any attachment to place, such attitudes were a necessary component of permanent settlement. The greater sense of permanence that followed industrial consolidation ultimately moderated the improvisation and haste that had made the West Coast goldfields a raw and dangerous place. 'Rushing' was a risky enterprise, and May speculates that accidental deaths on the Otago and West Coast goldfields 'probably exceeded European casualties' in the New Zealand wars.[49] On the West

47 Philip Ross May, *Gold Town, Ross, Westland*, Christchurch, Pegasus, 1970.

48 May, *Gold Town*, p. 37.

49 May, *West Coast Gold Rushes*, p. 292.

Coast, death by drowning was predictably the most common cause of sudden death. The rush to be rich created a recklessness that made every river a 'likely grave'. In the three years from November 1864, rivers and streams accounted for nearly half (47 per cent) of the 239 deaths, and a further 20 per cent perished in mining accidents.[50] The high mortality rate reflected, in May's view, the spirit of the times. As mining moved beyond the simple creek and gully stage, the West Coast goldfields had become more rather than less dangerous. On the deep ground at Ross, tunnel collapses and shaft cave-ins were at first frequent. The more stable communities of the 1870s imposed new standards and gradually expunged the mentality of rushing, but improvisation remained at the heart of West Coast life.

The combination of harsh conditions and hardheaded, practical men produced a peculiar political landscape. As noted earlier, unlike the Victorian political motherlode, the West Coast goldfields produced no Peter Lalor, no republican charter, no Eureka rebellion, and generated no flag under which a powerful and myth-sustaining legend might flourish. By May's account, several things worked against this: New Zealand benefited from bringing up the tail of the gold rush that rippled through the Pacific borderlands (California, Australia and New Zealand); and New Zealand had legislation (Gold Duty Act, Gold Fields Act) in place before the major rushes occurred. After 1860, all who possessed the miners' right, provided they met a residential requirement of three months, were eligible to vote. With a few subsequent modifications throughout the 1860s, this was a framework that proved workable. Such friction as occurred in hammering out the details of licence fees, size and tenure of claim and water rights was minimal. Where such matters were concerned the miners were a litigious lot but not a riotous one. Political activity on the Coast was less dramatic, couched in milder terms and directed at more immediate ends.

The democracy of the diggings was that of the small, independent capitalist. A part of both the Nelson and Canterbury provinces, the 'West Coast' was a hybrid political being. Boundary lines bore no relation to the pattern of gold discoveries, created additional costs for the miners, led to law enforcement difficulties and produced squabbles over the collection of customs duties. The heartland of May's gold rush saga, however, was

50 May, *West Coast Gold Rushes*, p. 292.

'West Canterbury'—that bit of the 'West Coast' south of the Arnold and Grey River junction—and its political history was inevitably bound up with the expectations of the landowning elite that determined Canterbury provincial politics. Fearful at first that a rush 'over the Hill' might upset the social and economic balance of their province, Canterbury's political leaders were ambivalent in their attitude to their remote goldfields and created a goldfields administration that maintained order without becoming a drain on provincial finances.

Criticism of the remote provincial administration was the stuff of emergent goldfields politics. George Sale, the resident Commissioner, was the immediate target. As 'King' Sale, he became the butt of caricature and was compared unfavourably, by the diggers, with his counterpart on the Nelson South-West goldfields, the flamboyant and democratically inclined T.A.S. Kynnersley. Sale was, in many respects, the archetypal imperial administrator. Born at Rugby in the English Midlands, he had attended the middle-ranking public school that took its name from the town and was to pass it on to a form of football. A day boy in 1845 when the rules of the rugby code were first written down, he was among the game's founding fathers in Dunedin, where, in 1870, his firsts in classics from Cambridge had provided his passage to the inaugural chair of classics at Otago University.[51] As a loyal Rugbeian and Cambridge man, he was keen to head off the rival code of Victorian Rules that had crossed the Tasman with the thousands of diggers who had learned the Australian game in Melbourne or on the goldfields at Ballarat and Bendigo. With this pedigree, Sale moved more easily among the political leaders of the Canterbury establishment than among the bulk of the diggers, or so it seemed to many on the diggings. Whatever his dictatorial inclinations, as Commissioner of the West Canterbury goldfields, 'King' Sale was the representative of a political system that could not last. He had been given wide powers but lacked the resources to meet the myriad demands of a rapidly expanding and mobile population and was, as May put it, a 'powerless servant of a distant and alien Government'.[52]

51 Sean O'Hagan, *The Pride of Southern Rebels: On the Occasion of the Otago Rugby Football Union Centenary, 1881–1981*, Dunedin, Pilgrims South Press, 1981, pp. 14–15.
52 May, *West Coast Gold Rushes*, p. 268.

Whatever the level of digger unrest on the West Coast goldfields, it was not, as the Canterbury establishment suggested, the work of a 'big Irish minority'.[53] In dismissing this view, May cites, with approval, the judgement of a Roman Catholic priest: 'the Irish miners in Westland came from well-to-do classes at home … sons of well-to-do farmers'.[54] He presents evidence that the number of Irish to appear before the courts was in keeping with their proportion of the population. In the years of the rush the West Coast Irish were, as May points out, 'less evident in business circles, except as small storekeepers and publicans'.[55] Over time, as a recent historian explains, their greater numerical strength among the earliest arrivals allowed them to become part of a 'diverse "charter group"' that exercised 'a powerful role in defining the nature of local community life'.[56] When revisiting West Coast history in *Vanished Kingdoms* (1990), Pat O'Farrell puts it more bluntly; in many ways, the West Coast Irish Catholics became the establishment.[57] As such, they found their place in all sections of the economy in a manner that 'matched regional patterns of occupational attainment and general prosperity' elsewhere.[58]

As diggers, the Irish were unremarkable. Their sheer number, however, created a visibility and produced, as we have seen, fertile ground for the perpetuation of old-world prejudices. The same concentration provided the critical mass necessary for the public display of political and sectarian loyalties to Irish causes. As May put it, 'Trouble in Ireland rather than trouble on the West Coast' provided the fuel for a spate of 'polemico-mining'[59] disputes and donnybrooks. In 1867, a Fenian uprising in Ireland that sought an Irish Republic totally separated from England was the catalyst for a brief surge of sectarianism. Fenian sympathies had been in evidence at Ōkārito in 1866 when £243 8s was sent to Dublin to assist the families of Irish prisoners in the hands of the English. And, in November 1867, John Manning, an adventurous and literary Irishman whose articles in the *Ballarat Times* had led to a charge of high treason,[60] commenced publishing the *New Zealand Celt* 'apparently with the intention of

53 May, *West Coast Gold Rushes*, p. 307.

54 May, *West Coast Gold Rushes*, p. 285.

55 May, *West Coast Gold Rushes*, p. 311.

56 Lyndon Fraser, *Castles of Gold: A History of New Zealand's West Coast Irish*, Dunedin, Otago University Press, 2007, p. 51.

57 O'Farrell, *Vanished Kingdoms*, pp. 260–72.

58 Fraser, *Castles of Gold*, p. 54.

59 May, *West Coast Gold Rushes*, p. 308.

60 Richard P. Davis, *Irish Issues in New Zealand Politics 1868–1922*, Dunedin, University of Otago Press, 1974, p. 12.

setting things right in Ireland from Hokitika'.[61] Its spiritual 'godfather' was Father William Larkin, a missionary priest from Queensland, who made much of Irish grievances in building his congregations at Waimea and Staffordtown. In William Shaw, the politically ambitious, Irish-born Orange Protestant proprietor of the *West Coast Times*, the *Celt* found a rival also prepared to cast moderation aside.

Local sectarian skirmishes fed off grievances generated in the old world. In 1868 three Fenians were executed in Manchester for the accidental killing of a police sergeant, and in Sydney one Henry James O'Farrell attempted to assassinate the Duke of Edinburgh while visiting Australia. On the West Coast the two events were to provoke what came to be called, rather grandiosely, the 'Fenian Uprising'. The Hokitika Town Council refused the local Irish community permission to place a wooden Celtic Cross in the local cemetery as a memorial to the 'Manchester Martyrs'. During a subsequent mass demonstration, the protesters removed the locked cemetery gates from their hinges, entered the cemetery and, after a service conducted by Father Larkin, planted the cross. As more details of O'Farrell's abortive assassination reached the Coast, tensions grew; the inflammatory outbursts by the *West Coast Times* and the *New Zealand Celt*, and a procession of loyalists, led to civilian military units being formed and hundreds of special constables enrolled. Manning and Larkin were arrested along with five others on charges of 'riot' and subsequently charged also with seditious libel. On the first charge they were fined £20, and on the second, imprisoned for a month.

May's prime interest in the Irish was as a part, and a significant part, of the gold rush community and only secondarily in their future role in the consolidation of that community. The ramifications of 'Fenianism' lay beyond the scope of his study.[62] He does not see episodes of sectarian conflict as indicative of deep-seated animosities likely to reverberate through West Coast history. Rather, he endorses the description of Thomas Kynnersley, the Commissioner of the Nelson South-West goldfields, that on his patch at least the 'Fenian riots' were little more than 'a miserable street row'. To May, the origins of the Hokitika affair lay in:

61 May, *West Coast Gold Rushes*, p. 533.

62 May, *West Coast Gold Rushes*, p. 309.

> An odd conjunction of circumstance, some irresponsible newspaper reporting, and too much ready liquor [that] brought the threatened troubles to the West Coast in 1868 when the boom days were over and people had time to discover grievances.[63]

The historian of the years immediately after the gold rush subsided thought that the 'Fenian' affair revealed underlying 'social and economic cleavages': the creditor/debtor relationship between the big wholesale merchants and commission agents of Hokitika (who were generally of English, Scots or German extraction) and the small shopkeepers and miners of the Waimea diggings, many of whom were Irish Catholics, 'exacerbated' 'religious differences'.[64] The 'suppression' of the 'Fenian' movement added to the ingrained hostility of the goldfields towards Hokitika and ensured that the Irish vote and sectarian differences maintained a persistent presence in the politics of county and province (1868–76) and beyond.

Put simply, the West Coast defied the neat categories of the systematic colonisers. Gold populated the wilderness and defined attitudes to the land itself. Mineral rights belonged to the Crown; the right to exploit them was parcelled out in a system of licences that categorised 'claims' by those who paid £1 a year for a miners' right, according to the type of deposit—alluvial, river, creek, beach or quartz. Defining non-auriferous land and assigning values to it was, from the beginning, contentious. The land regulations of the Canterbury settlement had imposed a uniform price of £2 per acre on rural land and the cost of town lots reckoned on clear land. The first was designed to encourage agriculture and prevent the dispersal implicit in pastoralism, the latter to encourage concentration of settlement and thus provide the nucleus of civilised urban culture. As a blueprint for development, the regulations matched West Coast realities even less than they did the sheep lands of Canterbury. A cluster of buildings was giving shape to Hokitika before the regulations had been framed, and the price of rural land took no account of clearing bush, estimated to cost between £30 and £40 per acre. To prospective West Coast landowners the land price was seen as a revenue-raising device to offset the cost of running the goldfields and especially the building of the Otira Road.[65]

63 May, *West Coast Gold Rushes*, pp. 308–9.

64 Bernard Conradson, 'Politics and Penury: County and Province, 1868–1876', in Philip Ross May, ed., *Miners and Militants: Politics in Westland 1865–1918*, Christchurch, Whitcoulls for the University of Canterbury, 1975, p. 32.

65 May, *West Coast Gold Rushes*, p. 402.

May's interest in the dilemmas that surrounded land is primarily related to the unfolding of the gold rush. His narrative also provides a glimpse of the future as it explores how the germ of a West Coast community emerged, as it were, from within the tide of events that collectively comprised the gold rush. Agriculture developed slowly, with 540 acres under crop by 1868.[66] Small market gardens on land leased for five shillings per acre and subject to cancellation if gold was subsequently discovered near the main townships. Cattle made an early appearance on a few river flats, but pastoralism was equally slow to take root. By 1867 some 5,000 acres had been freeholded, predominantly to the north of Greymouth and most promisingly on the elevated tableland of Ahaura and Totara Flat, and only 215 acres taken up south of the confluence of the Grey and Arnold rivers. Within a decade, pioneer farmers had taken up land along the most fertile river flats between Arahura and Jackson Bay. By the end of the nineteenth century these farming pockets had developed sufficiently for a cluster of dairy factories, firstly in Totara Flat (1895) and subsequently at Kokatahi, Arahura, Kumara, Whataroa, Waitaha and Hokitika. Only after the opening of the Otira tunnel in 1923 was dairying able to expand beyond its local market.

The reliance upon shipping, as a means of provisioning and providing a source of income, was long to hamper development. Not even timber proved capable of overcoming isolation. The early timber industry catered for a purely local market and profited from some creative responses to the dilemmas of shifting heavy or bulky merchandise through dense bush. Among the most inventive was the wooden tramway. Quickly built, they made relatively poor auriferous land rich by reducing the costs of provisions, provided employment for luckless diggers, a foundation for later permanent roads and quick profits for the merchant-dominated companies that financed their construction. As May put it, the 'tramway fever was as active as the gold-bug'.[67] Fifty per cent annually was considered a fair return for a pathway to a gold deposit that might be worked out in a few years. Cradles, sluice-boxes, fluming, waterwheels fashioned from rimu and kahikatea trunks provided the basis of a less speculative sawmilling industry. By 1866, local 'sawn' timber was competing with the imported product for local construction. Timber continued to be logged,

66 May, *West Coast Gold Rushes*, p. 498.
67 May, *West Coast Gold Rushes*, p. 372.

however, at a faster rate by goldminers clearing land than by sawmilling operators, and more timber was consigned to the flames, or simply left to rot, than was converted by axe or saw.

In 1868 the first four cargoes of white pine were despatched to Melbourne. It was the Australian market that by the mid-1890s allowed the West Coast to become a net exporter of rough sawn timber and New Zealand's leading sawmilling region, producing 20 per cent of national production in 1916. Only after the completion of the Otira tunnel in 1923 did Canterbury surpass Australia as the largest single market for West Coast timber. The tale of the timber merchants underlined the fundamental West Coast dilemma. The riches produced by gold were not used to lay the foundation for the future. There were, as contemporaries were quick to point out, other more promising and safer avenues of investment and most of them in Australia. Looking back from the vantage point of 1960, May traces how the ownership of the timber industry was quickly dominated by merchants from elsewhere in New Zealand. In that year, just under three-quarters of West Coast timber mills were owned by outside interests, some 38 per cent in Canterbury hands and the rest distributed between Auckland, Dunedin and Wellington (16, 14 and 5 per cent respectively).[68] It was a pattern repeated in the early development of coalmining where it ultimately required the intrusion of the state in the 1940s to overcome the difficulties of maintaining the industry.

Gold had peopled the place but did not provide the impetus for future development. 'No other part of New Zealand', May suggests, 'exported its substance, its pioneers and the sons of its pioneers so freely.'[69] Too many rush merchants and professional men, who had prospered during the expansionary years, moved on as the rush receded, taking with them their capital and experience. Those who remained had to find a way to sustain the place. Around them, already visible as they faced the future, were the familiar signs of exploitation and decay that set mining regions apart. In 1962 as May completed *The West Coast Gold Rushes*, it seemed that the coalmining townships of the Grey Valley were beginning to resemble the fading goldtowns they had replaced.[70] It was precisely this juxtaposition of vigorous exploitation and gradual decay that lies at the heart of the 'West Coasts' that Pat O'Farrell and Bill Pearson created.

68 May, *West Coast Gold Rushes*, p. 501.
69 May, *West Coast Gold Rushes*, p. 501.
70 May, *West Coast Gold Rushes*, p. 501.

In 1969 May returned to this theme in *Gold Town*, a lovingly sketched and illustrated history of Ross, his hometown. Here, May traces the post–gold rush experience of a single mining community. The deep leads of Ross had made it the 'Ballarat of Westland' and gave it a permanence unusual for an alluvial goldfield. Until the 1870s it was one of New Zealand's most stable and productive fields, but a long and steady decline set in after 1872. Seasoned hands reckoned that the influx of more Chinese miners on old alluvial ground reworking tailings and leaner gravels abandoned by European miners was a sign of a goldfield entering its death throes.[71] Water was the problem: pumping it out of the deep leads had become increasingly costly and the transition to hydraulic mining even more so. But, in May's words, it was 'time to abandon the essentially Victorian technique for the more efficient and appropriate Californian'.[72] In this way, the high gravel deposits resting upon 'Old-man bottom' could be flushed out by heavy and uninterrupted floods of water.

The advent of hydraulic mining brought in its wake something of an industrial revolution and transformed the physical environment. Within 30 years Jones's Flat, at the heart of the Ross diggings, had become a huge amphitheatre worked to a depth of nearly 100 feet by hydraulic nozzles, bucket elevator and incline tram and underground drainage adit. By 1885 more than 110 miles of water race took water to 320 sluice heads, and the hills were pocked with 49 dams and 29 reservoirs.[73] Twenty years later, the industry employed fewer than 30 in Ross and the town was casting about for a new economic base. Goldmining had stimulated a local market for timber. But, in a region where bush was everywhere, Ross was poorly placed to compete. Until a rail link to Hokitika was established in 1909, sawmilling found its natural home along the Hokitika–Greymouth railway and between the northern town and Lake Brunner as the Midland line was pushed eastwards. With the completion of the Otira tunnel in 1923, Ross was better able to find a place in the West Coast timber industry. Thus, as May wrote in 1969, 'Old gold town was converted to young timber town and miners' sons to millers',[74] who now made up more than 50 per cent of the male workforce. Something of the hardrock mining tradition persisted in the quarrying of limestone from the terraces beyond the town by a farmers' cooperative. One historian has characterised this

71 May, *Gold Town*, p. 47.
72 May, *Gold Town*, p. 49.
73 May, *Gold Town*, p. 57.
74 May, *Gold Town*, p. 97.

process of adaptation as evidence that in regions where runholders and merinos did not dominate, the 'stayers' among the miners of the 1860s provided the basis of a property-owning democracy of independent artisans and miners. By easing their way onto small subsistence farms and grazing a cow and maybe a horse, they provided the core of a lasting community.[75] The difficulty for Ross, as for the region as a whole, as May was well aware, lay in two related aspects of the West Coast experience: more diversified as the local economy might be, its future depended upon wasting assets. Few writing in the 1960s would have been brave enough to predict a future economy built on farming and tourism.

75 Erik Olssen, 'Lands of Sheep and Gold: The Australian Dimension to the New Zealand Past, 1840–1900', in Keith Sinclair, ed., *Tasman Relations: New Zealand and Australia 1788–1988*, Auckland, Auckland University Press, 1987, p. 46.

4

PATRICK O'FARRELL

The Reds and the Greens

The publication of *Vanished Kingdoms* by the University of New South Wales Press in 1990 did not attract the attention it deserved in New Zealand. Partly this reflects nothing more than the tendency of Australian publishers to neglect the New Zealand market. It is also a reflection of how quickly some twentieth-century experiences of New Zealand life have already become if not invisible then as faded as the snapshots of family photograph albums. Yet Patrick O'Farrell's personal excursion gives us a unique insight into a slice of West Coast history in the 30 or so years after the end of World War I. By chronicling his parents' journey from Borrisokane (Tipperary) to Puketahi Street in the heart of Greymouth's Catholic community, he opens up both the dynamics of the Irish diaspora and confronts again the peculiarities of the West Coast experience that had first troubled him some 30 years earlier. It is a story that unfolds around two events that were to reverberate through the twentieth century—the Russian Revolution and the Irish Rebellion. In the Grey Valley, the contradictory impulses of international Communism and assertive Catholicism were to give a sharper edge to the fragile alliance of the Reds and the Greens that had been stitched together by a community in which, as O'Farrell puts it, a 'worker ethos'[1] prevailed.

1 O'Farrell, *Vanished Kingdoms*, p. 140.

Figure 2: Patrick O'Farrell in 1956 when completing his doctoral thesis at The Australian National University.

Source: Courtesy O'Farrell family.

The roots of the unholy alliance, as its conservative and Protestant critics dubbed it, were to be found among the coalminers, waterside workers, railwaymen and labourers whose employment depended upon the coal trade. To O'Farrell, the miners were the 'closest and most complex of working communities'.[2] His mother found the West Coast variety of

2 O'Farrell, *Vanished Kingdoms*, p. 142.

the species almost frighteningly so. Set apart from the river port towns of Greymouth and Westport, the 'rough and temporary'[3] settlements at Runanga, Blackball, Denniston and Millerton seemed to newcomers like the O'Farrells to resemble a band of strange outsiders living precariously on a 'grimy coastal platform held hard against storm and sea'.[4] Compared with the ordered world they had left behind, the Coast seemed crude, primitive and newborn. It was a mix that had already produced a thrusting and assertive working-class community. Attitudes and traditions, first shaped at the coalface in the old world, expressed themselves in different forms in an environment where improvisation and creativity were needed. In this respect, the unions were agencies of colonialisation. Pragmatic and tough-minded in outlook, the colliers who built unionism anew on the Coast learned quickly that new circumstances required a new unionism. In this they had begun to wrestle with the very same problems that were to preoccupy O'Farrell as he began his exploration of how the Irish migrants of late nineteenth- and early twentieth-century Australasia adjusted to their new environment. What of the old ways of doing things remained essential to their new circumstances?

At the heart of the colliers' experience of the new world was the need to re-establish in the mines the status they had been attempting to construct in the old. As workers whose lives were at risk every time they ventured underground, the miners had sought to develop a protective web of customs and practices that offered some sense of security at the coalface. Over time the appeal to custom might, in favourable circumstances, allow the men at the sharp end of the production process—the hewers—to assert greater control over the way coal was mined. They assumed the status of 'independent collier'[5]—free to manage their own workplaces in ways that allowed them to regulate the pace and pattern of their labour. The transfer of the traditions of the coalface from one mine to another, even within a single coalfield, was often a tortuous process; on the embryonic coalfields of settler societies like Australia and New Zealand, such traditions needed to be built anew. And, for both the coaltowns that developed on the Coast and the unions that stood at their heart, improvisation and tradition proved to be a potent mix. The communities that grew up around the mines that gave them life on the Grey Valley and

3 O'Farrell, *Vanished Kingdoms*, p. 142.
4 O'Farrell, *Vanished Kingdoms*, p. 140.
5 The term 'independent collier' is discussed in Royden Harrison, ed., *Independent Collier: The Coal Miner as Archetypal Proletarian Reconsidered*, Sussex, The Harvester Press, 1978.

Buller coalfields, in the 50 or so years after the creation of the Denniston Miners' Union in 1884, were to play a role in the national history out of all proportion to their size and numerical strength and in ways that were variously condemned and celebrated by a wider community largely ignorant of the miners and their concerns.[6]

It was precisely the newcomer/outsider status of the miners within a society still in the throes of shrugging off the trappings of colonialism that interested O'Farrell. The vagaries of coal seams and the capitalist mode of production together made migrants of the miners. On New Zealand's West Coast they confronted a double separation: they were cut adrift from both the familiar union structure of home and from the embryonic colonial labour movement. In combination, these twin prongs of isolation fanned the ingrained sense of protest that was deeply embedded in mining culture and a powerful ingredient in the ideology of the aspiring independent collier. These were forces that produced a closed and intense enclave of workers preoccupied with the grievances of particular pits yet at times able to launch a wider assault on the coal owners and the capitalist system more generally. Did the peculiarities of the West Coast environment make easier the transition from the narrower concerns of time and place to the more inclusive considerations of occupation and class that might lay the basis of a regional or national labour movement? Or, as O'Farrell asked of May's goldminers in his 1969 review of *The West Coast Gold Rushes* (second edition): did the 'cheerless rotting damp'[7] defeat colliers and coal owners alike?

The first chapter in this contest between migrant miners and colonial environment had its genesis in the attempt to exploit the rich coal deposits of the Buller coalfield. Even by West Coast standards, the coal seams of what was to become Denniston required ingenuity and persistence before they would yield their rich resources. No amount of colonial improvisation was going to overcome the need for experienced labour. And thus it was that the British colliers recruited for the task came as a community apart, newcomers marked out by occupation and an accent that was even then uniformly discordant. It was the miners' collective presence as unionists that was to mark them out as a people apart. Their efforts to consolidate unionism on West Coast coalfields in

6 See Len Richardson, *Coal, Class & Community: The United Mineworkers of New Zealand, 1880–1960*, Auckland, Auckland University Press, 1995.

7 O'Farrell, 'Review: P.R. May, *The West Coast Gold Rushes*', p. 90.

the 1880s came at a time when the colonial economy was contracting, labour/capital relations were hardening and sensitivity to any disruption of shipping was increasing. The initial skirmishes between the miners and coal owners injected the language of class war into an environment where the rhetoric of boosterism and pioneering prevailed. By common consent, the difficulties of the West Coast frontier were obstacle enough without the added complication of colliers whose workplace practices were a mix of ideology, customs and traditions fashioned in the old world. The coal masters of the new world, bent upon establishing an infant industry in circumstances where the odds seemed stacked against them, sought to prevent these attitudes from taking root in their pits. It was this struggle for influence at the point of production that lay behind the first round of labour disputes on the West Coast coalfields.

O'Farrell was less interested in the push and shove of industrial relations than in the world views that underlay them. And the miners who established unionism in the West Coast pits in the 1880s brought with them not only the pragmatism of the pits, grounded as it was in custom and tradition, but also some of the notions that collectively have been labelled by historians as utopian socialism. They were to prove a heady mixture. The belief that society could be transformed by cooperation and rationality without the need for conflict lay at the heart of these beliefs. It was embedded in the cooperative nature of mining and informed the entrenched sense of their own history rooted, as it was, in the grievances of the pit. The miners who assembled at Denniston and Brunner carried with them, from the specific mines they had experienced, historical memories encased, as it were, in a litany of injustices generic to that which bound miners together as a people apart. It was a powerful ingredient and one that at times was capable of converting the pragmatism of the workplace into the realms of wider social protest.

Grievance and protest were the stuff of which the early history of mining unionism on the Grey and Buller coalfields was made. The initial years witnessed a struggle for acceptance as the new arrivals sought to establish the collective right to organise so as to protect long-established work practices. A rash of industrial skirmishes followed as the mine owners sought to limit the influence of old-world unionism in their pits. In these disputes, as O'Farrell notes, the unionists faced difficulties, overcoming the 'individualistic disposition' and restless capitalist impulses of the goldminers whose 'usually hopeful poverty was at such an ebb' that they 'appeared from their lonely gullies'[8] to become strikebreakers. The introduction of new workers with little if any experience underground compromised, in the view of the miners, the safety of the men in the pits. Attempts by unionists to vet all newcomers were rebuffed by the coal owners as intruding upon the prerogatives of management. Unwilling at first to test the miners' resolve, the initial efforts to bring in unskilled labour were abandoned by owners who recognised that in colonial circumstances skilled British colliers were indispensable.

The primitiveness of the West Coast environment provided a setting in which the combined forces of tough-minded pragmatism and utopian idealism might fuse. Methodism was an important conduit between these apparently mutually limiting attitudes of mind. John Lomas, a Methodist lay preacher from Barnsley in southern Yorkshire, became the defining voice of the West Coast mining unionism. From his unlikely Denniston base, he launched New Zealand's first attempt at a national mining organisation. To Lomas, the miners' demands were as rational and just as their rejection by the coal owners was unconscionable and perverse. The union's function, as he saw it, was to give wider expression to the cooperative impulses made necessary by the dangers of mining. Such cooperation might, he believed, be the basis for a wider organisation of labour that might prevail upon employers to see the future in less antagonistic terms. It was a conclusion hastened by the consolidation that was taking place among employers.

In 1888 the Union Steam Ship Company assumed monopoly control of the Grey Valley and the Buller coalfields. To avoid being played off against each other, it now became imperative for the miners to meet combination with combination. To achieve this end the colliers needed to construct novel forms of mining unionism as they knew it. For mining unionism to be effective in the West Coast environment it was essential not only to assert an influence in the pits but also to educate and organise the district's labour force that lacked a tradition of unionism. And the all-embracing tentacles of the 'southern octopus' that was the Union Steam Ship Company drove West Coast miners to seek combination with their Australian counterparts. In 1888 Lomas made his way to Creswick, Victoria, and aligned the West Coast miners with the Amalgamated

8 Patrick O'Farrell, 'Noble National Myths, Bitter Local Reality: 1890 in New Zealand's Grey District', in Jim Hagan and Andrew Wells, eds, *The Maritime Strike: A Centennial Retrospective, Essays in Honour of E.C. Fry*, Wollongong, Five Islands Press, 1992, p. 32.

Miners' and Labourers' Association of Australasia. Over the next two years he became a veritable 'apostle of unionism', preaching the gospel of unionism throughout the colony's coalfields. As such, he became the face and voice of the miners as colonists began to recognise that they had what contemporaries called a 'labour problem'.

At one level, Lomas presented a conciliatory presence in the events that led to the colony's first labour/capital crisis, the Maritime Strike of 1890. Yet there was a steely resolve in his consistent rejection of a market economy that was determined by the untrammelled fluctuations of the law of supply and demand. It was a resolve that was to bring opprobrium upon the miners; what could working men know about how the economy functioned? Newspaper commentators were quick to paint the miners as putting their own petty and parochial concerns ahead of the interests of the colony.[9]

The confrontation that was the Maritime Strike came too soon for the embryonic labour movement. Confronted by a determined phalanx of employers and a government prepared to stand and watch, defeat was inevitable. The utopian socialist impulse that lay behind the miners' first foray into colonial and intercolonial prominence withered in the 1890s. In addressing the issue of what the men of the Grey Valley thought and believed at the time of the Maritime Strike, O'Farrell is characteristically blunt: they 'thought little, believed dreams' and possessed a 'naïve and passive confidence in the omnipotence of combination'.[10] When pushed to explain their actions, the men of the Grey described their actions as 'fighting for a principle' and believed there was something in the very struggle 'that lifts up'. Reflecting upon this, in 1990, O'Farrell thought the justifications seemed 'lame, absurd' but added that in 'a Utopian age, men must have dreams'. The cost of the 'warm glow of (false) commonality and the illusion of shared strength'[11] was, he considered, immense. By the late 1890s:

> Brunner was dead—breathing, but yet an economic and psychological corpse … and its role in the 1890 Strike reads like bad melodrama, desperately sad, ruled by dark and largely impersonal forces, with the human actors shadowy and

9 Richardson, *Coal, Class & Community*, pp. 41–51.
10 O'Farrell, 'Noble National Myths', p. 34.
11 O'Farrell, 'Noble National Myths', p. 34.

> uncomprehending, caught in the grip of their fates. It is a grim play, now badly dated, hard to believe, of no inspiration save for endurance, a performance which will never be staged again.[12]

The pressing problem was to preserve the traditions of the pit in the face of employers determined to deny unionism a presence. This had long been the everyday preoccupation of the miners, and at the coalface this concern was always going to provide the basis for union regeneration in each particular mine. The process was smoothed by legislative and political changes at least in part products of the wave of union activity that had seen the miners emerge as a significant industrial organisation. The Maritime Strike played a significant role in the reconfiguration of colonial politics and the building of what came to be known as the 'Lib–Lab' alliance. It was a realignment that had immediate consequences for West Coast miners. The introduction of the *Industrial Conciliation and Arbitration Act 1894* (ICA Act) allowed the miners to regain the recognition in the pits they had all but lost in the aftermath of the Maritime Strike. The Denniston miners were the first workers in the colony to register under the new legislation that compelled employers to negotiate with the union and provided a process whereby disputes might be resolved by an independent umpire. Surrendering the final word to an arbitrator sat uneasily alongside the desire of the hewers to control work at the coalface. For the moment, however, acceptance of the ICA Act offered a safeguard when the exercise of their industrial muscle at the point of production proved inadequate. It was a compromise grounded in the pragmatism of men unwilling to defer to others on matters that determined the safety of life in the pits.

Revisiting these events 100 years on, and from the perspective of the Grey Valley, O'Farrell offers a grim picture of West Coast realities:

> [T]he workforce was fluctuating and migratory to a degree destructive of all organisation, it was naïve and ill-informed to a degree innocent of and antipathetic towards all ideology, it was bereft of leadership or strong personalities, it was internally competitive and company-ruled to a degree undermining all solidarity, and it was the constant victim of a wider and depressed inter-colonial economy whose vagaries, together with local weather factors, ruled both employers and employees. In this environment, the 1890 Strike was … another destructive incident

12 O'Farrell, 'Noble National Myths', p. 35.

> in the individual worker's experience of a continuum of intense depression and uncontrolled economic anarchy. Each element in this repressive structure had to be seriously weakened, if not shattered, by new men and new ideas, and, not least, by time and economic improvement, before labouring men began to be released from the prison of the 1890s.[13]

So restricted were the employment prospects of the Grey Valley that down on their luck goldminers had no option but to seek work on the roads, wharves and railways where they constituted an unstable and unpredictable element of a coal-oriented workforce or, as O'Farrell puts it, 'inveterate wanderers, with fluid and basically capitalist social ideals, and no commitment to geographic place'.[14]

The destabilising influence of the diggers was to fade as the exploitation of coal grew in the opening decades of the twentieth century. Even then, as O'Farrell writes, the fluctuation of the trade cycle on the Buller and Grey Valley coalfields 'was never boom but often bust'.[15] In union building, however, the opening decade of the new century witnessed a shift in the centre of gravity from the Buller to the Grey Valley. Blackball and Runanga miners became the driving force as a new generation of miners brought new ideas and new forms of organisation to the coalfields. It was a conjunction of time and place that was, in O'Farrell's view, to 'change the history of New Zealand'.[16] The newcomers were a more diverse lot than the British colliers who crafted unionism at Denniston in the 1890s. The new settlement that sprang up at Runanga, for example, reflects the new order. There was a sprinkling of families from nearby Brunner, the Grey Valley's oldest coaltown, hoping to shake free of the shadow of tragedy that hung over a community devastated by a tragic pit explosion in 1895, which left 65 miners dead. Others came from smaller South Island pits in the hope of finding more regular work. Still others—probably the majority—came from British coalfields in response to the urgings of friends or family.

What distinguished the second wave of migrant miners from that of the 1880s, however, was its 'new world' leavening. The arrival of men from across the Tasman—principally from Victoria—led commentators to describe it as an 'Australian invasion'. Whatever Runanga's precise

13 O'Farrell, 'Noble National Myths', pp. 31–32.
14 O'Farrell, 'Noble National Myths', pp. 31–32.
15 O'Farrell, 'Noble National Myths', pp. 31–32.
16 O'Farrell, 'Noble National Myths', p. 35.

character, it was, like the new mining towns on the Buller coalfield at Millerton, Stockton and Granity, rough and temporary in nature. To newcomers in the Grey Valley, like O'Farrell's parents who established themselves in Greymouth in the 1920s—a decade after Runanga and Blackball had become synonymous with Red Fedism—they appeared to have been put together with a frontier-like randomness. They were the antithesis of an 'ordered society', a 'jumble of unknown individualists bouncing off each other in random unpredictable ways'.[17]

Disordered, complex and chaotic in composition as it was, this Grey Valley briefly thrust itself into colonial consciousness in ways that were to have dramatic consequences nationally. The workplace grievances that formed the basis of the new radicalism emanating from the Grey Valley were both historic and particular to time and place. Historic in the sense that they derived from the traditional hewers' concern to exert as much control over the pace and pattern of life at the coalface as they could. The particularities added by the Grey coalfield mirrored those that had provided the context for the first wave of mining unions on the Buller field. Runanga and Dunollie, Blackball and Roa were as primitive in their provision for miners and their families as Denniston and Coalbrookdale, if not as spectacularly remote. What distinguished the southern coalfield was its different pattern of ownership. Its most striking feature was the involvement of the state. To Lomas and the mining leaders of the 1880s, coal was a national resource best exploited as a public enterprise. The monopoly of the West Coast coal supplies that the shipowners possessed in the 1880s and 1890s reinforced the miners' preference for a nationalised coal industry. The decision of the Seddon Government in 1901 to involve the state directly in the mining of coal, in competition with private coal owners, was welcomed by miners who calculated that a state colliery presented an opportunity for the men at the end of the pick to establish a greater level of control in their own workplaces. More than this, the venture might conceivably set new standards in working conditions that could become the benchmark for all other pits in the colony. Whatever the calculation, as O'Farrell noted, Runanga quickly 'took the lead in workers' affairs'.[18]

17 O'Farrell, *Vanished Kingdoms*, p. 144.

18 P.J. O'Farrell, 'Politics in Westland', in Rupert A. Kay, ed., *Westland's Golden Century 1860–1960: An Official Souvenir of Westland's Centenary*, Christchurch, Westland Centennial Council, 1959, p. 45.

The state mine at Runanga, 8 kilometres from Greymouth, offered men with programs an opportunity for putting them into practice. Socialists of various hues arrived determined to put the new tenets of industrial unionism to the test; among them, youthful men from Australia as different in temperament as Robert ('Bob the Ranter') Semple, Patrick (Paddy) Webb and Pat Hickey, a New Zealand–born radical, recently returned from the United States where he had been in touch with the syndicalist-inspired Industrial Workers of the World (IWW or Wobblies). The apostles of socialism carried their message about the West Coast coalfields with a proselytising zeal that was to strike a chord among the hastily thrown together community that developed in Runanga and adjacent Dunollie, and beyond to the nearby mining township that was taking shape at Blackball. O'Farrell was the first historian to explore in depth the story of how this socialist vanguard took their message beyond the coalfields and thrust themselves to the forefront of the New Zealand labour movement.

> Here in microcosm, so it seemed, was the classic Marxist technique with "the most advanced and resolute section" of the working class asserting its historic role. The avowed object was the formation of the 'proletariat' into a 'class', the overthrow of 'bourgeois' supremacy, and the acquisition of political power by the proletariat. The language was that of the *Communist Manifesto* of 1848: the setting was the draughty tin-roofed halls of Greymouth and Runanga, the sunless Brunner streets and the dusty confines of a Blackball coalface.[19]

It was this collision between rhetoric and the bitter reality that attracted and retained O'Farrell's attention for nearly half a century. There was drama in the jostle of ideas and personalities. Semple emerges as the most colourful of activists:

> His spare build gave the impression of tallness. High prominent cheek-bones and a drooping moustache accentuated sunken cheeks. He held himself erect, shoulders a little back, the stance of a boxer … he was to stand out in the Grey district as industrial radicalism personified, the core of worker protest and action, the giver and receiver of vitriolic abuse … he was 'Bob the Ranter', 'the demon of dissension'.[20]

---

19 P.J. O'Farrell, 'Politics and Coal: The Socialist Vanguard', in Philip Ross May, ed., *Miners and Militants: Politics in Westland 1865–1918*, Christchurch, Whitcoulls for the University of Canterbury, 1975, p. 102.

20 O'Farrell, 'Politics and Coal', pp. 103–4.

Hickey had imbibed at 'the bitter springs which nourished the extremism in the American Labour movement', and these 'harsh American years', especially his experiences as a member of the Western Federation of Miners, the 'toughest, most hard bitten of American unions', were 'written on his face': 'the thrusting aggressive chin, the sour down-turned mouth, the challenging eyes'.[21] The 'already partially bald' Paddy Webb, who like Semple had crossed the Tasman from Victoria, possessed 'a look of maturity much in advance of his twenty three years'.[22]

The story of how this socialist vanguard refashioned the Grey Valley labour movement and created arguably the nation's most radical industrial organisation, the Red Federation of Labour, has become deeply imbedded in left-wing mythology. O'Farrell's pioneering exploration of the burst of activity that reverberated well beyond the coalfields was concerned primarily with its political manifestations. Writing well before the attention of labour historians began to turn more closely to the workplace dimension of worker radicalism, O'Farrell's preoccupation was essentially with the political ideas that propelled action. His explanations of the relationship between place, politics and pit recognise both the cohesiveness of mining communities in general and the newness and rawness of the Grey district. The latter provided radicals with a fresh stage upon which to perform, a platform less encumbered by existing hierarchies. In short, Runanga, Blackball and their camp-like offshoot settlements full of youthful miners ready for a scrap were receptive to the muscular socialism of the emergent Red Fed radicals. Nonetheless, for all the speed with which the radicals thrust themselves to the forefront of coalfields unionism, their emergence took much of its vitality from the ongoing tradition of pit socialism—the desire of the hewers to eke out as much freedom as they could at the end of the pick.

The convergence of this traditional attempt by the most skilled segment of the underground workforce to maximise their independence in the pits and the more overtly political and revolutionary objectives of the radicals produced, as O'Farrell recognised, a radical fragment of immense energy and intensity. Its initial achievements were local ones. There were improvements in the hewing rate at Runanga. At Blackball in 1908, however, the socialists successfully engineered a local strike that won them a 30-minute crib time (tucker time). The success of the strike catapulted

21 O'Farrell, 'Politics and Coal', p. 108.
22 O'Farrell, 'Politics and Coal', p. 110.

the socialist leadership onto the national stage and, as we shall see later, established Blackball's claim to a pre-eminent place in the history of the New Zealand labour movement. The critical significance of the strike for the socialist leadership, however, lies in the damage that the strike did to the central pillar of industrial relations, the arbitration system. The notion of compromise and the adjudication of a notionally impartial umpire implicit in the ICA Act of 1894 sat uneasily with most miners. Accepting the judgement of a court-appointed arbitration system was, in their view, placing too much reliance upon a system that lacked real knowledge of the issues it was being asked to decide. No arbitration system and no arbitrator appointed by the state could be truly impartial. Discrediting the system required them to demonstrate firstly to the miners that it was possible to achieve more by direct action—striking—than could be negotiated within the arbitration system.

The victory at Blackball emboldened the radical leadership to pursue more vigorously their plans for a wider assault upon the capitalist system. Here the doctrines of syndicalism were to prevail. Its central objective was creating one big industrial union that drew together the entire labour movement so that the workers' most powerful weapon—the general strike—might be more easily mounted. After the events of Blackball, the question for the more ideologically driven miners was not whether there should be a crack at the capitalist system but when and where it should happen. The initiatives of the Grey Valley miners led directly to the establishment of the Red Federation of Labour and a campaign designed to persuade the colony's trade unionists to cancel their registration with the arbitration system and endorse the direct action philosophy of the syndicalists. Such a campaign took the activists away from the coalfields and, as O'Farrell made clear, ran the risk of distancing the radicals from the pit socialists—those miners left with the realities of life in the coaltowns. What eased the tension between the wider interests of the ideologues and the particular concerns of the men in the pits was, as O'Farrell saw it, a combination of the traditional and hardbitten quest for independence at the coalface and an urgency lent by the rawness of a coalfield 'situated at world's end'.

Flushed by the dramatic events at Blackball, the formation of the Red Federation of Labour and the successes their threatening presence produced in disputes around the colony, the radicals were irritated when there was no headlong rush on West Coast coalfields or anywhere else to proclaim a general strike. Runanga and Blackball in the Grey Valley continued to adopt a more radical stance; at Brunner and in the older Buller communities, the memories of the defeat in 1890 induced a greater caution. In some pits there was a belief that as useful as the threatening posture of the radicals was, throwing away such protection as the arbitration system offered was foolhardy. This pragmatic wariness was strongest among the hewers and those closest to the perils of work at the coalface where any change was weighed carefully. It was nonetheless clear that after the exhilaration of the Blackball dispute the Grey Valley coalfields were, as one commentator put it, 'jumpy'. The heightened expectations aroused by the initial euphoria of the Red Fed victories, the energy and enthusiasm of the socialist vanguard and an environment that nurtured grievance and generated protest was a powerful combination.

To impatient radicals the hiatus was frustrating. A loss of momentum allowed employers time to regroup politically and industrially. It also bred uncertainties. The five years between Blackball and the eventual proclamation of a general strike in 1913 were played out elsewhere. The proselytising zeal and belligerence of the peripatetic Red Fed organisers, as they sought to swell the ranks of militant labour, produced alarm in boardrooms throughout the colony and hastened the unravelling of the political alliance born in the aftermath of the Maritime Strike. The new alignments produced by this disintegration were to take on a special significance in the Grey Valley. O'Farrell saw the Grey Valley as providing an environment in which it was possible for these political shifts to occur in advance of, and more dramatically than, anywhere else in the colony. Politically, the Grey Valley was Liberal Party territory. In large part this attachment reflected support for the premier, Richard John Seddon, the rambunctious publican from the goldmining town of Kumara who had become synonymous with the mixture of state activity, modest social reform and colonial boosterism that characterised the Liberal Party.[23] The opening of the state coalmine at Runanga in 1902 was seen as strengthening the bond between the miners and the government. But Seddon's death in 1906 loosened this link and strengthened the hands of the socialists already beginning to direct their attention to attacking the arbitration system, the central pillar of the Liberal's industrial relations

23 On Seddon, see Janice Lockwood, 'Personality and Politics: Seddon and His Electorates, 1879–90', in Philip Ross May, ed., *Miners and Militants: Politics in Westland 1865–1918*, Christchurch, Whitcoulls for the University of Canterbury, 1975, pp. 48–79. On Seddon and the Liberal Party, see Tom Brooking, *Richard Seddon: King of God's Own. The Life and Times of New Zealand's Longest-Serving Prime Minister*, Auckland, Penguin, 2014.

and the cornerstone of its political alliance with organised labour. Calls for an independent labour political organisation that had surfaced on the coalfields before Seddon's death now gathered momentum.

It was several decades before the ghost of Seddon ceased to hover over the political scene. His son T.E.Y. Seddon defeated the mayor of Hokitika to follow him as the Member of the House of Representatives (MHR) for the adjoining seat of Westland. Within a year of the premier's death the first shot had been fired and the construction of the Otira tunnel had begun; the great dream of a rail link with the east was finally underway. Local Liberals continued to incorporate other visible additions to the Greymouth townscape into a permanent Seddonian legacy. A new post office at the corner of Tainui and Guinness streets, completed in 1908 and hailed by the *Grey River Argus* as an example of 'English Rennaissance architecture', soon took on 'its own symbolic significance' and was 'read as a memorial to Seddon's political achievements'.[24] A courthouse completed nearby in 1912, less imposing in its public face, further greened the memory. Not to be left out of the commemorative urge and more than a little perturbed at Greymouth's expansion, Hokitika-interests successfully thwarted moves to transfer more government offices to the northern coaltown. And, in front of the new offices, they erected a memorial statue to a premier they believed, justifiably, belonged more to them than their Greymouth counterparts.

The eclipse of political Liberalism on the Coast coincided with the rise of Greymouth and a corresponding decline in the fortunes of Hokitika. As the Liberal MHR for Westland, Tommy Seddon was to witness the shift and to suffer the political consequences of an electoral redistribution that added Greymouth to his electorate. In his autobiographical *The Seddons* (1968), he recaptures contemporary thinking on the shifting fortunes of the two towns:

> Edinburgh feels itself superior to Glasgow, and Hokitika and Greymouth are critical of each other's progress. Hokitika remembers its romantic past when the port of Hokitika rivalled the ports of Wellington and Auckland in importance. Hokitika remembered the agitation to free Westland from the fetters of Canterbury—Hokitika remembered that there sat the Provincial Council. A superintendent lived in Government House. Hokitika was

24 Peter Richardson, 'An Architecture of Empire: The Government Buildings of John Campbell in New Zealand', MA thesis, University of Canterbury, 1988, p. 163.

> proud to call itself the Capital of Westland. Greymouth's interests were once tied up with the interests of Nelson. To Hokitika, to goldfields nearby, swarmed the goldseekers from the ends of the earth. When the gold petered out, coal in the hinterland from Greymouth became a very valuable asset. Greymouth's port was improved by guiding walls of stone, Hokitika's port filled with the debris from sluicing claims. Greymouth was advancing with greater speed than the southern town, Hokitika.[25]

The dynamic behind the shift was unmistakably linked to coal. The miners accordingly bulked large in the local labour movement and their organisation was such that they possessed the numerical strength to shape labour's entry into the political arena. But theirs was neither the only voice nor, as O'Farrell reminds us, always the most significant one locally. Organised Catholicism was beginning to make its presence felt alongside the miners, watersiders and sawmillers—the manual workers who encapsulated the physicality of work in the Grey Valley. In Greymouth, as we have seen, the dominantly Catholic community had already staked out its segment of the town and politically attached itself to the rising star of Liberalism. If Seddon was its West Coast face, its local Liberal Catholic standard bearer was Martin Kennedy (1839/40–1916). Part of the first wave of Irish migration to the West Coast, he became one of the most influential layman in the New Zealand Irish Catholic community of his day.[26] His pathway to Greymouth had been a familiar one: the goldfields of Victoria, then a storekeeper on the Otago fields before moving to the Coast in 1868. As a merchant and businessman, he made his mark quickly; in 1870 he founded the Greymouth Gas Company. Within a decade he had earned the sobriquet 'West Coast coal magnate', as sole proprietor of the Brunner Coal Mine and owner of a fleet of colliers. In the process, he had dabbled briefly in politics—unsuccessfully contesting the superintendency of the newly created Westland in 1874; he won the Grey Valley seat in the 1876 election but retired to concentrate on business two years later. By the beginning of the Liberal reign in 1890 he had sold his coal interest to the Union Steam Ship Company and moved to Wellington. His departure, as both Greymouth's Liberal-aligned newspapers (the *Greymouth Evening Star* and the *Grey River Argus*) sensed, raised the possibility that the 'Liberalism of the Grey' might be

25 Seddon, *The Seddons*, p. 185.

26 Hugh Laracy, 'Kennedy, Martin', in *Dictionary of New Zealand Biography*, first published in 1996, updated 7 April 2006, *Te Ara—the Encyclopedia of New Zealand*, teara.govt.nz/en/biographies/3k9/kennedy-martin.

undermined by an unholy alliance of the Reds and the Greens. It was a connection that came easily to the pen of editorialists. Irish Catholics loomed large among the railwaymen, sawmill workers, watersiders and general labourers, and were thus seen as providing a home for Red Fedism in the town. Whatever the reality, this perception was strengthened by the politics that surrounded the rise of radical unionism.

The death in 1913 of Sir Arthur Guinness, the Liberal member for Grey since 1884, provided a testing ground for the shifting politics of the day. A barrister and solicitor, Guinness had set up practice in Greymouth in 1867. As a loyal acolyte of the colourful Seddon, he had been rewarded for his loyalty by appointment as Chairman of Committees (1893–1903) and Speaker (1903–13). An uneasy representative of the alliance between organised labour and the Liberal Party, he had struggled to contain the growing demands for an independent labour voice in the electorate. In the 1911 general election the miners had campaigned unsuccessfully, under the banner of the Grey District Industrial and Political Council, to unseat Guinness. Their candidate was Paddy Webb, now President of the State Miners' Union at Runanga. Guinness survived the socialist foray into politics (by 3,667 votes to the 2,539 of his nearest opponent) but it was clear that Labour had arrived as a political force in the Grey. The by-election in 1913 to find a replacement for Guinness thus marks in local terms the passing of the old regime and the construction of a new set of political loyalties more aligned to the community that Greymouth had become in the near 30 years Guinness had been the district's parliamentary voice.

The political scramble for the Grey that followed reflected the consolidation of the district's major social groups. Webb was once more the choice of organised labour. The Liberals chose Michael Hannan, a Greymouth lawyer and Catholic; the newly created party of colonial conservatism, Reform, nominated an initially reluctant Hokitika businessman, sometime mayor and prominent Mason, Henry Michel. Thus, the three-way contest straddled the fault lines of the community. No candidate gained a clear majority. The *Second Ballot Act 1908* required that the bottom polling candidate drop out and electors asked to choose between the two highest-polling candidates. It was the Liberal and Catholic Hannan who was squeezed out by the rival and increasingly polarised forces of industrial labour and the alliance of urban and rural property that made up the Reform Party. Disappointed Liberals were now forced to choose between Webb, the voice, so conservatives would have it, of revolutionary labour bent upon destroying the fabric of capitalist society as they knew it, and a party of property with historical roots in the thinking of the neoclassical economists of the nineteenth century. The electors of the Grey district would have probably seen the choice in more parochial and pragmatic terms: that between a coalminer from Runanga—a 'Paddy' by name and ancestry if not by inclination—a product of the Grey as it now was and an outsider from Hokitika of establishment and plainly Protestant hue.

The campaign was marked by scare tactics and sectarianism. Reform interests painted Labour as the 'Red Terror' and threatened that the Massey Government would close the state mine at Runanga and cease construction of the Otira tunnel if the electors returned Webb. Employers declared their support for Michel and hinted that workers who voted for Webb could face dismissal. An anonymous report circulated in Greymouth suggested Webb's supporters would descend from the mining centres and wreak havoc upon the town's business premises should the Reds be rejected at the polls. 'Is the Grey electorate to be placed in the grip of the monster?' was the question put to a meeting in the Greymouth Town Hall on the eve of the poll as Reform campaigners strove to frighten waiverers and drive a wedge between Webb and Catholic Liberal voters thought to be transferring their vote to Labour. It was a strategy that produced vitriolic outbursts, unruly behaviour and a few ruffled feathers. It also flew in the face of changing social and political realities.

With the demise of Seddon and his protégé Guinness, loyalty to the political regime that had delivered state coalmines and, if more slowly, railways was diminishing as impatient newcomers added their voices to those who had already sunk roots in the district. The Catholic vote alone, if it could be assembled, would not have given Webb victory. But many Liberals would have clung to the hope that the socialist Webb was a preferable heir to the old liberalism that they traced back to Sir George Grey in the 1870s than the conservatism of the propertied classes represented by the Reform Party. However much defeated conservatives might bemoan the unholy alliance of the Red Feds and the Greens, the political verdict of the Grey electorate in 1913 was an endorsement of a town on the cusp of embracing a future in which coal and Catholicism would play an even more significant part. And, in this sense, the district's verdict was, as Webb's supporters claimed, a victory of democracy.[27]

27 See O'Farrell, 'Politics and Coal', pp. 101–27; Len Richardson, 'Politics and War: Coal Miners and Conscription', in Philip Ross May, ed., *Miners and Militants: Politics in Westland 1865–1918*, Christchurch, Whitcoulls for the University of Canterbury, 1975, pp. 128–55.

O'Farrell's first foray into the history of the Grey Valley effectively ended as the curtain was drawn on the old liberal period with its foundations anchored in the nineteenth-century gold rush and its aftermath. But his involvement with the history of the Grey district moved almost seamlessly on as he took up a research scholarship at The Australian National University in Canberra and began work on a life of Harry Holland. A militant socialist born in 1868 at Ginninderra, near modern-day Canberra, Holland had crossed the Tasman at the urging of the Red Federation of Labour in 1912 anxious to use his talents as a propagandist during the Waihi Strike, widely seen by local socialists as a precursor to a general strike. His revolutionary reputation preceded him. His role in the 1909 Broken Hill metal miners' strike earned a conviction for sedition and he served five months of a two-year jail sentence. He left Australia under threat of further imprisonment after failing to register his son for compulsory military training and refusing to pay the fines imposed. In New Zealand he quickly added to his image as a troublemaker. With 'Ballot Box' and R.S. Ross he had written *The Tragic Story of the Waihi Strike* (1913), a work that was to become a landmark in the history of the New Zealand labour movement.[28] During the 1913 General Strike, he was convicted of seditious utterance, sentenced to 15 months and spent two and a half months in prison.

If the defeat of the General Strike revealed to Holland the limits of industrial unrest as the harbinger of capitalism's collapse, the election of Paddy Webb as the Social Democratic Party member for Grey in 1913 opened up the prospect of building a genuine socialist labour party, as it were, from the ground up. The outbreak of world war in August 1914, in Holland's view, signified the imminent collapse of capitalism and made it more urgent that labour should be organised politically and industrially so as to take power when the end finally came. The introduction of conscription in 1915 strengthened his conviction that the war was a capitalist one and made political consolidation of labour's ranks even more critical. In July 1916 he threw his support behind the formation of the New Zealand Labour Party (NZLP) and stepped up his campaign against conscription.

28 H.E. Holland, R.S. Ross and 'Ballot Box' (Francis O'Flynn), *The Tragic Story of the Waihi Strike*, Wellington, The Worker Printery, 1913.

The Grey Valley became a hotbed of opposition to conscription. The reorganisation of mining unionism after the calamitous General Strike of 1913 brought a harder edge to union affairs as miners sought to shore up their influence in the pit. The war and the dislocation of the coal trade that it brought with it strengthened their negotiating hand industrially. In these circumstances, opposition to military training grew into a campaign against the conscription of manpower for military purposes and was seen as a precursor of industrial conscription. Catholics in the Grey, as elsewhere, were drawn into the issue by the treatment of the religious orders in the ballots for military service introduced in the *Military Service Act 1916*. The legislation allowed no blanket exemptions and as a consequence individual seminarians were called before the various appeal boards to make their case. Many Catholics saw this procedure as yet another example of Protestant insensitivity. The repression of the Irish Rebellion in 1916 stirred Irish nationalist sympathies and, in Grey Valley terms, drew Reds and Greens to a shared platform of dissent. The miners' anti-conscription campaign spearheaded from Runanga and Blackball during 1916–17, the rejection of conscription in Australia in two plebiscites and the role played by the vociferous and belligerent Melbourne Archbishop Daniel Mannix in this campaign provided the backdrop against which the West Coast thrust itself once more onto the national stage.

O'Farrell was drawn to the political dimension of this transformation. In the 1914 general election, Paddy Webb had held the Grey seat for the Social Democratic Party despite a 'khaki campaign' that saw conservatives question the loyalty of a party that had links to Berlin. He was called up for military service in 1917. He resigned his seat forcing a by-election which he fought on the issue of conscription, intending to argue that if elected his rejection of conscription had received a mandate from the electorate. The wartime coalition government undermined the strategy by refusing to run a candidate in the by-election. Webb then refused the non-combatant role offered him, was court-martialled, sentenced to two years hard labour and deprived of his civil rights for 10 years. The Labour Party chose another Australian, Harry Holland, as its candidate in the by-election that ensued in 1918. If Webb was the genial face of socialism, Holland was its unsmiling and revolutionary one. Holland's credentials were impeccable for a campaign that was to test the embryonic alliance between the Reds and the Greens. Holland had played an important role in fostering what amounted to an alliance between the NZLP and

Catholicism. In 1916 he had written a series of articles on the historical foundations of the Irish Easter Rebellion. A year later he toured the country delivering a series of lectures on Irish topics. His championing of the Irish cause rested upon a 'distaste for imperialism and oppression of minorities' and shunned violence. His selection to contest the Grey seat provided radical Protestantism with a target.

Six months earlier, in July 1917, Protestantism had launched an offensive against 'Romanism' and formed the Protestant Political Association (PPA) to fight Catholicism in New Zealand. Irish nationalists used the pages of the *Green Ray*, the organ of the Maoriland Irish Society, to announce their support for Labour: 'We sincerely hope that every man and woman of Irish blood, irrespective of class or creed, shall unite in returning the labour candidate for the Grey [and] give the militarist, capitalist and shoneen cliques a smashing defeat'. After a vitriolic campaign, Holland shed most of Webb's near 1,000 majority to sneak home by 148 votes. That almost one-third of potential voters abstained made the result a difficult one to read. Did Holland alienate sections of the moderate Labour vote? Did the urging of the PPA frighten off Protestant voters who might otherwise have voted Labour? O'Farrell was in no doubt that Irish voters did support Holland. He notes with satisfaction the celebration of a Mrs O'Donnell of Runanga: 'The way the Irish rallied round our Labour candidate was grand. We certainly are "children of a fighting race" especially when the fight is for liberty and freedom as was Mr Holland's policy'.[29]

In a number of ways the more important consequence of the 1918 by-election was that it consolidated such linkages as were being drawn between Irish nationalists and the Labour Party. Firstly, the election witnessed the purchase of the *Grey River Argus* by the local labour movement. During Holland's campaign, the party had purchased column space in the paper. Traditionally seen as the miners' paper, the *Argus* was much more than this. Its pages reflected the perspectives of its hybrid nature. For the miners, politics was something of an optional extra—important when all other avenues of achieving their objectives seemed closed off. Except to the activist few, its committees and bureaucratic procedures were at odds with the general impatience of the many. The heart of the political Labour machine was in Greymouth and thickly represented among its custodians were working-class Irish Catholics. As a group their political

29 O'Farrell, *Harry Holland*, p. 93, citing the Maoriland Irish Society's *Green Ray*, 1 June 1918.

flavour was, as O'Farrell has described, right wing. And the 1918 electoral redistribution consolidated their influence. Greymouth became part of the Westland electorate; the mining towns of Runanga and Blackball, north of the Grey River, part of the Buller electorate. In all other respects the mining towns were tied to Greymouth, but the loosening of direct political representation was to alter the delicate balance that existed between the rival factions that made up the Grey Valley labour movement.

If the immediate realignment of local politics owed a great deal to the war and events in Ireland, the future was to reflect the working-out of the forces unleashed by arguably the most dramatic event of twentieth-century history—the Russian Revolution. To radicals on the coalfields, the image of the seizure of power by the masses was a seductive one. It raised again the prospect of revolutionary activity with the miners leading the way. Men with agendas flocked once more to the Grey. And, in 1926, the Communist Party of New Zealand shifted its headquarters to Blackball. Its activist core became more assertive, organised a 'Miners' Page' in the *Grey River Argus*, organised their own paper, the *Worker's Vanguard*, and, to counter the influence of the Boy Scouts among the young, established a Young Comrades group with its own newspaper and uniform. As a young man who grew up as these new forces played themselves out, O'Farrell was drawn to seek an explanation of the world around him. His immediate explanations came in the form of academic articles about the formation of the New Zealand Labour Party, the impact of the Bolshevik Revolution, a biography of Harry Holland and, retrospectively, in the tour de force that was *Vanished Kingdoms*.

The biography of Holland provides a convenient bridge between these two radical surges. It also brings to the fore what were to become O'Farrell's lasting and productive preoccupations—religion and politics. These themes formed the core of a perceptive review by Noel McLachlan, an Australian historian about to complete a PhD at the London School of Economics. It appeared in the *Times Literary Supplement* in 1965 and, as was then customary, anonymously. In McLachlan's opinion, O'Farrell had produced a 'merciless anatomy of Holland's heart and mind and their confusions', and told the story of a militant materialist socialist whose heartbeats followed a deeply emotional and religious rhythm. As such, it was remarkable, McLachlan believed, that 'a biographer who evidently has so little sympathy for his subject understands him so well'.[30] As a young man, Holland had abandoned the Salvation Army in response to its failure to deal with evident poverty, and put his faith in a socialist army that promised salvation on this earth. He became disillusioned as the young Australian labour parties made the compromises thought necessary to win electoral support, becoming parties of social reform rather than socialism, and he increasingly viewed industrial action as offering a short-cut to a revolutionary destination. In 1912 he was drawn to New Zealand by the prospect that the revolutionary potential exhibited by the Red Feds offered a more promising environment for his socialist aspirations.

O'Farrell's account of Holland's second bite at the socialist cherry goes straight to the kernel of Holland's dilemma: the same proselytising zeal that made him, as leader of the New Zealand Labour Party from 1919 until his death in 1933, the party's socialist conscience made him increasingly irrelevant to the political manoeuvring that was involved in making Labour a credible electoral alternative. Two years after his death, the leaders of the New Zealand Labour Government, flush with Holland's socialist mates who like Holland had crossed the Tasman to spearhead the Red Fed assault upon the capitalist citadel, erected a monument above Holland's grave: a small central figure stood naked, 'holding the fruits of the earth, looking up sightlessly into the heavens'. It was, O'Farrell wrote, 'a harsh commentary on Holland's endeavour' and a symbol of the Labour Party's preference for the 'mild Liberal tradition of Seddon' rather than the 'militant socialist tradition of Holland'.[31]

Greymouth and the West Coast form little more than the backdrop against which O'Farrell analyses Holland's political career. He was the member for Grey for little more than a year. When the 1918 electoral redistribution placed the mining communities on the north bank of the Grey River in the Buller electorate, Holland moved with them. He took up residence in Westport and it was from there that he led the New Zealand Labour Party from 1919 until his death in 1933. Holland's decision to live in Westport rather than Wellington was based on democratic and moral principles: he saw himself as the representative of the electors and believed he should experience their lot in life first hand. It was an attitude that flowed naturally into his views of political leadership. A more ego-driven leader of the NZLP would have preferred to be in Wellington—

30 *Times Literary Supplement*, 30 December 1965, p. 1212.

31 O'Farrell, *Harry Holland*, p. 213.

closer to the manoeuvring that the quest for political power encouraged. With the support of the miners, his tenure as the member for Buller was secure. A staunch and informed miners' advocate in parliament, as a local member he tended his patch diligently and remained a familiar figure in the Grey Valley coaltowns of Blackball and Runanga. Nowhere was Holland's immersion in community life better demonstrated than on Burns Night celebrations in Blackball where he spoke on the Scottish poet Robert Burns.[32]

The battles that preoccupied the party's Greymouth activists with whom Holland rubbed shoulders were, at one level, immediate and practical ones but, at another, deeply ideological. A new generation of coalfield radicals found in the Communist Party a new gospel of hope. In 1926 the party's national headquarters transferred to Blackball and briefly the township became the frontrunner in industrial politics. The remote township had its attractions for a party whose members and sympathisers might be numbered in the tens rather than the hundreds, and whose immediate strategy was to consolidate its base among the traditionally militant industrial workers. Moreover, the *Grey River Argus*, the nation's pioneer labour daily, recently purchased by the local labour movement, offered a means of spreading their message beyond the West Coast.

In O'Farrell's biography of Holland, relations with the communist cells on the coalfields are presented largely in the context of their impact on national politics. Thirty years on, in *Vanished Kingdoms*, he dwells more upon how the ideological push and shove taking place in the Grey Valley sat in the local environment. If the Communist minority set the political pace in Blackball, in Greymouth the prevailing political ethos was increasingly set by a small group of right-wing Irish Catholic activists whose agenda was firmly focused on improving the here and now. From their perspective, the political epistles emanating from Blackball were as unwelcome as the cold edge of the notorious 'Barber', a chilly, katabatic wind that snaked its way down the Grey Valley as an all-enveloping mist. The greeting 'comrade' favoured by radical activists from Blackball and Runanga marked out the ideological divide between the contending factions. Intended to conjure up notions of international brotherhood, it was seen, by labour reformists in Greymouth, as a 'distancing title, an ideological declaration rather than an affirmation of bond and common

32 Harry Holland, *Robert Burns: Poet and Revolutionist*, edited by Dougal McNeill, Wellington, Steele Roberts Aotearoa, 2016.

cause'.[33] It symbolised an almost unbridgeable gulf between an 'army of dedicated fanatics' and a Greymouth 'Labour Party that was just that; Greymouth—local'.[34] To O'Farrell, the coalfields radicalism of the 1920s lacked the dash and sparkle of its predecessor, possessing neither the 'fiery Americanism' of a Pat Hickey nor the 'noisy larrikinism' of a Bob Semple. What remained was 'dour and tough' and doctrinaire.

The struggle between the rival strands within the Grey district labour movement took place largely away from the public gaze, in miners' halls and union offices. If the Grey Valley labour movement had a meeting place it was the *Grey River Argus* building. The *Argus* had been established at the height of the gold rushes in 1865 as a private publication and by the time it was taken over by the local labour movement in 1919 its presses were ageing and the building that housed them wore a dilapidated air. It sat less than 50 metres from the wharves and the rakes of coal wagons waiting to be emptied into the steamships tethered in the Grey River. During moments of high tide or when heavy rain had swelled its waters, the coal steamers rode proud above street level and squeezed the murky waters of the Grey across the streets, threatening to submerge the ancient presses. It was here that the ideological push became shove as the rival factions sought column space. The new generation of radicals from Blackball and Runanga established a 'Miners' Page' and used it to provide analyses of the worsening economic fortunes of the coalfields locally and internationally. Such commentaries frequently sat awkwardly alongside more cautious editorials or articles by Harry Holland providing summaries of the historical background to world events or a talk on Robbie Burns to the Scottish contingent at Blackball.

The Greymouth-based, Irish Catholic arm of the local labour movement was able to maintain a precarious ascendency in this struggle for influence. It was from among its number that James O'Brien emerged to squeeze out T.E.Y. Seddon as MP for Westland in 1922.[35] The son of the great Liberal premier clawed his way back in 1925, but the engine driver from Runanga reclaimed the seat in 1928 and held it until his death in 1947. O'Brien was one of the so-called 'Irish invasion' of the first decade of the twentieth century. He came to prominence through the Westland Engine Drivers' Union and fit within what a British writer, Richard Hoggart,

33 O'Farrell, *Vanished Kingdoms*, p. 262.
34 O'Farrell, *Vanished Kingdoms*, p. 263.
35 See Seddon, *The Seddons*, pp. 348–49.

described as 'the earnest minority'[36] of the working class: activists who were seeking to improve the here and now through self-improvement and voluntary representation of their communities in a range of organisations. For O'Brien, this had meant playing a central role in bringing the cooperative store to Runanga and serving on both the Greymouth and Runanga borough councils. He had been imprisoned for sedition in 1917 while opposing conscription. In the early 1920s he had become chairman of directors and manager of the *Grey River Argus*. By temperament and inclination he was thus a fit custodian of the interests of the Irish Catholic community and the pragmatic majority of the mining towns bent upon establishing a permanent place for themselves in the Grey Valley.

To O'Brien and the group of reformist and dominantly Irish Catholic activists from whose ranks he had emerged, the Communists in the coaltowns seemed not so much to promise better things to come as to imperil the precarious nature of survival in the Grey. O'Farrell characterises the tussle between the rival Catholic and Communist arms of the Greymouth labour movement in terms reminiscent of the struggles between Don Camillo and Peppone, the fictional Catholic priest and Communist mayor of Giovannino Guareschi's *The Little World of Don Camillo.*[37] In O'Farrell's Grey Valley, James O'Brien and Paddy O'Farrell stand as the representatives of Catholicism. Their communist bête noire was 'bloody Jack Doyle'. Of Irish Catholic descent, he had come to the Grey Valley from Napier to join an underground cell of Irish bent upon avoiding conscription during World War I. When the Communist Party set up its headquarters in Blackball in 1926, Doyle and his wife Sophie became among its most active disciples. Their combined zeal maintained the production of the party organ, the *Workers' Vanguard*. Together with the talented Angus McLagan, a young Scot who was to become secretary of both the Communist Party and the national union of coalminers, the United Mine Workers of New Zealand, they spearheaded local radicalism. When the Communists withdrew from Blackball, McLagan aligned the United Mine Workers with the NZLP; Doyle's status as the Communist Party's most dedicated disciple assumed, in the minds of many, almost demonic proportions. O'Farrell paints a vivid picture:

36 Richard Hoggart, *The Uses of Literacy*, London, Chatto and Windus, 1957, p. 318.

37 See Giovannino Guareschi, *The Don Camillo Omnibus*, London, The Companion Book Club, 1955.

> His distinctive mode of cycling, leaning forward grimly into whatever the gales that lashed him, with bulging eyes and total dedication to piston-like pedalling encapsulated his confrontationist political attitude. He and his velocipede were hurtling with total commitment towards the beckoning final barricades … [with] the humourless intensity of the totalitarian zealot …[38]

To the moderate men of the Greymouth labour movement, Doyle was a maverick wrecker, a troublemaker, a political liability but still exasperatingly a part of the local scene. It was precisely this bellicosity and physicality that made him the idol in the physical world of bush, pit and wharf that shaped the lives of young men of his day.

The political world of the Grey was, as O'Farrell saw it, masculine in its ethos, as directly physical as its landscape. His father, 'Paddy', had embraced both; in 'the black rainstorms that hurled so often from a tumultuous Tasman into a Greymouth huddled in creaking timber and tin houses clinging to the foot of a mountain range, it was easy enough to cast oneself as an intrepid battler at the world's edge'.[39] In *Vanished Kingdoms* he contrasts this response to the Grey with that of his mother. After the ordered and structured life she had known, the Grey she confronted for the first time in 1920 was chaotic and raw. The miners appeared 'a strange lot of dark and silent folk who seemed of a piece with their coal and timber economy and their incessant grey rain'.[40] At first even the local Irish fragment of the town lacked much resonance with what she had known. To her ear, 'the natural Irish cadences of the colonies were raucous and beery, or heavy with false sentiments of rebellion and violence'.[41] It was years before she was able to shrug off the feeling that she was caught up in a 'barbaric place'.[42] Instead of the familiar tight communal life of the Irish village, Greymouth seemed thin and crude. Colonial life with its 'pervasive, chilling, contagious Protestantism'[43] bore heavily upon her.

It is a fundamental tenet of O'Farrell's treatment of Irish migration that the construction of an essentially Irish culture as a means of easing the transition from old world to new was simply impossible. There was little

38 O'Farrell, *Vanished Kingdoms*, p. 263.
39 O'Farrell, *Vanished Kingdoms*, p. 137.
40 O'Farrell, *Vanished Kingdoms*, p. 140.
41 O'Farrell, *Vanished Kingdoms*, pp. 84–85.
42 O'Farrell, *Vanished Kingdoms*, p. 142.
43 O'Farrell, *Vanished Kingdoms*, p. 87.

left to pass on. It had already been lost. The great cultural tragedy had already occurred. Gaelic Ireland, the real Ireland with its ancient stone face, had been largely obliterated during the eighteenth century. Famine had completed the rout, physically dispossessing those already in the throes of cultural dispossession. Thus it was that his mother, Mai O'Farrell, a child of late nineteenth-century Ireland, could not wrap herself in Irish culture as a means of easing the shock of the new. What she could and did do, as *Vanished Kingdoms* makes eloquently clear, was immerse herself in the Catholic Church. It was a decision that reached back to Ireland for its validation. The link was the Sisters of Mercy by whom she had been taught in Borrisokane. More than anyone else it was contact with the nuns at Borrisokane who were to provide the reassurance needed to cope with the strange colonial world she found herself in. The Mercy order had been in Greymouth since 1882 and to the Mercy Convent adjacent to St Patrick's Church, just a five-minute walk from the O'Farrell's home in Puketahi Street, there came young nuns Mai had known in Borrisokane. In their company and that of a small cluster of lay helpers, Mai shared in the rich prayer world of Catholicism. Its rosaries, litanies, devotional prayers and religious ceremonies offered an imagery and vocabulary that had the capacity to enrich the mind and expand the intellectual horizon. Its dense tapestry helped to counter the overwhelming colonial thinness and rampant masculinity.[44]

This perceptive recreation of the inner world of his mother, in many respects, encapsulates O'Farrell's ongoing contemplation of the West Coast. He came to describe himself as a New Zealander of Irish descent and Australian citizenship. The order is of course an accurate statement of a demographic reality; it might also be read as defining the terms of his engagement with the past. Together they form the critical vantage points from which he recreated the making and remaking of the Grey Valley from the last days of the gold rushes until the middle of the twentieth century. As collective markers of his identity, they embrace the world of ideas as refracted through the prisms of Catholicism and socialism and the communities each helped shape within Australasia. The rubbing together of these offshoots of European intellectual life, as virtual wilderness confronted industrial capitalism and colony struggled to become nation, is at the heart of O'Farrell's thinking about the Grey Valley and its people.

44 O'Farrell, *Vanished Kingdoms*, pp. 76–77; and see also Patrick Morgan's review of *Vanished Kingdoms*, 'The Irish in Australasia', *Quadrant* (Sydney), vol. 35, no. 3, March 1991, pp. 72–76.

5

BILL PEARSON

1908 and All That: *Coal Flat*

Whether by coincidence or design, Bill Pearson's *Coal Flat* is set in 1947. To Pat O'Farrell, the year had marked the demise of his father's generation of political activism. From his Puketahi Street home in the Catholic quarter of Greymouth, he had been at the heart of working-class political organisation that had derived its energy from an alliance of the 'Reds and the Greens'. By 1947, whether looked at from Greymouth or Blackball, the tension between the two factions, once creative and energising, now seemed more likely to inhibit activity than to encourage it. Men and women whose political aspirations had both helped shape and been shaped by the evolution of the New Zealand Labour Party were beginning to draw up their individual balance sheets. To some, the achievements of the first Labour Government represented a fair if not formidable return; the state now provided a system of social welfare that offered to take the rough edges off capitalism, the coal barons had been stripped of their mines, the Reserve Bank now regulated the behaviour of the trading banks, the tyranny of the landlord was curbed by a state housing program and access to education and health provision had both been greatly improved.

Figure 3: A studio portrait of Bill Pearson shortly before the publication of *Coal Flat* in 1963.

Source: Courtesy Paul Millar.

To others, the full social dividend remained to be paid out. The trading banks had escaped nationalisation and the promise of free health provision remained just that. Nor had the Labour leaders honoured the party's opposition to military conscription. They had introduced compulsion sooner in World War II than the non-Labour coalition had during World War I. As the Cold War set in and the major powers lined up behind capitalist and communist banners, New Zealand labour leaders alienated many of their supporters by introducing conscription in peacetime. And, in their efforts to prevent a repetition of the rampant inflation that followed World War I, they had persisted with economic controls that seemed better at restraining wages than prices or the profits of employers. In sum, these tensions were irritants rather than matters likely to catapult the Grey Valley into ferment, as had happened in 1908, during World War I and in the 1930s. Yet, as always, irritants offered fertile ground for men with programs.[1]

Bill Pearson's *Coal Flat* presents a community still working out the expectations of 1908.[2] In an environment that bred precious few heroes, the brief historical moment that was the 'Tucker Time' or 'Crib Time' Strike quickly assumed mythical status. The achievement of a 30-minute meal break by the Blackball miners emboldened coalfield radicals and led directly to the creation of a national union of miners and the Red Federation of Labour. Syndicalist in tone, the 'Red Federation', as it was soon dubbed, spoke the language of class warfare and promoted the general strike as an instrument of social transformation. When the state struck back with a vengeance in 1913, politics looked even more attractive. Paddy Webb, an Australian-born member of the 'Blackball Seven'[3] who defied the Blackball mine manager, had been elected as the Social Democratic Party (SDP) member for Grey in 1913 before the crushing of the Great Strike. With progress on the industrial front for the moment blocked, the miners focused their attentions on coalface issues and threw their weight behind initiatives designed to produce a united working-class party. In this sense, the formation of the Labour Party in July 1916[4]

1 Len Richardson, 'Class, Community and Conflict: The Blackball Miners' Union, 1920–31', in Len Richardson and W. David McIntyre, eds, *Provincial Perspectives: Essays in Honour of W.J. Gardner*, Christchurch, University of Canterbury, 1980, pp. 106–27.

2 Nolan, '"The View from Over the Hill"', pp. 1–27; Brian Wood, *The Great '08 Blackball Coalminers' Strike*, Greymouth, Bright Print, 2008.

3 The others were J. Goldsmith, H.J. Fox, T. Milligan, G.R. Hunter, W. Bromilow, P.C. Webb and P.H. Hickey.

4 The definitive history of the New Zealand Labour Party is Peter Franks and Jim McAloon, *The New Zealand Labour Party, 1916–2016*, Wellington, Victoria University Press, 2016.

became a crucial part of the mythology of 1908. In 1935 M.J. Savage formed the nation's first Labour Government. Webb became Minister of Mines, and when he was joined in 1941 by another Blackball miner, Angus McLagan, the township nestled on the slopes of the Paparoas could claim to be more than bit players in the nationalisation of the mines that followed. The *Coal Flat* that Pearson presents is a community living out the realities that lay behind the myth.

Blackball had never, as Pearson knew well enough, been short of activists whose agendas extended well beyond the preoccupations of the coalface. In Paddy Webb and Angus McLagan it had produced the nation's most influential coalminer-politicians; one a product of the first wave of early twentieth-century industrial radicalism, the other inspired by the Bolshevik Revolution and the surge of international socialism that followed the end of World War I. An unlikely pairing, with Webb as genial as McLagan was intense, they were the voice of the coalfields in the Labour Cabinets of the 1940s. Familiar figures still in the mining towns with which they had once been almost synonymous, their mana as men who played their part in battles long ago was considerable. They returned to Blackball as miners who had got themselves into a position where they could implement two of coalmining unionism's fundamental objectives—a national workplace agreement and the nationalisation of the nation's major coalmines. If this stopped short of introducing pit committees to allow the men who worked at the coalface to share in the day-to-day running of the mines, to most miners two out of three was not a bad return for a generation of struggle.

Webb and McLagan were products of the communities they now represented, and as such they were explicable and acceptable. Idealists who stood outside the mining fraternity were a different matter. Like many a mining township, Blackball attracted a range of individuals for whom the decision to live among the miners was born of a mixture of faith, hope and compassion: faith in the potential of the collective and communitarian nature of the isolated mining towns to serve the interests of 'the people'; hope that the miners' struggle might engender a wider commitment to social justice; and compassion expressed in a desire to enrich the lives of the communities they entered. The 1920s brought a number of such visitors to Blackball. The miners' opposition to compulsory military training and their anti-conscription campaign during the 1914–18 war had led military defaulters to seek sanctuary in the bush beyond the township. After the war, the convergence between the 'No More War Movement' and the Communist Party brought individuals from both groups to Blackball.

Alfred William (Fred) Page best illustrates the former. He had grown up in a Quaker, pacifist and prohibitionist family that was arguably the fulcrum of the middle-class radicalism that flourished in the Christchurch labour movement during the first two decades of the twentieth century. In 1918 his elder brother Robin, a university student at Canterbury College, was imprisoned as a military defaulter after his appeal against call-up on conscience grounds was rejected. Too young for call-up, Fred supported his brother by visiting him weekly in prison and 'frequently expressed the wish that he [too] could have suffered in the cause of peace'.[5] To Page and his family, who stood at the hub of Christchurch's middle-class radical community, the anti-conscriptionist stance of the miners provided a point of closer contact with union leaders from the coalfields. The arrest and imprisonment of Paddy Webb, the MP for the Grey, as a military defaulter in 1918 personalised the sense of common cause with the miners.

Among the pacifist, socialist circle in which Page moved, the coalfields possessed a reputation as a sanctuary for defaulters 'on the run'. Early in 1918, with his brother Robin and a group of friends, Page had cycled through the West Coast and saw something of the mining communities first hand. This personal experience was reinforced in 1919 by the publication of a Board of Trade Report on the coal industry that painted a grim picture of life in mining towns and drew particular attention to the primitive and sometimes squalid nature of housing, especially that available for single men.[6] Two aspects of the report struck a responsive chord within the socialist movement: its support for nationalisation of the coal industry and the support it provided for greater attention to the environment in which the miners lived. The interest in the mining community as an entity embodied in the report was shaped, in large part, by Samuel Hurst Seager.[7] He had presented a blueprint for reform that reflected the thinking of the American garden suburb movement and

5 Jim Gardner, 'Tradition and Conscience: Canterbury College and R. O. Page, Conscientious Objector, 1918–1919', *History Now*, vol. 9, no. 2, May 2003, p. 8.

6 'Board of Trade Report', *AJHR* (NZ), 1919, H44A; Richardson, *Coal, Class & Community*, pp. 181–84.

7 Ian J. Lochhead, 'Seager, Samuel Hurst', in *Dictionary of New Zealand Biography*, first published in 1996, updated May 2002, *Te Ara—the Encyclopedia of New Zealand*, teara.govt.nz/en/biographies/3s8/seager-samuel-hurst; Richardson, *Coal, Class & Community*, pp. 181–84.

would have required the destruction of existing coaltowns and the creation of model communities supported by the amenities of a middle-class utopia—library, theatres and debating clubs. The idealism that infused this program of reform was common currency among Christchurch's middle-class radicals who saw municipal and state intervention as necessary to moderate the worst excesses of capitalism. And it was a mixture of pacifist principle and socialist idealism that led Page to the Grey Valley in 1925. A science graduate, he had taught for a while at Christchurch Boys' High School, but resigned his position after the school refused to accept his request to qualify his taking the mandatory oath of allegiance with the phrase 'so long as this undertaking continues not to conflict with the dictates of my conscience'.[8] After a period as a 'University coach',[9] he became a trucker in the Blackball mine.

Page brought to the pits the fitness of tramper and athlete, an understanding of the techniques of mining and a keen sense of his own practical limitations:

> I thought at first that the work just about suited my level of intelligence, but found later that a good deal of science was involved. It is quite a nice point to know when to put a spurt on in order to surmount a rise in shoving the empty trucks, and when it is safe to let the loaded ones go at full speed ...[10]

Of more concern to Page 'than the dark and dirt and heat and bad air of the mine', was a 'monotony ... so deadly' as to 'become insufferable'. With 'no educational advantages' and 'very few interests', the miner, in his view, had little choice but to take his leisure in the pub. To counter the attractions of the bar rail, Page arranged social gatherings and organised a debating society whose meetings discussed 'important public questions' and drew audiences of 'fifty to sixty'.[11] The vitality and idealism of Fred Page is clearly exhibited as he leads a Blackball social gathering in song and, to the tune of 'On the Ball', coaxes them through:

---

8 Elsie Locke, *Peace People, A History of Peace Activities in New Zealand*, Christchurch, Hazard Press, 1992, p. 76.

9 Alfred William Page, *'He's for the Morning': Alfred William Page, His Journal; also Some Recollections of His Life by His Aunts, Ellen, & Ann Saunders*, Christchurch, A.Wildey, 1939, p. 49.

10 Page, *'He's for the Morning'*, p. 49.

11 Page, *'He's for the Morning'*, pp. 49–50.

Oh, Workers, no more be content to be led,
Just think for yourselves or you'll fall,
Education's the way to bring nearer the day
When each man gives his best to help all.

Chorus:
Come the day!
Come the day! Come the day!
When Class has been banished away,
And we dig at the coal for the good of the whole
Working for joy not for pay.

We'll work for a system where everyone helps
And chances for all are the same;
Where no man will fight, but all nations unite
To make brotherhood more than a name.[12]

The particular form of idealism that propelled Page to Blackball was the product of a unique set of personal circumstance. Other individuals came imbued with different hopes and expectations. Among those to arrive at much the same point in the 1920s as Page was a cluster of communist activists, whose objective was to build a headquarters for the New Zealand Communist Party. Blackball appealed as a launching pad for the party's campaign to establish a stronger base within the organised labour movement. Standing apart from the main body of unionist ideologues was a young Scot and sometime student of the University of Edinburgh, Allan Eaglesham (1902–1935).[13] A son of the manse, he had been born in Dumfriesshire and his socialism was grounded in an amalgam of democratic Protestantism, the intensely moral socialism of the Independent Labour Party and the revolutionary ferment associated with the 'Clydeside Reds'. While a student at Edinburgh University, he was drawn to the revolutionary strand of Scottish politics that surrounded John Maclean (1879–1923). A Glaswegian schoolteacher and university graduate, 'The Fighting Dominie' traced his family heritage back to the Highland clearances. Dismissed from teaching after denouncing World War I as an imperialist war, Maclean thereafter immersed himself in introducing Glasgow workers to Marxist theory. His radical analysis drew upon what he called the 'communism of the clans' and he came increasingly to argue that the Scottish working class possessed greater revolutionary

12 Page, '*He's for the Morning*', p. 51.

13 Gavin Bowd, 'Comintern Cadre: The Passion of Allan Eaglesham', *Socialist History Society Occasional Paper*, no. 22, 2006.

potential than the workers in England or Wales. Only by going 'back to communism' would Scotland move 'forward to communism' and ultimately to the Communist Republic of Scotland.[14]

This was the heady environment in which the 18-year-old Eaglesham joined the Communist Party and committed himself to a life of activism that was to lead him first to Australia and subsequently to New Zealand. The road to Blackball was very much that of the itinerant party man familiar in the annals of radical activism, with periods spent working as seaman, wharfie, agricultural labourer, railway navvy and coalminer. He arrived in the Grey Valley in mid-1926, as part of the New Zealand Communist Party's attempt to establish its headquarters in Blackball and, like Page, worked in the mine as a trucker. With at least a quarter of the party's 120 members, the coaltown became a virtual 'Little Moscow'. Within that community, Eaglesham's proselytising zeal was channelled into 'educational work'. He wrote copiously for the *Workers' Vanguard*, the mouthpiece of the Communist Party, printed by the miners' daily newspaper, the *Grey River Argus*, and for 'Young Comrades', a roneoed magazine designed to counter the influence of both the Boy Scouts and the capitalist comic and provide suitable socialist activities for the young.

If, as O'Farrell suggests, the energising force behind the moderate wing of the Grey Valley labour movement emanated from Greymouth's Catholic quarter, the socialism of predominantly Protestant Blackball did not flourish in a Mecca of non-conformist radicalism. The heavily Presbyterian Scots undoubtedly injected an element of democratic Protestantism, but Pearson's *Coal Flat* accurately presents a community in which the churches maintain a fragile presence. The Presbyterian minister lived outside the coaltown in Ahaura, 'a settlement on the river flat several miles up the Grey Valley' where a 'few prosperous farmers ran sheep',[15] and visited the coaltown fortnightly for Sunday services. The only link drawn between union and religion is attached to Arthur Henderson, an elder in the Presbyterian Church, secretary of the school committee and writer of the 'Coal Flat Notes' for the *Grey River Argus*. These roles bring him into contact with the 'improvers' and place him outside the political or industrial mainstream of union activity. There is not the slightest trace of socialist evangelism about him. He is depicted as something of 'a social

14 James D. Young, *John Maclean: Clydeside Socialist*, Glasgow, Clydeside Press, 1992.

15 Pearson, *Coal Flat*, p. 310.

and psychological misfit'[16] and is taunted by the younger men as the 'village queen'. Similarly, Catholicism's presence in *Coal Flat* is as a marker of difference rather than as a contributor to coalfields radicalism. The Catholic Herlihy family are presented as 'outcasts', living on the fringe of Coal Flat and each deeply troubled. The priest is an infrequent and at times unhelpful visitor. There is no Catholic school and the nearest Catholic church is across the Grey River in Ngahere.

Blackball was not only Red, it was also Tartan. From the early twentieth century, Scottish coalfields contributed a significant portion of the newcomers entering the township. Of their number, Angus McLagan has left the clearest historical footprint. His road to Blackball and his experience of it illustrate a pattern familiar on coalfields everywhere. Born in Mid-Calder, Midlothian, in 1891, he had entered the pits as a 14-year-old. Six years later he joined the exodus of young mobile miners seeking employment on the newer and expanding coalfields of Canada, the USA, Australia and New Zealand. By 1911 he was in Blackball working as a trucker. In the aftermath of the 1913 General Strike he lost his place in the Blackball mine, spent a period in a variety of labouring jobs and, after the death of his mother, sailed for Scotland in 1919. His return to Blackball in the early 1920s came as poverty was becoming widespread on the Scottish coalfields. Emigration was no longer dominated by the young and mobile but increasingly presented the best option for entire families and extended families. It was an exodus that was stimulated further by the wholesale retrenchment that followed Britain's disastrous 1926 General Strike. For this second infusion of Scottish miners the timing was unfortunate. The golden weather of the late 1920s that brought a brief burst of activity gave way to the 'troubles' of the 1930s and the impoverishment of the town. And, if most of the newcomers were more familiar with Burns than they were with Marx, they were a familiar and receptive audience for Scottish radicals like Eaglesham and McLagan who sought to nurture a 'Little Moscow' in the shadow of the Paparoas.[17]

The times were to become increasingly out of joint for idealism, whatever its variety. The New Zealand coal industry had at first been sheltered from the worst of the downturn that beset the coalfields internationally, but as the decade ended pit closure, the rationing of available work and

16 Kenneth Prebble, 'Coal Flat', *Comment: A New Zealand Quarterly Review*, no. 18, January 1964, p. 37.
17 See Richardson, 'Class, Community and Conflict', pp. 106–27.

unemployment brought poverty and shrinking expectations. As young men with little mining experience, Page and Eaglesham were among those culled from the pits. Page left to become the first secretary of the No More War Movement, a pacifist organisation in search of a new, socialist-orientated international order, and died in 1930 in Paris where he had linked up with the War Resisters' International. After a period in Wellington, Eaglesham returned to Britain, continued his work for the Communist Party and was sent to Moscow in 1930 to attend the Anglo-American E-Section of the International Lenin School, assuming the underground name of William Murphy, a former comrade in New Zealand.[18] After contracting tuberculosis, he returned to Britain and died in Scotland in 1935.[19] Thus the departure of the two idealists and the withdrawal of the New Zealand Communist Party's headquarters from Blackball in 1928 coincided with the end of a phase of heightened expectations and the onset of perhaps the grimmest years that Blackball miners experienced.

The idealism that had attracted 'outsiders' to Blackball in the 1920s had been based, in different ways, in a belief in the capacity of mining communities to hasten social change. In the 1930s there was little in Blackball to attract observers, idealistic or otherwise. The one notable newcomer who has left his impressions of the place was a young medical practitioner, Dr F.O. Bennett.[20] In the straightened economic circumstances of the late 1920s, he was attracted to Blackball by the financial security of a position as salaried medical provider for the Blackball Medical Association: 'A roof and five hundred pounds a year'.[21] His expectations were few and his first glimpse of main street Blackball dispiriting:

> less of a street than a rough road with deep ditches on either side. The houses were small, unpainted and all with tarred roofs. Weeds were often window-high and the scrub and gorse filled the many vacant sections … Halfway up on the left was a street of high rusted pylons, relics of an earlier aerial railway for coal.[22]

---

18 Locke, *Peace People*, pp. 75–76.

19 Bowd, 'Comintern Cadre'.

20 See Geoffrey W. Rice, 'Bennett, Francis Oswald', in *Dictionary of New Zealand Biography*, first published in 2000, *Te Ara—the Encylopedia of New Zealand*, teara.govt.nz/en/biographies/5b24/bennett-francis-oswald.

21 Francis Bennett, *A Canterbury Tale: The Autobiography of Dr Francis Bennett*, Wellington, Oxford University Press, 1980, p. 124.

22 Bennett, *A Canterbury Tale*, p. 124.

The township was connected by pathways of 'crushed cinders';[23] 'soot' and a 'sulphurous smell' were everywhere.[24] Bennett's five years in Blackball were years in which the township was sucked into the coal crisis that engulfed the coalfields of the Western world and brought intermittent employment and mine closure. Work-sharing schemes that attempted to give most work to those with families meant high levels of youth unemployment and only short-term relief. Disputes about union strategies brought division. A dissident fraction broke ranks and returned to the pits on terms rejected by the union leadership. A police contingent was stationed in the township to ensure those returning to work could do so.

The 'troubles',[25] as these events came to be called, provided Bennett with a unique perspective on the functioning of the township. He witnessed first-hand the failure of employers to engage in any way with the miners' efforts to build a community:

> The Company paid the wages and nothing more … All the town possessed in the way of amenities—medical association, doctor, domain, football team, football grounds, swimming baths, miners' hall and pictures twice a week, debating clubs, sickness fund—had come from a scraping off the wages.[26]

Moreover, the coal proprietor's presence in the township was as limited as its contribution to community well-being:

> [They] came to Blackball only at intervals of a few years when the contract would need renewing. They would pick their way through the cinders to the miners' hall and there confronting the executive across the table would thrash out a new agreement and then make for their car at the door.[27]

Such indifference bred appalling industrial relations. In Bennett's view, the miners brought 'a deep implacable hatred' and a 'fervently uncompromising' attitude to their dealings with their employers. Politics were played out in 'black or white, with rarely a hint of grey'[28] and class warfare kept 'surging' to 'battle plans' that had been 'drawn up by Karl

23 Bennett, *A Canterbury Tale*, p. 126.
24 Bennett, *A Canterbury Tale*, p. 127.
25 For a fuller account of the 'troubles', see Richardson, 'Class, Community and Conflict', pp. 106–27.
26 Bennett, *A Canterbury Tale*, p. 131.
27 Bennett, *A Canterbury Tale*, p. 131.
28 Bennett, *A Canterbury Tale*, p. 130.

Marx'.[29] Such a world view rarely bred compromise, and conflict became as 'inevitable'[30] as it was frequent. The 'miner as a citizen', 'zealous custodian of his little cottage' and 'staunch family man' was more attractive, to Bennett, than 'the miner as a unionist'.[31] A neat distinction, it was nevertheless not one the miners would have recognised. The union was more than an instrument for and of industrial relations, it was a vehicle for the negotiation of life's circumstances as they confronted them here and now. It was precisely this connection between life and work that gave their collective solidarity its stubborn and unyielding edge.

Thus it was that, when Pearson sat down in Hampstead Heath, London, to conjure up Coal Flat, he was entering a terrain as familiar in Blackball as it was on unionised coalfields everywhere. How did idealism stack up against the harsh realities of time and place? What space was there in the collectivity of unionism that would at bedrock insist upon loyalty and label as 'a scab' anyone who deviated from union policy? It was a question that Pearson explored in a somewhat different manner in arguably one of the most sustained pieces of polemical writing of his generation, 'Fretful Sleepers'. In this essay, he argues that during the 1951 waterfront dispute the gullible nation was led by the radio pep-talks of a prime minister, cynically determined to exploit the communist bogey, to accept actions that were potentially fascist. In this apparent willingness to conform to the dictates of authority, Pearson detected a reluctance within the wider community of the 1940s and 1950s to tolerate dissent or difference. *Coal Flat* was largely written before the events of 1951, but it has been seen by commentators as the working out of a similar set of concerns. Its essence is an individual at odds with a community whose central values he shares.

Unlike Page and Eaglesham, Paul Rogers, the central character of *Coal Flat,* is not so much an outsider as, to employ Richard Hoggart's words, an 'anxious' and 'uprooted'[32] individual set apart, by education and opportunity, from a community to which he returns. Accepting a position as a teacher in the local primary school brings with it a set of expectations within the community. Rogers has to demonstrate that his status as a representative of 'authority' has not blinded him to his roots. Pearson depicts this tension as a clash of ideas and ideals in which the

29 Bennett, *A Canterbury Tale,* p. 129.
30 Bennett, *A Canterbury Tale,* p. 130.
31 Bennett, *A Canterbury Tale,* p. 134.
32 Hoggart, *The Uses of Literacy,* p. 291.

mining community is presented as 'a hard puritan society, materialistic to the point that it was afraid of ideas because ideas were not material'.[33] To Rogers, the young idealistic teacher, this pragmatism was buttressed by an ingrained suspicion of all that came from outside their own community. The miners' children he was about to teach had, he believed, been 'brought up to sneer at authority and vaunt their intransigence'. In this respect they were preferable to country children who accepted 'their parents' beliefs as unquestionable'.[34] To Rogers, this opened up the possibility that they might be moulded in accordance with the ethical foundations of his particular brand of socialism. It was indeed only when these values—tolerance, service of the common good, consideration for others, self-sacrifice—were widely held that real socialism would, he believed, be possible.

Pearson's central character, in this sense, is a recognisably Blackball one. Rogers stands comfortably in the tradition of Page and Eaglesham. Set apart by occupation, he takes his place within the larger community without joining his idealistic predecessors alongside the miners in the pits. Pearson was later to explain that, as he wrote the novel, Rogers became of less interest to him than the community of *Coal Flat*. It is also recognisably a West Coast one. As writer, Pearson tells us, he had been aware that there was an 'expatriate' dimension; Hampstead Heath was a long way from the Paparoas. And, at times, Pearson has recalled, writing of the bush, gullies and creeks that made up the Blackball he knew made the writing process a 'labour of love'.[35] Critics have uniformly emphasised the dominance of 'the Coast' and pointed to the 'finely evoked … insistent, laborious detail' with which its 'personality' dominated all in a 'uniform, panoramic'.[36]

It is perhaps just as pertinent to note that the bit of Pearson's 'West Coast' that the critics singled out for praise was not the coaltown in which *Coal Flat* is set but its antithesis: the unspoiled, thinly populated, rural wilderness of South Westland. As 'mere land and seascape, few parts of New Zealand can have as concrete and credible an existence in literature as Bill Pearson's South Westland'.[37] It is here that Pearson sets, in a 'serene

33 Pearson, *Coal Flat*, p. 9.

34 Pearson, *Coal Flat*, p. 9.

35 Alex Calder, 'An Interview with Bill Pearson', *Landfall 150*, vol. 47, no. 1, April 1993, p. 57.

36 Stuart Johnston, 'Review: *Coal Flat*. Bill Pearson', *Landfall 67*, vol. 17, no. 3, September 1963, pp. 299–301.

37 Allen Curnow, 'Coal Flat Revisited', in Cherry Hankin, ed., *Critical Essays on the New Zealand Novel*, Auckland, Heinemann Educational Books NZ, 1976, p. 121.

chapter', a whitebaiting sojourn. It stands, as one reviewer put it, apart from the action of the novel, 'placed as (one imagines) a composer might place a contrasting lyrical movement or passage in a symphonic work'.[38] And its descriptions of the 'hard-slogging of the journey, the hut life by the Maori Creek mouth' and the 'labour of netting, of setting and emptying the whitebait traps' were interpreted as offering a 'redemptive' and contrasting setting to the tyranny of the pits and the harshness of the coaltown.[39] Thus, Pearson's 'West Coast' offers hope, or at least a part of it does. Pearson was later to reveal that the interlude was in part an attempt to redress what was thought by some to be the unflattering image given to the only Māori in the initial drafts—Mrs Palmer, a matriarchal and bossy individual.[40] In this sense the whitebaiting expedition draws upon the notion that the Māori offer a wisdom and alternative path to the suffocating normality that predominated in the coaltown and nation.

In *Coal Flat*, however, mine, union and pub shape existence. The narrative brings them together in a way that is reminiscent of Pat Hickey's celebrated recounting of the Tucker Time Strike of 1908. A group of Pearson's fictional miners decide, almost casually, as they make their way along an underground roadway to the coalface, to boycott the pubs until they abandoned a projected increase in the price of beer.[41] This 'spontaneous' decision provides the framework around which the place of unionism is explored. To Rogers, the idealistic socialist seeking a higher purpose for the industrial muscle of the miners, the issue was comic: 'A town sulking over an extra penny a glass'.[42] He rationalises his initial decision to ignore the boycott: had he been a miner, he would have happily abided by 'a union ruling';[43] as a teacher, he considered himself free to regard the issue as a conscience one. His attempt to support the collective and democratic decision of the miners' union to engage in 'peaceful communal action' while himself acting in ways that undermined the effectiveness of such action provides a dramatic tension that suits Pearson's purpose as novelist. It also raises a spectre of the recent past. Little more than a decade earlier, in the midst of the Depression, Blackball had been torn apart as the union was unable to prevent a dissident faction from within the town setting up

38 Curnow, 'Coal Flat Revisited', pp. 119, 121; Frank Sargeson, 'Conversation in a Train', *Landfall 21*, vol. 84, no. 4, December 1967, p. 361.
39 Curnow, 'Coal Flat Revisited', p. 121.
40 Pearson, *Coal Flat*, p. 14.
41 Pearson, *Coal Flat*, pp. 206–7.
42 Pearson, *Coal Flat*, p. 213.
43 Pearson, *Coal Flat*, p. 213.

a 'tribute' company and thereby threatening the integrity of the union and working conditions in the mines.[44] Pearson draws in part on the residual animosities of these past battles as he explores the relationship between union, community and the individual. In Mrs Seldom he creates a tragic embittered by-product of such a conflict living in self-imposed isolation, an ever-present reminder of troubles past.

The boundary between union and community is a shifting one. As an idea the union permeates all that occurs in *Coal Flat* and Pearson understands its dynamics. The formal decision to boycott 7d beer is taken at a bathhouse meeting as the miners sit in their pit-clothes ready to begin their shift, 'their batteries on their belts and lamps on their helmets'.[45] The good-natured banter of the meeting contrasts with the stark reality of work underground:

> Down below you took on the mentality of citizens whose sleep might at any time be disturbed by an air-raid siren, who had lived like this for years. Extracting the earth's frozen power, you lived at enmity with it. At any time it might fall and bury you. A random spark might strike off an explosion, or a race of boxes run loose downhill. You were always on the alert; though you had worked here without a scratch for twenty years and though you hardly acknowledged the thought you never knew that you would see the sun again that afternoon. The town that lived off raiding the earth carried its casualties—Alec, carpentering on the surface, limping because of his heel torn to the bone by a winch-cable; Sandy with three fingers bitten off where two trucks collided, reared from their bumpers and kissed where his hand tried to hold one of them back; Fred with an eye torn out when a badly-aimed sprag flew back from the spoke of a downhill truck; and the graves in Karoro, from falls of stone, and explosions. Underground you had to settle your habits into realizing that you were a cog in a lumbering inefficient machine for gutting the earth and that any mistake you made might cause a breakdown or an accident to other men. An error of judgement was a sin, an oversight inexcusable. When you were broken into the mine mentality you had what they called pit sense.[46]

44 Richardson, 'Class, Community and Conflict', pp. 106–27.
45 Pearson, *Coal Flat*, pp. 205–8.
46 Pearson, *Coal Flat*, pp. 205–8.

Mining unionism gained most of its gritty hardness from these realities, and Pearson's union leaders have no difficulty placing the beer boycott squarely in the tradition of legitimate working-class activity: 'We don't want any scabbing in this thing. Either we're all boycotting the beer, or we take no action at all. Not some *in* the pubs and some out'.[47] The younger men, writes Pearson, 'were glib about it' but 'knew they would have to abide by their decision'.[48]

Pearson's interest in the union is, of course, bound up with his preoccupation with the individual who attempts to stand out from community norms. Rogers understands the historical loyalties that bind the miners to their collective decisions but finds himself caught up in the fringes of the political struggles that both shaped and were shaped by the union. Pearson presents these struggles in both generational and ideological terms. Representative of the district's radical, if not heroic, age is Bernie O'Malley, now an ageing member of parliament. Once a fellow-traveller of Red Fed firebrands, he had been imprisoned during the anti-conscription campaigns of World War I. He was now losing touch with the younger men whose ideological framework had been honed by different circumstances and different ideas. And among the 'Clydeside, Yorkshire and Tyneside accents' that reverberate throughout Pearson's *Coal Flat*, the voice of Jock McEwan is that of the 'damp, filthy, disease ridden warrens' of the Gorbals, whose notorious backlands had been noted by Friedrich Engels in his celebrated *Condition of the Working Class in England* (1845). He is the representative of the 'Clydeside Reds' and, in 1940s Blackball, as elsewhere, this was a phrase that continued to conjure up images of the Glasgow rent strikes of 1915 and what one recent historian has described as 'the nearest thing to a revolutionary situation seen in twentieth century Britain'.[49]

It was a moment when 'a few strategic moves by the Red Clydeside leaders *could* have led to a local seizure of power by workers'.[50] Thus, in *Coal Flat*, McEwan's voice carries the conviction that experience confers and conveys a 'toughness' that was, in its origins, a reflection of historically harsh working and living conditions. To this historical legacy newer arrivals in the 1920s added the lessons drawn from the nine-day General

47 Pearson, *Coal Flat*, p. 209.
48 Pearson, *Coal Flat*, p. 209.
49 Sean Damer, *Glasgow: Going for a Song*, London, Lawrence & Wishart, 1990, p. 117.
50 Damer, *Going for a Song*, p. 117.

Strike of May 1926 that had taken British coalfields into a winter of starvation. The ultimate terrible defeat in December had ended the industrial militancy of the 1920s and smashed the Miners' Federation of Great Britain (MFGB) as any kind of force for more than a decade. This was the 'miners' history' that shaped the lives of many in the community that Pearson describes. Grounded, as it was, in an instinctive recognition of the nature of capitalist exploitation, it was a history that peppered 'pit talk' and took its place alongside and helped shape a rich and sometimes inspiring local tradition. And, like idealists of the real world who had gone before (Page and Eaglesham), Rogers struggles to find a way of putting the collective authority of the miners' union to work for improving purposes. His dilemma, as one commentator reviewing *Coal Flat* remarked, is that of a 'priest without a religion' attempting to use the miners' union as a substitute Church.[51]

This is clearly demonstrated when Rogers attempts to persuade a meeting of a Labour Party branch addressed by Bernie O'Malley, the local member of parliament, to take some action to limit the sale of comics in the town. His suggestion that the comics, 'full of war and crime; sex, violence and cruelty',[52] would cause a lot of harm came during question time after a knock-about meeting in which O'Malley and local Communists had confronted each other. To O'Malley, the Labour program was imperilled by a changed international situation: 'half of Europe lived in terror of the iron heel, the secret police, forced labour, the knock on the door at three o'clock in the morning'.[53] Describing his opponents as 'power-hunting hirelings of Joe Stalin' bent upon breaking up the meeting, he asks his *Coal Flat* audience whether they wanted the 'world to be submerged in the system of atheistic communism—the system that denied God and Christianity'—and the work of the Labour Government imperilled by industrial disputes engineered by the Kremlin.[54]

Rogers was caught in the crossfire. He had rejected the red-baiting tone of O'Malley's speech and then, in the manner of the middle-class academic, had argued that there was 'plenty of evidence to suggest that Russia has betrayed the principles of socialism'. The socialist cause was not advanced by 'the grey monolithic state imposing itself on the lives

51 Prebble, 'Coal Flat', p. 35.
52 Pearson, *Coal Flat*, p. 115.
53 Pearson, *Coal Flat*, p. 111.
54 Pearson, *Coal Flat*, p. 112.

of ordinary citizens'.[55] In a burst of point scoring, he drops in the names Arthur Koestler and Ignazio Silone—two of six ex-Communist, left-wing writers who after the war had contributed to *The God That Failed*. An explicit reference to Koestler's *Darkness at Noon* (1940), with its powerful exposé of Stalin's show trials, brought a stern rebuke: 'You can't argue from a work of fiction'.[56]

In tone and in substance, Rogers's intervention affirms his marginality in *Coal Flat*. His introduction of the comic question is an artless and clumsy afterthought coming as it does after the ideological cut and thrust of the clash between O'Malley and the Communists. The miners had manoeuvred the politician into promising that a seven-hour shift would be introduced in the mines before the end of the year and most stood up and prepared to leave 'without clapping', dismissing the evening's performance from their minds.[57] In the dialectic of the meeting and the sound of the miners 'clapping half-heartedly', Allen Curnow, writing in the mid-1970s, detected the origins of Labour's 'modern labour dilemma'. As a political party, he argued, it was torn 'between apologising *to* or *for*, the more militant spirits of its past' and 'its present power-base in industry'.[58] For Pearson, the meeting, and especially the exchange between Rogers and the Communists, established the fragile nature of the young teacher's idealistic socialism.

The pub even more than the mine is the hub of the story. One of two in the town (the other, 2 miles away in Paparoa), its function is clearly established. It acts as a boarding house for two of the primary school teachers and allows them to stand, as it were, slightly apart from both the miners and their families and the single miners in their huts. Pearson invests talk in the bar with a 'greater range' of subject than was the norm.[59] The pace and pattern of its day is set by the shifts of the miners as much as by the strictures of the licensing laws. Commercial viability rested upon after-hours trading and, as one publican explained to Licensing Commissioners, a coalfields pub acted as a meeting house where men had

55 Pearson, *Coal Flat*, p. 114.

56 Pearson, *Coal Flat*, p. 114. *Darkness at Noon* (1940) was the second of Arthur Koestler's trilogy that dealt with idealism going wrong. The other two were: *The Gladiators* (1939) and *Arrival and Departure* (1943). *The God That Failed* (1949) brought together six testimonies by journalists and writers who had become disillusioned with Communism.

57 Curnow, 'Coal Flat Revisited', pp. 105–27.

58 Curnow, 'Coal Flat Revisited', p. 112.

59 Pearson, *Coal Flat*, p. 23.

an opportunity to have a drink. Few miners came directly to the pub at the end of a shift. Most drinkers attended to 'a lot of household duties', had a meal and headed for the pub sometime after 6 pm. In short, the coalfields public house was cast, at least in the operation of its bars, in the English rather than the colonial mould. That it could function in this way required a gentleman's agreement—a commonsense set of conventions that saw the bar operate until 10 pm.[60] Local practices notwithstanding, the miners collectively supported the proposition that just as the mine in which they worked had been nationalised so, too, should the nation's liquor industry.

That the issue around which Rogers's idealism is put to the test should be a 'beer boycott' serves to highlight the dilemma of the 'improvers'. Among local communists there was a cynicism about the cultural question. The humanists and communists shared the belief that the lure of the bar-rail blinded workers to the all-pervasive capitalist oppression and weakened the capacity of unions to use the strike as a weapon of anything other than last resort. They nonetheless shared the hope that the working-class community could liberate itself. As thoughtful corporals in the class war, they were, of course, anxious to hasten the process. Men like Eaglesham and Page had, in the 1920s and 1930s, been at the forefront of left-wing educational activities. They arranged the publication of extracts from left-wing literature in the pages of the *Grey River Argus*, organised discussion classes for the Workers' Educational Association and maintained after 1939 a 'freely patronised' library of over 150 books for the Left Book Club as part of an attempt to make literature available to 'even the humblest worker'.[61] Pearson contrasts this cultural socialism with the more rigid attitudes of 'Marxism-Leninism-Stalinism' for which class struggle is the only 'justifiable activity' and to whose exponents 'community centres and play-acting and all the rest of it are all very well … after victory'.[62]

The tension between these competing forms of socialism reflect an underlying and fruitful tension in Pearson's depiction of Coal Flat. On the one hand, as we have already seen, the mining community is presented as being impervious to and afraid of ideas; on the other hand, the debates between the miners are rooted in a variety of ideological positions.

60 The wider Westland community was divided in its attitude to the nation's drinking laws; in 1949, 4,764 voted in favour of retaining 6 pm and 4,475 wanted 10 pm closing.

61 Rachel Barrowman, *A Popular Vision: The Arts and the Left in New Zealand, 1930–1950*, Wellington, Victoria University Press, 1991, pp. 68–72.

62 Pearson, *Coal Flat*, p. 75.

Ideas were in fact a central part of life on the coalfields. The great majority of miners may not have picked up ideas in study groups or reading clubs, but rather in the jostle of ideas that peppered union meetings and were never far from the surface in everyday life. To a degree, Rogers comes to recognise this and redefines his conception of unionism and its role in Coal Flat. His faith in the ability of unions to give effect to a broad socialist agenda—never so much described as alluded to—is tested during the winter of 1947. He had invested a great deal of emotional capital in the ability of union officials to provide, if not intellectual leadership, then direction. In short, he believed that the way ideas were received and spread was very much in the hands of a small elite—the socialist vanguard—that had risen through union ranks. It was their task to raise the awareness of the majority. It was this high sense of purpose that was offended by the beer boycott that, as we have seen, he viewed as a comical if not cynical abuse of union power. He came to accept that the boycott was a legitimate exercise of the collective solidarity of the miners and acknowledges that the wider social reconstruction he seeks is simply not something the union can be expected to initiate.

This is most clearly revealed in Rogers's reaction to the birth of workingmen's clubs throughout the Grey Valley. On 1 October 1947 the Grey Valley Licensed Victuallers' Association announced that the price of beer would increase to 7d a glass (softening the blow by suggesting they would introduce a 12 oz glass also to sell for 7d) and that the price of a glass of spirits would be reduced. The Central Organising Committee appointed by the Westland Trades and Labour Council to coordinate the boycott called for the nationalisation of the liquor industry and the creation of workingmen's clubs. Meetings at Blackball, Runanga, Brunner, Reefton, Waiuta, Greymouth and Hokitika endorsed the argument that the new clubs would break the hold of the beer barons and provide a more congenial environment for community activities. Long a feature of life on British coalfields they were an extension of the self-help principle that had fostered the cooperative society. Designed 'to provide recreation, a place for talk and reading and some education, for working-men', by the mid-twentieth century these objectives were 'still formally alive, though little more than that'. They continued to serve as 'pub-cum-club' for more than 2 million members in 3,000 separate clubs and remained defiantly proud of being run for members and 'not … for the benefit of the profiteers'.[63] From an idealist perspective, the embryonic clubs of the

63 Hoggart, *The Uses of Literacy*, p. 151.

Grey Valley could be, and were, promoted as an example of independent working-class activity and also as institutions through which educational and cultural objectives might be realised.

Pearson presents these issues in a discussion between Rogers and an orthodox Marxist, Dr Alexander. The pair assess the potential of a workingmen's club in the process of being established in a local billiards room in Coal Flat. Alexander expresses confidence in the leadership potential of the educated, socialist professional within working-class communities. It was possible to 'identify with the workers', he tells a disillusioned Rogers, without having to become one.[64] He suggests Rogers move into adult education and that in such a role it would be possible to develop the workingmen's club as the hub of community activity. Rogers is sceptical:

> The climate's not favourable. No one wants to learn anything. Everyone's too comfortable having a sleep, even the miners. You wouldn't even get the horse to water, let alone make him drink. And people don't learn that way. They learn best from their own experience and what the miners learn will be from their collective experience, from disputes and action and settlements of disputes, not from classes in history and politics and literature … What's the use in stimulating activity when no one feels the need for it? All they feel the need of in the new club is beer and billiards and forty-fives … Drama groups, reading and discussion groups in Coal Flat! It would be as phoney as glee clubs or marching girls … Union meetings in the day, crime films at night.[65]

That the union had wittingly been the instrument of this 'escapism'—the Blackball Miners' Union Hall and Welfare Society organised film showings and redirected the profits from them into community projects and individual welfare—had long been a contentious issue among coalfield ideologues. The Miners' Page of the *Grey River Argus* had periodically denounced the silver screen as 'one of the strongest props of the present system of exploitation'.[66]

In this outburst, Rogers confronts the dilemma of the idealist who has invested in mining unionism a potential for progressive reformism that was beyond its capacity to deliver. Dismissing the prospects of the

64 Pearson, *Coal Flat*, p. 415.
65 Pearson, *Coal Flat*, p. 416.
66 *Grey River Argus*, 1926.

workingmen's club ever becoming more than a 'co-operative society for the purchase and sale of beer' is too harsh. In historical terms, the clubs had come to New Zealand coalfields, as we have seen, late in the piece, as coaltowns were beginning to fragment and their populations were ageing. Better transport was already making it possible for miners to live at greater remove from their workplace. The Labour Government's housing program was providing affordable housing in the larger towns of Greymouth and Westport. Consequently, the old community that worked and lived together was slowly being dismantled. In a trend that first became evident during the 1920s and 1930s and quickened sharply after the war, young men (and especially those who had entered the mines to take advantage of the protected industry status of the wartime coalmining industry) were moving away from the coaltowns. The tradition of son following father was similarly being broken down as opportunities widened. In terms of community coherence and creativity, the birth of the workingmen's clubs came at a time when their potential for providing an impetus for change and self-improvement was limited.

As an example of community action, the creation of the Grey Valley workingmen's clubs was nonetheless impressive in both its speed and ingenuity. After little more than two months, plans had been finalised for clubs in Blackball, Brunner, Greymouth, Runanga and Hokitika. Brunner's was first to open. 'Rough and ready' premises were opened on 21 December 1947, on land leased from the Brunner Borough Council at the rear of the Dobson mine, and as men finished their shift and began their walk home they could now go straight to the club. Two further clubs had opened before Christmas. Runanga miners raised the money to purchase from the state a property that had previously housed the district mine manager. In Greymouth, the combined resources of miners, watersiders and railwaymen were sufficient to purchase a two-storey house on Alexander Terrace. Elsewhere the process was slower, but within two years Blackball, Reefton, Hokitika and Westport each had a workingmen's club. The legal position was initially shaky. In theory, the clubs were unable to offer beer for sale across the bar until they achieved the status of a chartered club. With this achieved, the Workingmen's Clubs and Mutual Schools of Arts, to give them their full title, became a feature of coalfields life. Some were bemused by the grandiose title; the only 'art' was 'in the drinking'.[67]

67 *Greymouth Evening Star*, 12 March 1994.

The communitarian possibilities of the workingmen's clubs, as envisaged by the more idealistic in the late 1940s, were never fully realised. Yet there can be little doubt that, for many, life was enriched by their presence. Perhaps the greatest beneficiary of the clubs was sport, an activity barely visible in Pearson's *Coal Flat* and introduced as a symbol of conservative values, past glories and physicality. Football (and for Pearson this means rugby union) is suggested by a Catholic priest as a more appropriate activity for Rogers than political activism.[68] 'Mr. Tribe', the ubiquitous 'Mr. Fat', whose pep-talk to wavering members of the Westland Branch of the Licensed Victuallers' Association is a caricature of Cold War capitalism's unlovely face, is a 1923 All Black and one of the new army of business functionaries rallying behind a resurgent National Party. To the generation who looked backwards to a past stocked with images of resilient gold seekers and the pyrotechnics of pugnacious socialists, periodic sporting success and military heroism—'All Blacks did well on an overseas tour, or a war came and perhaps a local lad got a V.C.'[69]—remained markers of vitality, if not regeneration.

Yet if, as Peter Simpson has written, we are to see Pearson's novel as a fictionalising of mainstream New Zealand, a place where 'coal mines, saw-mills, pubs and football clubs' pass for normality, then sport, as one ingredient of that normality, is largely missing from the community in which Paul Rogers moves.[70] Whether this was a conscious decision or merely a by-product of literary artifice is unclear. One of Pearson's obituarists tells us that throughout his life Pearson remained 'sports numb' and that he had taken a perverse pleasure in noting that 'his Herne Bay home had been built a century ago by the famous All Black captain Dave Gallaher, while his nephew, Fred Goodall, had become one of our best known cricket umpires'.[71] Whatever the reason for the marginal role played by sport in *Coal Flat*, it would have been impossible, in the Blackball of 1947, to ignore the sport of rugby league.

68 Pearson, *Coal Flat*, p. 133.

69 Pearson, *Coal Flat*, p. 323. Samuel Frickleton worked in the Blackball mine, 1913–15, before enlisting. He was awarded a Victoria Cross for bravery shown at Messines on 7 June 1917.

70 Peter Simpson, 'Bill Pearson's New Zealand Then and Now: Testimony of an Internal Rapporteur', *Landfall 194*, no. 3, Spring 1997, pp. 214–15.

71 Paul Millar, 'William Harrison Pearson: 1922–2002', *Journal of New Zealand Literature*, no. 20, 2002, pp. 164–69.

As Geoffrey Moorhouse has written, Blackball had been in the 1930s and 1940s a 'nursery of footballers'.[72] The game of rugby league had come to the West Coast during World War I as part of a missionary expedition from Christchurch where the code had established a solid base in the aftermath of the pioneering tour to Britain by the 'All Golds' team in 1907–08. Blackball miners played their first game on 16 June 1915 on the local domain against a visiting side from Canterbury. After the game a club was formed. The timing was significant; it coincided with the genesis of the anti-conscription campaign by the Miners' Federation and the conjunction of events had the effect of attaching the game to a radical and oppositional culture. Among conservatives it was seen as evidence that, in their sport as in much else, the miners were 'troublemakers'. In the 1930s Blackball miners had played their part in making the West Coast the nation's pre-eminent rugby league province.

During the early 1940s the club had become arguably the dominant South Island club, being six times (between 1940 and 1947) winner of the Thacker Shield—the symbol of Canterbury–West Coast club rugby league supremacy.[73] In 1947 seven members of the 25-strong Kiwi side to tour Great Britain came from the West Coast, four of them from Blackball: Bob Aynsley, Ray Nuttall, Ken Mountford and Charlie McBride.[74] At the heart of the rise of the local club were the brothers Mountford. Two, Ken and Bill, were to play for the Kiwis. In 1947 Ken, as a loose forward for the touring Kiwi side, found himself chasing brother Ces around Central Park, Wigan, where he had become something of a local hero while studying at Wigan's celebrated Mining and Technical College for a manager's certificate. Whereas in Pearson's *Coal Flat* it is the two schoolteachers who board at the Palmer's pub, in 1947 two of Blackball's most famous league players, Charlie McBride and Bill (Ginger) McLennan, had adjacent rooms at the hotel.[75] But the flow of rugby league players from the Blackball mines was already beginning to slow. There were two further Thacker Shield victories—1950 and 1953—but thereafter the ability of the township to retain the young men needed to keep the victories coming slowly withered.

72 Geoffrey Moorhouse, *At the George and Other Essays on Rugby League*, London, Hodder and Stoughton, 1989, p. 140.

73 The exact years were 1940, 1942, 1943, 1945, 1946 and 1947.

74 The other three West Coasters were Jack Newton and 'Nippy' Forrest, both miners from Runanga, and Artie Gillman, a policeman from Hokitika.

75 Peter Kerridge, 'Obituary: Bill McLennan', *Press* (Christchurch), 18 August 2007.

The absence of sport from *Coal Flat* goes to the heart of the dilemma that Pearson created for Paul Rogers. In part, such a dilemma is founded upon the separation of culture into popular, or mass, and high culture (the arts and literature). Rogers's efforts to bridge this gulf meet not so much resistance as indifference. Part of the problem, then, in constructing the dilemma is that it does not confront the bit in between—in short, those elements of the community experience that fall outside Pearson's *Coal Flat*. In the fictional world this does not matter much. But it does indicate the self-imposed limits of Pearson's interest in the 'wider community'. It is also in tune with the prevalent belief that New Zealand's attitude to sport was 'colonial' or 'primitive', and therefore to be, if not shunned, then at least shuffled off into another category of experience. Sport was, therefore, an inescapable part of the national landscape that helped make sense of the present, but one that more sophisticated folks hoped might find a lesser place in the future.

It is a perspective recognised and, in some degree, accepted in John Mulgan's celebrated *Report on Experience*:

> Our main pursuits were only cultural in the broadest sense. They were horse-racing, playing rugby football, and beer drinking—especially playing football ... This phenomenon is greatly deprecated by a lot of thinkers who feel that an exaggerated attention to games gives the young a wrong sense of values. This may well be true and, if it is true, the majority of New Zealanders have a wrong sense of values for the whole of their lives. But to be frank, and since we live in a hard world, and one that has certainly not in my time got any softer, I found in wartime that there was a considerable virtue in men who played games like professionals to win, and not, like public-school boys and amateurs, for exercise. So that perhaps it would be more correct to say that the virtues and values of the New Zealanders were not so much wrong as primitive, and to this extent useful in the current collapse of civilisation.[76]

That Mulgan had rugby union rather than rugby league in mind when he made his comments speaks of both his own social position and the lower place in national consciousness of what was then, and very largely remains, a working-class sport. By omitting league from his depiction

76 John Mulgan, *Report on Experience*, Wellington, Pen & Sword Books and Victoria University Press, 2010, p. 40.

of his fictional community, Pearson is simply sticking to more familiar terrain. The sporting preoccupations of the miners could be regarded as an affirmation of physicality and one further example of the presentism that prevailed within the community; above all, they were a distraction in the same way as the cinema, to which miners retreated after union meetings. In literary terms, ignoring such a significant slice of coalfields life is explicable and scarcely inconsistent. Historians, sociologists and anthropologists were only beginning to turn their attention to working-class leisure. But even studies such as Richard Hoggart's *The Uses of Literacy* (1957) and Norman Dennis, Fernando Henriques and Clifford Slaughter's *Coal Is Our Life* (1956), which recognise the importance of sport in working-class culture, did not pursue it very far.[77] Nor were there many literary precedents. David Storey's celebrated *This Sporting Life*[78] was not published until 1960, by which time *Coal Flat* had taken its final shape. Indeed, as we have seen, it is very much a book of the late 1940s. It is also an 'expatriate work' written, as Pearson has explained, at some distance from New Zealand and from the coaltown it depicts. If it was, as Pearson wrote in 1960, the 'difference in atmosphere between London and New Zealand that generated "Fretful Sleepers"', then the same framework shaped *Coal Flat* and had little place for sport.[79]

A West Coast coalminer, writer, playwright and actor from a later generation, Mervyn Thompson, addressed the relationship of sport and art directly. He endorsed Pearson's view that New Zealanders were 'viciously addicted to the habit of glorifying sporting heroes while insulting or ignoring its artists'.[80] Nonetheless, in his autobiographical *All My Lives*, Thompson sought to balance the charge with a spirited denunciation of the 'anti-sport lobby':

> Too many people in the theatre world—and the arts generally—are totally snobbish about sport. Alienated from the land they live in and in many cases looking rather wistfully towards old Europe, they never tire of telling anyone who will listen how much they despise 'Kiwi philistines' and their 'common' pursuits ... With their superior sensibilities you'd think they'd know better.[81]

77 Hoggart, *The Uses of Literacy*; Norman Dennis, Fernando Henriques and Clifford Slaughter, *Coal Is Our Life: An Analysis of a Yorkshire Mining Community*, 2nd edn, London, Tavistock Publications (Social Science Paperback), 1969.

78 David Storey, *This Sporting Life*, London, Longmans Green & Co., 1960.

79 Peter Simpson, 'Bill Pearson's New Zealand Then and Now', *Landfall 194*, Spring 1997, p. 205.

80 Mervyn Thompson, *All My Lives*, Christchurch, Whitcoulls, 1980, pp. 50–51.

81 Thompson, *All My Lives*, pp. 50–51.

Nonetheless, when he reflects upon the Runanga of the 1940s and 1950s, he attributes the appeal of football squarely to a physical environment that was 'a testament to man's ability to survive at the lowest ebb of his existence'.[82] So harsh and unyielding was the state coaltown that it led young miners, he believed, to prize above all else 'physical dominance over others'. Thus, Thompson seems to suggest that while football as a sport possessed the potential to exhibit the finer elements of human achievement, in its Runanga or coalfield setting, it exhibited a crudity that approached barbarism.

Others saw the place of sport in mining towns more positively. Dr Francis Bennett, who as we have noted experienced Blackball in the grim years of the 1930s, thought the establishment of a domain, football ground and football club a testament to the township's communitarian spirit and civic pride. The 'scraping off the wages'[83] that made such amenities possible was an expression of a resilient citizenship that spoke of a future. In much the same way as the union had provided a generation of ideologues with a pathway into national politics, Blackball provided its most talented rugby league men with a platform from which to launch themselves onto a national and, for a select few, an international stage. And beyond football there was a range of organised sporting activities sustained by the town: wrestling, boxing, soccer (though never as successfully as the Buller coaltowns of Millerton and Stockton), cycling and quoits. May Day sports in Blackball rivalled in enthusiasm, if not in scale, the St Patrick's Day celebrations in Greymouth. All, to a greater or lesser extent, added to the threads of a shared experience that set individual coaltowns apart from each other and from other communities.

Sporting clubs did not in Blackball, any more than they did anywhere else, dominate community life. A Caledonian Society flourished among the sizeable number of Scots who had come to Blackball in the 1920s and especially after Britain's 1926 General Strike. They sustained a pipe band that was to be an ever-present symbol of a Scottish presence at the head of demonstrations in Blackball and represented the town in competitions and gatherings throughout the South Island. Their celebration of Burns Night was a feature of the social calendar. Despite Rogers's assertion in *Coal Flat* that a drama society would be 'as phoney as glee clubs or

82 Thompson, *All My Lives*, p. 13.
83 Bennett, *A Canterbury Tale*, p. 131.

marching girls',[84] Blackball at various times had sustained one. A debating club peopled by the 'earnest minority' addressed such topics as 'whether the rebel or the constitutionists have done more for the advancement of humanity'. Whatever else these activities tell us about Blackball, they point to a diverse range of community activity.

It could be said, of course, that *Coal Flat* is played out at the withering end of this communal creativity. In Blackball, as elsewhere on the coalfields, the celebrations that greeted the nationalisation of the pits had been muted. The demise of the well-compensated coal barons did not so much come at the height of a capitalist peak but as the Blackball mine neared the end of its productive life and the coal industry was in retreat. Since the troubles of the late 1920s, the bonds of community had struggled to thwart the long slide into the oblivion into which the old goldtowns had descended. The building of a new primary school in 1930 had been hailed as the forerunner of a high school.[85] The same confident flush encouraged the Miners' Union Hall and Welfare Society to explore with the Western Electric Talking Pictures Company the prospect of bringing 'talkies' to the town. By 1936, as calls for assistance grew and contributions withered, the society closed its books. A decade later the society purged its rolls of unfinancial members, borrowed £200 from a private individual and reduced the annual grant for the children's picnic from £25 to £5.[86]

Nothing better captures the ambiguous and contradictory nature of Blackball's predicament in the late 1940s than the circumstances confronting the Miners' Hall. A product of the optimism of the early 1920s, it stood at the head of Main Street alongside the hotel and opposite the billiards rooms soon to become the workingmen's club. Like the bulk of the township, it had been built on land leased from a London-based trust. Paying the rental had been a recurring reminder of capitalism's ubiquitous presence. The 21-year lease expired in 1947 just as nationalisation of the pits became a reality. Was there another 21 years in the coal seam? Canny union leaders began with an abortive attempt to derive more income from hall rentals. The major tenant, the company that operated the picture theatre, was struggling to remain viable and had

84 Pearson, *Coal Flat*, p. 416.

85 *Grey River Argus*, 25 October 1930.

86 Blackball Miners' Union Hall and Welfare Society Minute Book, 1946, ms, private collection, p. 21.

cancelled Saturday afternoon sessions.[87] The visible signs of communal endeavour under stress were apparent as the library and reading room of the Hall fell into disrepair.

Literary critics detected something similar in the final passages of *Coal Flat*. To some the final words of the novel seemed 'bleak and laconic, if not fatalistic', and indicative of a surrender to the contingencies of time and place:

> and the school-bell rang for playtime. In the mine men paused to swig from the thermos-flasks, and the postboy's whistle piped a small signature to the sudden quietness as the dredge stopped for smoko. In the distance a motor-bike started up, and a delivery van pulled up in front of the grocer's; a heavy truck loaded with barrels stopped outside one of the pubs. It occurred to Jessie, feeling the freshness of the hills and the cicadas singing, that it would be about as good a summer as they'd ever had on the Coast.[88]

Pearson rejected such a reading of the passage as based on an ignorance of just how good a West Coast summer could be and at odds with his intention.

In writing *Coal Flat*, he later explained, he had been attracted by the artistic symmetry involved in leaving his story very much as he had entered it—an idea he attributed to Koestler's novel *Arrival and Departure*.[89] Thus, when readers first meet *Coal Flat* it is on 'a sunny February morning throbbing with cicadas';[90] they leave on a 'sunny November morning' where 'already the air was singing with grass cicadas'.[91] Life goes on much as it always had, seemingly untouched by the crises that had enveloped the lives of the individuals at the centre of the novel. Its central character, Paul Rogers, whose estrangement from the community provided the dynamic of the narrative, comes to accept much of what Pearson calls the 'hopes and beliefs'[92] of the majority. Communality might thus be seen as the handmaiden of conformity. It might also be seen as an arbiter of the levels of diversity that seemed appropriate to the circumstances of time and place.

87 Blackball Miners' Union Hall and Welfare Society Minute Book, 1946, p. 146.
88 Pearson, *Coal Flat*, p. 419.
89 Pearson, 'Beginnings and Endings', p. 21.
90 Pearson, *Coal Flat*, p. 6.
91 Pearson, *Coal Flat*, p. 418.
92 Pearson, 'Beginnings and Endings', p. 21.

6

BEYOND THE 1960s I

Literary Reflections

The following two chapters explore the West Coast's literary and historical writing that built upon the foundations laid by the centennial generation. Coalminers and their communities stand at its centre. We begin by tracing the literary antecedents that portrayed coalfields life and played a significant role in shaping attitudes and assumptions. This sets the discussion against a backdrop provided by Pat O'Farrell's finely and imaginatively drawn recreation of his family's experience of the Grey Valley in the middle years of the twentieth century that forms the core of *Vanished Kingdoms*. Commentators most frequently, and rightly, praise the book's contribution to the literature of the Irish diaspora. Less often remarked is O'Farrell's unequivocal restating of the Grey Valley's unequal and unrelenting nature as it confronted the changing forms of modern capitalism. It is this theme that stands at the centre of the discussion that follows.

As different as the 'West Coasts' of Pearson, O'Farrell and May were, their perspectives set the terms upon which the Coast took its place in the unfolding national story. Pearson's mix of realistic analysis and literary artifice deeply connected to the natural world presented the omnipresent bush as imposing timelessness upon events and inducing among its people an introspection that both fostered community and defined its limits. O'Farrell's 'Coast' is similarly imagined: a tragic, isolated place where life is played out in a 'cheerless rotting damp' and the human spirit is stretched to its limits. Neither the acquisitive, individualistic instincts unleashed by the discovery of gold, nor the insatiable demands of industrial capitalism provided the basis for an enduring equilibrium between people and place. By figuratively standing on the slopes of Scandinavian Hill alongside 'Jimmy the Slogger and Liverpool Bill, Gentleman George and Yankee Dan', Phil May sought to understand the rush of '65 in its own terms. The result was a closely textured and rich account of the interaction between the diggers and the land over which they swarmed. May's historical perspective possessed a comparative dimension rooted in the diverse nature of the experiences that diggers brought to the quest for instant riches. The balance sheet he drew up on the endeavours of its foundational generation acknowledged achievement and innovation and counted the cost for individuals and region within a framework that remained defiantly optimistic.

In the late 1980s when O'Farrell revisited his literary Grey Valley, he did so with a perspective enhanced by an unsurpassed understanding of the Irish diaspora and the adjustment and adaptation critical to the process of migration. There is a noticeably more vigorously expressed analysis of the conflict between mine owners and organised labour. The emphasis is now upon the tragic dimensions of an unequal struggle between the remote forces of international capitalism and migrant miners whose communal environment was so raw and devoid of resources that it left them, collectively and individually, cruelly exposed to the demands of prolonged industrial battles with their employers. The efforts to establish the customs and working practices of the old world, which supported the expansion of industrial unionism in the new, were imbued, O'Farrell now suggests, with a 'utopian idealism'. Theirs was a 'naïve and passive confidence in the omnipotence of combination' that induced a 'warm glow of (false) commonality and the illusion of shared strength'.[1] The belief was that they were 'fighting for a principle'—an abstract idea that, no matter how imperfectly understood, betokened a widespread sense that right was on their side.

'Men must have dreams',[2] is O'Farrell's judgement of this late nineteenth-century Grey Valley coalfield idealism. The immediate aftermath, in his view, was closer to nightmare: the newly created unions were swept aside amid mass dismissals and widespread impoverishment. Before the community could reconstruct itself, on 26 March 1896, 65 miners were killed in an explosion at the Brunner mine, the worst mining disaster to that date in the colony's history. Reflecting upon the combined impact

1 O'Farrell, 'Noble National Myths', p. 34.
2 O'Farrell, 'Noble National Myths', p. 34.

of industrial defeat, economic stagnation and mine disaster, O'Farrell is struck by the grimness of life in the Grey Valley. Brunner's tale, of dream and disillusion followed by disaster, read 'like bad melodrama, desperately sad, ruled by dark and largely impersonal forces, with the human actors shadowy and uncomprehending, caught in the grip of their fates'. It was, O'Farrell suggests, 'a grim play, now badly dated, hard to believe, of no inspiration save for endurance, a performance which will never be staged again'. By the late 1890s, he laments, 'Brunner was dead—breathing, but yet an economic and psychological corpse'.[3] Brunner's misfortune was to be in a struggle with unrestrained monopoly capitalism as the familiar coalfields life-cycle of expansion, contraction and decay neared its nadir.

O'Farrell's reprise of his earlier account of the Grey Valley came in the 1990s as capitalism, in its corporate garb, was pursuing a neoliberal agenda that allowed 'dark and impersonal forces' to prevail once more. Against this background, O'Farrell now invoked what had become the dominant metaphor of West Coast writing, historical or fictional: the quest to build community against insuperable odds. Its concerns were those common to pioneering literature: the absence of the recognisable tangible and intangible forms of social cohesion and the physical and climatic obstacles that stood in the way of its achievement. As coal and timber proved incapable of providing a viable basis for a flourishing local economy, the celebration of past achievement that coloured Coast literature takes on the more sombre tones characteristic of the literature of nostalgia. The emphasis is upon the withering of community as a pervasive neoliberal political agenda allowed the market to dictate the future and made little allowance for the ability of the regions to adjust to the new political economy.

O'Farrell's perspective on the foundation years of Grey Valley mining communities has its roots in the challenges they mounted to the political economy of the late nineteenth century. In contesting the supposed sanctity of the law of supply and demand upon which the expansion of a largely unregulated industrial capitalism depended for its legitimacy, Brunner miners were reluctant followers of the Denniston miners, newcomers from British coalfields.[4] Both communities were cruelly exposed in this contest with international capitalism. The apparent futility of their struggle forms the essence of O'Farrell's treatment of nineteenth-

3 O'Farrell, 'Noble National Myths', p. 35.

4 Richardson, *Coal, Class & Community*, pp. 17–51.

century coalfields communities. It is a historical perspective that echoes the popular literary responses to the Coast that had flowered briefly on the coalfields in the early years of the twentieth century. Described variously as proletarian, working-class or socialist, such writing forms part of an essentially moral response to the economic transformation that followed the Industrial Revolution.[5] As imperial offshoots of the 'workshop of the world', West Coast coalfields provided a challenging environment for industrial capitalism.

The first literary interpreters of life in West Coast coaltowns came from within. They were migrant miners fresh from British coalfields and hopeful that they had left the evils of industrialisation behind them. The most well-known of them was Edward Hunter (1885–1959), a young Scot, who came to the West Coast as part of the influx of British and Australian coalminers drawn to the expanding New Zealand coalfields in the first decade of the twentieth century. He came as a committed socialist influenced by Keir Hardie and Bob Smillie of the Independent Labour Party. West Coast workers first made Hunter's acquaintance as readers of the mouthpiece of New Zealand radicalism, the *Maoriland Worker*. As 'Billy Banjo', he articulated, in verse and in prose, the grievances of mining communities. His early writing drew upon his experience of the Scottish coalfields and the insidiousness with which the mines circumscribed the lives of those born to mining families. Sprawling pit frames and chimney stacks, he wrote, 'robbed the young of those daisy bedecked play-fields of childhood' and 'poverty drove … young boys into the pits where "boy life" gradually loses its cherished aim, "its meaning of worth" and "girl life" was woven into the "mills of greed" in distant city factories'.[6] It was a picture couched in old world terms and as such resonated with the historical sense of injustice and oppression that characterised the thinking of the British colliers who fashioned New Zealand coalmining unionism in the late 1880s.

Hunter and his family moved to Denniston in 1912. From within this remote enclave of British colliers, he began to articulate a more belligerent stance. When the 1913 General Strike was proclaimed Hunter welcomed it as a 'people's revolt'[7] against a social order he believed morally

5 Richardson, '"Billy Banjo": Coalminer, Socialist. Poet and Novelist', in Pat Moloney and Kerry Taylor, eds, *On the Left: Essays on Socialism in New Zealand*, Dunedin, University of Otago Press, 2002, pp. 73–86.

6 Richardson, '"Billy Banjo"', p. 75.

7 *Maoriland Worker*, 29 October 1913.

unconscionable. In Westport, as a member of the Buller Miners' Central Committee, he helped organise public demonstrations. At Newtown Park in Wellington, he was arrested and charged with sedition for allegedly telling assembled unionists that the Massey Government's violent response to the strike justified revolution.

Edward Hunter emerged disillusioned from the disintegration of radical unionism that followed the collapse of the 1913 General Strike. Placed on probation by the courts and blacklisted on the coalfields, he worked briefly in freezing works, on the waterfront and as an itinerant union organiser. In early 1915 his wife Mary died and the care of their four children absorbed more of his energies and precipitated his return to Scotland in the early 1920s. Two major publications appeared in this period: *Ballads of the Track* (1918), a collection of 32 poems, most of which had appeared previously in the *Maoriland Worker*; and *The Road the Men Came Home* (1920), a largely autobiographical novel about life on the coalfields of Scotland and New Zealand, mostly Denniston.[8] Literary historians have described Hunter's novel as belonging to a genre of naive social realism characterised by a 'crude mixture of biography and autobiography' spiced with a dash of 'explicit preaching'.[9] Within the mining towns and among the working class, Hunter's crusade against the evils of industrial capitalism captured the moral fervour of time and place. As a 'wandering minstrel'[10] of Britain's socialist left, he had made his way to the colonial coalfields, like many miners before and since, hopeful of building a better world. His unique form of 'social dreaming' envisaged mining communities remade and miners and their families freed to share fully in the fruits of progress.

Like many transient activists whose major works were published in their homeland, Hunter's outpourings faded into the colonial literary netherlands until rediscovery by New Zealand historians as they began to bring working-class experience more fully into the national story. Keith Sinclair, whose influential *History of New Zealand* elaborated a progressive and nationalist perspective that framed the historical agenda for a generation, had met Hunter in 1950 when visiting Labour Party

8 Edward Hunter, *The Road the Men Came Home*, London, The National Labour Press, 1920; Edward Hunter, *Ballads of the Track*, Auckland, The Cooperative Publishing Board, 1919.

9 Terry Sturm, ed., *The Oxford History of New Zealand Literature in English*, Auckland, Oxford University Press, 1991, p. 125.

10 Erik Olssen, *The Red Feds: Revolutionary Industrial Unionism and the New Zealand Federation of Labour*, Auckland, Oxford University Press, 1991, p. 101.

branches in Glasgow.[11] The old Red Fed had won his way onto the Glasgow City Corporation on the socialist ticket in 1937 and represented the Cowcaddens Ward until his death in 1959, shortly after he had become the corporation's deputy chairman. During this time, his literary activism was expressed in what he described as 'community musical dramatic plays'[12] that drew upon the talents of working people and expressed the grievances of those disfranchised by poverty and educational disadvantage. The literary outpourings of 'Billy Banjo', the 'wandering minstrel' of the coalfields, began to attract scholarly attention in the 1980s. As historians focused upon the regional and occupational communities, they discovered the rhythms, patterns and concerns of everyday life and the previously unheard voices giving expression to them.

If Billy Banjo and his literary heirs represent a response to the lingering convulsions of industrial capitalism, Jean Devanny's novels of the 1920s and early 1930s present an unflinching portrayal of women's lives, a socialist/feminist indictment of unrestrained capitalism's capacity to strip away human dignity.[13] She sketches its brutalising impact upon mining families cut adrift from mainstream society. Where Billy Banjo offered his readers a gospel of hope expressed in quaint and homely terms, Devanny laid bare, in bleak perspective, the crippling psychological and social cost of lives lived at the sharp end of colonial capitalism.

The eighth of William and Jane Crook's 10 children, Devanny was born in 1894, in Ferntown, near Collingwood. Some 20 years earlier her father, a boilermaker from Lancashire, had found work as battery manager at a goldmine and as a blacksmith and mechanic at various small coastal mines that characterised the Golden Bay coalfield at the South Island's northernmost extremity. The opening up of a new coal seam at Puponga, in the first decade of the twentieth century, brought new men and new ideas into a district that had been very largely unaffected by the first wave of coalfields unionism in the 1880s and 1890s. In its newer, more radical garb, unionism quickly took root among the 50 or so Puponga miners. Its arrival was signalled in 1904 by the construction of a miners' hall and by the formation of a small socialist study group. Rural in aspect and coastal in location, Puponga was typical of the West Coast coal communities

11 Sinclair, *Halfway Round the Harbour*, p. 128.

12 Richardson, '"Billy Banjo"', p. 85.

13 Carole Ferrier, *Jean Devanny: Romantic Revolutionary*, Melbourne, Melbourne University Press, 1999; Heather Roberts, 'Devanny, Jean', in *Dictionary of New Zealand Biography*, first published in 1998, *Te Ara—the Encyclopedia of New Zealand*, teara.govt.nz/en/biographies/4d13/devanny-jean.

in its isolation.[14] Miners and their families made up more than half its 600-strong community. It was among them that William Crook settled his family in 1909. He was already succumbing to miners' phthisis and, as his daughter later wrote, 'anaesthetised'[15] by periodic bouts of drinking.

In 1911, 17-year-old Jean married Hal Devanny, a 23-year-old hewer making his way within union ranks and an active member of Puponga's small socialist circle. These were the peak years of revolutionary socialist activity and the newly wed Devannys were soon moving among the rising generation of radicals we now know as 'Red Feds'. The platform pyrotechnics of these apostles of socialism stimulated enthusiasm and provided a framework in which individuals and communities could articulate protest. The arrival at Puponga of men unable to find work at Blackball in the aftermath of the 1908 Tucker Time Strike swelled the nucleus of union activists at Puponga. Within this cluster of radical miners, as housewife and mother, she began to explore the radical literature of the day. Like Edward Hunter, Devanny published her earliest writing in the *Maoriland Worker*. She explores the evolution of the family in a manner that reveals the influence of anthropological ideas then current within socialist writing. Under the capitalist system, married women, she wrote, were the economic, social and sexual property of their husbands. The notion that only a socialist state would allow women to achieve independence was fundamental to all her subsequent writing.[16]

The socialist community continued to nurture Devanny's literary development at a time when life on the coalfields was at its most turbulent. The closure of the Puponga mine, in July 1917, shattered the mining community and the search for work that followed disrupted family life. Hal scoured South Island coalfields looking for work. Jean and the three children stayed briefly in nearby Nelson with her husband's family before moving to Wellington where she joined Margaret Semple while husband 'Bob the Ranter' served his sentence for sedition in the Lyttelton Gaol. In 1918 the Devanny family was reunited after Hal found work at the Fairfield mine, some 6 miles south of Dunedin. Within two years, they were on the move again, this time to Wellington where Hal joined a group of tunnellers, led by Bob Semple and comprised largely of

14 Peter Dyer, *Coal Mines of Puponga*, Picton, River Press, 2003.
15 Ferrier, *Jean Devanny*, p. 15.
16 Roberts, 'Devanny, Jean', in *Dictionary of New Zealand Biography*.

displaced coalminers, working on the Orongorongo tunnel. Together the Devannys ran a guest house and became a part of the city's radical culture of young, itinerant labour activists.

It was from within this ever-changing community, where ideological distinctions between communist and radical Labour did not matter much, that Jean Devanny began to write. Her two coalfield novels—*Dawn Beloved* (1928) and *Poor Swine* (1930)—are set in Puponga and Denniston respectively.[17] An *Otago Daily Times* reviewer described *Dawn Beloved* as 'the first attempt to depict in fiction form the home life of the West Coast miners and to analyse the reasons for his communistic tendencies'.[18] It is the story of a young, artistic woman growing up in a mining community with a drunken miner-father and a mother with few resources other than her piano. Carole Ferrier's recent biography of Jean Devanny draws our attention to the similarities between her childhood as a coalminer's daughter and that of the most celebrated literary son of the Nottingham coalfields, D.H. Lawrence.[19] Ferrier doubts that Devanny had read *Sons and Lovers* (1913), but there is no doubt that *Dawn Beloved* and *Poor Swine* derive just as surely from within the constricted domestic world of the mining family.

Poverty had many faces on West Coast coalfields. Devanny had seen or experienced many of them: primitive homes, undernourished and inadequately clothed children, and violent behaviour. A minimal middle-class presence meant the absence of even the most menial of paid household labour that might have given women a semblance of economic independence and swelled family income. In Devanny's view, coalfields poverty had other, less tangible, consequences for women. Confined to their two- or three-roomed cottages with only the most basic household belongings, theirs were lonely and limiting lives, as barren intellectually as they were materially and physically. Devanny had become peculiarly sensitised to the narrowness of women's existence on the coalfields after she engaged with the socialist study groups alongside her union-activist husband. It was a liberating experience that awakened her to the inequalities of class and gender and their manifestation on the West Coast coalfields.

17 Jean Devanny, *Dawn Beloved*, London, Duckworth, 1928; Jean Devanny, *Poor Swine*, London, Duckworth, 1930.

18 Carole Ferrier, 'Jean Devanny, 1894–1962', *Kotare*, vol. 7, no. 1, 2007, p. 102.

19 Ferrier, 'Jean Devanny, 1894–1962', pp. 102–3.

The closure of the Puponga mine in 1917 and the move to Fairfield had opened the prospect of access to the wider opportunities of city life and sharpened her awareness of the enormity of coalfields deprivation. Subsequent family moves to Wellington (and later Sydney) provided the opportunity for sustained involvement within radical fringes of the labour movement and eventually led her into the Communist Party in Australia.[20] In her passage from Puponga to Sydney, the West Coast coalfields stood as a constant reminder of the ugly face of industrial capitalism.

Hunter and Devanny expressed two different strains of the literature of protest that emerged from early twentieth-century coalfields—the communitarian and the more personal. Hunter's quieter and often quaintly old-world voice strove for authenticity and conveyed commitment to the international mining community. The loyalty of class and occupation, rather than the bonds of Empire or the appeals of colonial nationalism, offered the surest path to combating capitalism and improving their way of life. Devanny's literary voice was just as surely directed at the perversions wrought by industrial capitalism. Her literary voice struggled at first to be heard—restricted as it was by the banning of *The Butcher Shop* in 1926, nominally for its likely detrimental impact upon the nation's immigration program. The immediate impact of Devanny's writing was thus minimal. What distinguishes her literary reputation from that of Hunter is its revival in the 1980s within a feminist and socialist rather than regional context.[21] Yet, in different and complementary ways, Edward Hunter and Jean Devanny may now be seen as frontrunners of a regional literature of protest grounded in the changing realities of time and place.

The 30 years between the polemically inspired writing of Hunter and Devanny and the publication of Bill Pearson's *Coal Flat* coincided with a major transformation of coalfields life. The creeping depression that spread across the coalfields of the Western world in the 1920s reached its nadir in the early 1930s. Despite a war-induced recovery in the 1940s, the decade that followed brought a gradual dismantling of the traditional coalfield community. The patterns of rise and fall that historians have subsequently sketched out became clear to contemporaries as mines closed and communities withered. The socialist idealism that informed

20 Stuart Macintyre, *The Reds: The Communist Party of Australia from Origins to Illegality*, Sydney, Allen & Unwin, 1988; Jean Devanny, *Point of Departure: The Autobiography of Jean Devanny*, edited by Carole Ferrier, St Lucia, Queensland University Press, 1986.

21 Jean Devanny, *The Butcher Shop*, edited and introduced by Heather Roberts, Auckland, Auckland University Press, 1981, pp. 7–26.

the industrial and social legislation introduced by Labour governments of the 1930s and 1940s was now losing its sheen. A new generation of coalfield radicals—fewer in number than their predecessors—sought answers, as Jean Devanny had done in the 1930s, within the Communist Party. It is this disintegrating and dispirited world of the Grey Valley that provides the inspiration for a diverse coalfields literature as redolent with protest as its precursors.

The hindsight that allows us to see more plainly the effects of one of capitalism's periodic convulsions upon the traditional Grey Valley coalmining communities is prompted by the onset of yet another some 40 years later. A generation of writers, alienated by a Labour Government acting as the handmaiden of corporate capitalism, looked backwards to an age when Labour seemed bent upon civilising capitalism. No one better exemplifies this literary continuity than Mervyn Thompson (1936–1992),[22] the coalfields' closest literary heir to the mantle of Edward Hunter. Unlike Hunter, Thompson's frame of reference was not so much that of international socialism but rather a uniquely personal amalgam of attitudes shaped in formative years spent in the Grey Valley coaltowns of Runanga and Reefton. 'Class'[23] is the cornerstone of all Thompson's work. He came to cast himself—somewhat melodramatically—as a 'working-class upstart' in combat with the 'privileged classes'.[24] It is a self-parody that allows Thompson to assert the social purpose of his writing and place himself at the forefront of a cultural popular front committed to achieving a national drama rooted in the New Zealand experience and sympathetic to the aspirations of the socialist left.

The West Coast took centre stage in Thompson's highly personalised attempt to play his part in the evolution of a distinctive national theatre. His forte was the solo song-play that 'harked back to the solo performers of gold rush days'.[25] *Coaltown Blues* (1984) mixes the autobiographical and the political. It traces the recurrent pattern of dream and disillusion that shaped the working lives of the generation of miners with whom he worked at Burkes Creek, near Reefton, in the 1950s. His rendering of the coalfield's past and left-wing hopes follows the contours of the deeply embedded oral tradition of the pits. It celebrates the heady days of the Red Feds and the birth of the Labour Party and places the miners in

22 Thompson, *All My Lives*.

23 Mervyn Thompson, *Passing Through and Other Plays, Introduction by Howard McNaughton*, Christchurch, Hazard Press, 1992, p. 6.

24 Mervyn Thompson, *Singing the Blues*, Christchurch, Blacktown Press, 1991, p. 53.

25 Thompson, *Passing Through*, p. 5.

the vanguard of New Zealand's socialist movement. The rise from the years of coalfield's despond during the Great Slump gives way to the triumph of Michael Joseph Savage's Labour. Now the miners had their own men at the heart of things. Bob Semple, Paddy Webb and Angus McLagan, men who had worked at the end of a pick at Runanga or Blackball, constituted a powerful triumvirate within the new government. Coalfield activists hoped that they would together put an end to the tyranny of the pits by nationalising the nation's mines and freeing New Zealand from the worst evils of capitalism.

The fading of this socialist dream in the late 1940s and early 1950s brings down the curtain on Thompson's *Coaltown Blues*.[26] On the coalfields, as elsewhere, the Labour Government's introduction of military conscription, and especially its continuation in peacetime, brought protest. To many on the Left, it seemed that Prime Minister Peter Fraser had become a Cold War warrior even before the real war had ended.[27] Ideological tensions gathered apace in a postwar economy in which the Labour Government proved, in the view of radical unionists, to be better at controlling wages than prices. The widening gulf between the militant unions and the Labour Government was a symptom of a more general disaffection with a leadership worn down by the problems of managing the economic transition from war to peace. The discontent was the backdrop to Labour's defeat at the polls in 1949 and the industrial upheaval of 1951.

To Grey Valley coalminers, their strike against the emergency regulations implemented by Sidney Holland's National Government in its dispute with the nation's watersiders in 1951 was legitimised by the principles of union solidarity. By appealing to the collective ethos of the workplace, they were setting out the terms of engagement for a struggle to defend their communities against a winding back of the government's commitment to the coal industry that they believed imminent. There was an air of inevitability about the manner in which the strike was embraced. Gone was the tragic mix of fatalism, naivety and utopian dreaming that O'Farrell detected in the Grey Valley miners' involvement in the 1890 Maritime Strike.

In its place was a more complex mix. The West Coast miners were no longer newcomers berated for their foreign twangs and dangerous ideas. They had played their part in creating a labour movement, elected

26 Mervyn Thompson, *Coaltown Blues*, Wellington, Victoria University Press, 1986.
27 Michael Bassett with Michael King, *Tomorrow Comes the Song: A Life of Peter Fraser*, Auckland, Penguin Books, 2000.

men to parliament and had become indispensable to the Grey Valley economy. Men from the coalface had helped remake the coal industry and strengthen inspection systems in ways that made them safer and gave the miners greater influence in the everyday operation of their mines.[28] Their strike in opposition to the emergency regulations was, in many ways, the 'last hurrah' of a coalfields generation that knew their communities were an endangered species. They invoked past struggle and celebrated achievement, but there was precious little naivety as they turned to defend union and community in time-honoured ways. In Grey Valley mining towns, 1951 assumed something of the status later afforded to the heroic struggle of British miners in 1984–85. The British Conservative Prime Minister Margaret Thatcher's determination to employ the comprehensive armoury of the state to destroy the National Union of Miners led by Arthur Scargill may have been more brutal than the implementation of Sidney Holland's emergency regulations, but each marked the imminent demise of the traditional mining community.[29]

An important ingredient in the reception of Thompson's *Coaltown Blues* was its timing. It was written and first performed in 1984, as Thatcher's battle to the death with the miners raged and as New Zealand's fourth Labour Government turned its back on its heritage and plunged headlong into a frenzy of free-market activity that was the envy of conservatives everywhere. David Lange's party won office in 1984 with strong support among a middle class increasingly alienated by the pugnacious National Party Prime Minister Robert Muldoon. In the face of mounting international opposition to South Africa's apartheid policy, Muldoon had resolutely plunged the nation into the divisive 1981 Springbok rugby tour of New Zealand. Now seen as marking a turning point in the nation's history, the protest and social dislocation that it wrought thrust issues of race and gender into greater prominence. Labour's electoral success owed much to its ability to construct a broad and progressive alliance that drew these forces, together with the anti-nuclear vote, into an unwieldy alliance with its traditional working-class base. It was a process that obscured Labour's economic intentions.[30]

28 Richardson, *Coal, Class & Community*, pp. 257–84.

29 David Howell, '"Goodbye To All That": A Review of Literature on the 1984/5 Miners' Strike', *Journal of Work, Employment & Society*, vol. 1, no. 3, September 1987, pp. 388–404; Dai Smith, 'The Longest Strike: In 1926 It Was the Employers; Now It's the State', *The Listener* (UK), 15 November 1984, pp. 11–12.

30 Jonathon Boston and Martin Holland, *The Fourth Labour Government: Radical Politics in New Zealand*, Auckland, Oxford University Press, 1987.

Thompson's emergence within the theatre world flourished alongside and, to some degree, within this evolving progressive movement. In 1980, while in his early 40s, he published a confessional autobiography, *All My Lives*, that made explicit and public the tensions he believed to be at work within the theatre world. His account is built around an intimate portrait of his West Coast coalfield origins and the extent to which this defined (and limited) his participation in the growth of a national theatre. Work and play are the physical core of the working-class culture that Thompson describes. And it is primarily through them that he comes to the understanding of community and identity that shapes his literary representation of the coalfields. Nowhere is this view put more strongly than when Thompson berates the middle-class theatre set for their condescending attitude to sport:

> Eyes clouded by distant cultural mists, they fail to see beyond the stereotypes of rugby, racing, beer, and plaster gnomes … This lack of interest in sport is, of course, evidence of virtue, and we are meant to admire them for their superior sensibilities.[31]

It was a caricature of the theatre set's attitude to sport and pitted an Anglophile, 'cultured' middle class against a vigorous and vital working class more at ease with its environment.

Thompson's quest for a national theatre that explored the nature of the relationship between people and place grew naturally from this dichotomy. It also drew heavily upon personal experience and a unique blend of nostalgia and optimism. In this respect it is a literary voice that contrasts sharply with that of Bill Pearson, whose concerns about the place of the artist in a national culture that, he believed, prized physicality and material culture lent an ambiguity to his attitude to the coalfields. Thompson, of course, knew the darker side of mining lives and, lest he be thought guilty of idealising the working class and its community, he took care to qualify his reflection:

> I do not deny the rot and the hollow … I merely suggest that our writers have spent rather too much time pretending that the rot and the hollow is all there is, that it is the whole truth. And have therefore failed to bring into theatrical life the positive life that resides in our people […] I am not asking for an idealised view of our lives, just a fuller one … There's life in these here isles! And a damn sight more particularity in our people than some of our writers will allow.[32]

31 Thompson, *All My Lives*, p. 50.

32 Thompson, *Singing the Blues*, pp. 66–67.

There is no sign of idealisation in Thompson's characterisation of Runanga where most of his West Coast life was spent. By any measure, his Runanga years were tragic and unhappy ones. He does not spare the town. It would, he wrote in *All My Lives*:

> have strong claims to enter the *Guinness Book of Records* as the ugliest and most depressing town on earth. Slovenly in posture ... The rain falls hard and often on the rough scrub-and-swamp terrain of the town ... people live, mainly in houses of such drabness that one wonders how anyone of even moderate self-esteem could dwell in them for more than five minutes.
>
> In Runanga the unpretentiousness of the Coaster is taken to the extreme where it becomes ugliness pure and simple. Barely anything has altered since the thirties—the slump came, the slump went, but Runanga sits there still as a visible reminder and symbol. It seems so temporary, but there is something indestructible about it all the same; another iceage might come and go but the town would still be there at the end of the aeons—a testament to man's ability to survive at the lowest ebb of his existence and to aspire to nothing, except perhaps physical dominance over others. A human race which lived as unpretentiously as Runanga lives would still exist in Neanderthal rock and slime.
>
> The town is laden with improbable paradoxes. It is full of hard-drinking men but boasts no pub [sic]. It is fanatical about sport but poorly equipped with sports grounds. It prides itself on its sporting heroes, the impressive number of its sons who have played rugby league for New Zealand, but it has built no monuments to them. It worships its women and will not tolerate swearing in front of them, but it drives them slowly mad.[33]

The unflattering assessment of Runanga found little support among Thompson's literary contemporaries. Writing at much the same time, Geoffrey Moorhouse, the celebrated English journalist, historian and writer, who had worked as a reporter for the *Grey River Argus* in the mid-1950s (1954–56), saw Runanga and the Grey Valley coaltowns very differently.[34] The son of a Lancashire clergyman, and a proud northerner, steeped in the 13-man code, he was a stalwart supporter of the Wigan

33 Thompson, *All My Lives*, pp. 13–14. A surprising claim given that it ignores the establishment of the Runanga Workingmen's Club in late 1947 in the aftermath of the 'beer boycott' of that year. It was this beer boycott that is drawn upon by Bill Pearson in *Coal Flat*. See Ch. 5, esp. pp. 103 ff.
34 Moorhouse, *At the George*, pp. 137–44.

club. And it was through rugby league that he first learned of the Grey Valley coaltowns. In 1946, the diminutive Blackball and West Coast stand-off half Ces Mountford had signed with Wigan. As a 19-year-old he had missed selection for the 1939 Kiwi side to Britain (abandoned after just two games against club sides—St Helens and Dewsbury) and has subsequently been thought, by many critics, to be the best player never to have played for New Zealand. At Central Park the 'Blackball Bullet', as he became known, quickly became a local hero, scoring 17 tries in his first season with the club. In 1947, when Wigan faced a touring Kiwi rugby league side, he took the field against his brother, one of six Grey Valley coalminers in a 25-strong touring side—four from Blackball and two from Runanga. The image of the Blackball Bullet loomed large in Moorhouse's thinking as he sailed for New Zealand in 1954 to see for himself the West Coast rugby league nursery.[35]

Moorhouse's subsequent reflections on his experience of the Coast appear in *At the George* (1989), a collection of essays on international rugby league. His concern is to capture the combination of people and place that made Grey Valley coaltowns such bountiful rugby league nurseries. When revisiting the district in the 1980s, Moorhouse writes, he experienced a sense of having come to the end of a world whose edge was 'just out there' beyond a Greymouth that seemed 'alien yet recognisable'.[36] There was, he wrote:

> a strange familiarity about it that had nothing at all to do with the fact that I once knew it pretty well … With its faint air of depression, of having seen better days, with its workaday and rather bleak dignity, with that loveliness of hills behind it and that blankness of ocean before, with its isolation from the rest of the country, with its taste for Rugby League and with, even, the simple utility of its name, Greymouth is the antipodean version of Workington.[37]

The bush environment of mining communities in the Grey Valley, Moorhouse believed, set them apart from Britain's coaltowns surrounded, as they typically were, by 'almost unrelieved urban and industrial

35 John Coffey and Bernie Wood, *The Kiwis: 100 Years of International Rugby League*, Auckland, Hachette Livre, 2007, pp. 118–23; John Coffey, *Canterbury XIII: A Rugby League History*, Christchurch, John Coffey, 1987, pp. 117–19.

36 Moorhouse, *At the George*, p. 144.

37 Moorhouse, *At the George*, p. 144.

sprawl'.[38] The 'forests of matai, kahikatea, pokatea, hutu, totara and other' natives that almost smothered the region, created a unique backdrop for the isolated mine settlements and their rugby league grounds. Blackball 'snugged down in a cleft of the Paparoa Range' was, he wrote, 'a paradigm of the tiny' Grey Valley coalfield towns. Wingham Park, rugby league headquarters, was evocative of the game and its environment. Its 'neat and well-kept grandstand' stood roughly midway between Runanga and Greymouth and possessed an 'unforgettable setting, lonely beside the highway in the middle of those bush-covered hills'. League grounds in Sydney 'might easily be in Brisbane' and 'one could envisage' others in Lancashire 'on the other side of the Pennines'. Wingham Park, however, 'could not possibly be anywhere else but where it is'. It symbolised a people as rooted to their environment[39] as were those in the West Riding heartland of the game.

Something of this sense of harmony between people and place is present, as we have seen earlier, in Pearson's *Coal Flat.* It is evident also in J.M. Ewen's *Far from the Sun.*[40] Published in 1966, three years after Pearson's *Coal Flat*, and somewhat overlooked in most literary surveys, it possesses an authenticity that derives from intimate connection with the Runanga community in which it is set. Like Phil May and Bill Pearson, Ewen attended Greymouth Tech. Born in 1932, a decade after Pearson, his high school years overlapped with May's but he left, aged 14, to begin work in the mines, as his father had done before him.[41] The community that he presents in *Far from the Sun* owed its very existence to the state experiments of the late nineteenth and early twentieth centuries. As the colony's first state coalmining community, Runanga and Dunollie possessed a symbolic importance to a generation of coalminers for whom nationalisation was the cornerstone of a socialism proudly proclaimed above the entrance to their now iconic Runanga Miners' Hall.

More than any New Zealand coaltown, Runanga exhibited the range of communal endeavour that underpinned mining communities in their new world environment. Co-op, miner's hall and workingmen's club defined the world outside the pits and offered the more serious-

38 Moorhouse, *At the George*, p. 139.

39 Moorhouse, *At the George*, pp. 138–44.

40 J.M. Ewen, *Far from the Sun*, Christchurch, Whitcombe & Tombs, 1966.

41 Carol Dawber, 'Voices of the West Coast: An Investigation into the Development of a Distinctive West Coast Character in New Zealand Fiction', PhD thesis, University of Canterbury, 2012, pp. 40–41, 152–55.

minded miners—if more rarely coalfield women—a variety of pathways to communal and individual self-discovery. For Jack Ewen it was the library of the Workingmen's Club that allowed him to immerse himself in the growing body of contemporary, left-leaning British literature and to realise through it his own literary talents. He later acknowledged A.J. Cronin's *The Stars Look Down* (1935), as the literary model for his attempt to capture the reality of life on the coalfields.[42] The social realism of *Far from the Sun* owes less to ideology than either *Coal Flat* or the West Coast–centred writing of Mervyn Thompson. Neither lament nor call to arms, it captures the mood of uncertainty that pervaded the Grey Valley in the early 1960s.

By contrast, Eric Beardsley's *Blackball 08* (1984) shares some of the political concerns that engaged Thompson.[43] A literary critic has considered it an exercise in reminding 'the 80s generation of young, politically aware activists about socialism and the formation of the New Zealand Labour Party'. Andrew Little, former leader of the New Zealand Labour Party, and son of 'High Tory' British parents, acknowledges *Blackball 08* as his 'first introduction into trade union history in New Zealand'.[44] To accept the view that *Blackball 08* is 'as much historical and political commentary as novel', is to place it alongside Edward Hunter's fictional but heavily autobiographical *The Road the Men Came Home* and Pat Hickey's *'Red' Fed. Memoirs*.[45] To group Beardsley's fictional version of events with these labour classics, however, risks ignoring the extent to which *Blackball 08* is shaped by considerations of place and community that go beyond the polemical.

Like Thompson and Moorhouse, Beardsley has also revisited his literary West Coast in autobiographical garb. In the pages of *Sliding Down the Hypotenuse*,[46] he sketches his West Coast 'experience'. Physically, his presence in the Grey Valley was brief and took second place to Christchurch as the place he called 'Home'. His father, a fitter and turner by trade, was

42 Dawber, 'Voices', p. 40; A.J. Cronin, *The Stars Look Down*, London, Gollancz, 1935.

43 Eric Beardsley, *Blackball 08*, Auckland, William Collins Publishers, 1984.

44 Simon Nathan, 'Five Books About Blackball', *Scoop Review of Books*, 5 August 2008, www.scoop.co.nz/stories/HL0808/S00056.htm; see also Diana Wichtel, 'Commentary: Interview: Andrew Little', *Listener*, no. 3712, 2 July 2011, pp. 22–26.

45 P.H. Hickey, *'Red' Fed. Memoirs: Being a Brief Survey of the Birth and Growth of the Federation of Labour from 1908 to 1915, and of the Days that Immediately Preceded It*, Wellington, New Zealand Worker Print, 1925; reprinted by Wellington Media Collective, Wellington, 1980.

46 Eric Beardsley, *Sliding Down the Hypotenuse: A Memoir*, Christchurch, Canterbury University Press, 2011.

made jobless as the Great Depression struck and took his young family across the Southern Alps for a job at a small sawmill at Bell Hill, 'smack in the middle of a valley of ancient rimu behind Nelson Creek'.[47] As one of a number of mill settlements that sprang up along the railway line to Otira, between Stillwater and Te Kinga, Bell Hill had much in common with the camp-like communities of the early coalfields. Beardsley recalls a settlement of 'ugly family cottages, knocked up with more haste than skill'.[48] A community had grown haphazardly around a noisy, 'ramshackle mill'. Accompanied by the 'hissing thud and chug of the steam engine', saws 'howled all day long' and 'sawdust and shriek filled the air'.[49] When there was no rain things became even worse:

> Sawdust heaps all over the valley kindled and glowed and there was a haze of blue smoke everywhere … fires broke out, striking fear into the bush settlements and producing smoke so dense the lowering sun looked like a burnished brass ball.[50]

Nothing was scarier to the young Beardsley than the 'semi-wild cattle foraging among the dry firewood and potato and apple stores under the house, setting up alarming vibrations as they bumbled about'.[51] These experiences confirmed for Beardsley that at Bell Hill his family had existed on the very margins of society. The Grey Valley mill communities were as much cut off from 'civilisation' as the better known and more pilloried coaltowns.

The times, however, were as out of joint for the timber industry as they were for coalmining. The widespread abundance of readily milled timber throughout the colony made it difficult for an isolated region that relied upon shipping its timber from notoriously difficult river ports. The early development of the local timber trade rested upon investment from outside the region and, by the outbreak of World War I, half the timber milled on the Coast was bound for the Australian market. It was not until the completion of the Otira rail tunnel in August 1923 that access to the Canterbury timber market became economically viable. But new attitudes to the management of the nation's forests were taking hold. The introduction of export quotas for indigenous timber, formulated after

47 Beardsley, *Sliding Down the Hypotenuse*, p. 18.
48 Beardsley, *Sliding Down the Hypotenuse*, p. 30.
49 Beardsley, *Sliding Down the Hypotenuse*, p .30.
50 Beardsley, *Sliding Down the Hypotenuse*, p. 32.
51 Beardsley, *Sliding Down the Hypotenuse*, p. 36.

the creation of the New Zealand Forest Service in 1919, constrained the development of the West Coast timber industry that exported some two-thirds of its rimu-cut to Australia. Worse still, as the troubled 1920s slid imperceptibly into wider economic depression, the Canterbury market for timber failed to materialise. By mid-1931 nearly 70 per cent of the district's sawmills were idle or operating fitfully, and roughly half the timber workers were jobless.[52] Timber stacks left to rot on the skids in the wet and damp as orders evaporated created a starkly surreal image.

The Beardsley family's experience at Bell Hill in the 1920s, as the mill community became part of a widening capitalist crisis, gave them an introduction to the world of radical activism. They had known little when they moved to the Coast of the mill settlements' reputation as bolt-holes for pacifists. As legend has it, during and after the Great War, the district was well-known, in Irish and socialist circles, as a refuge for men wishing to evade conscription and make common cause with local Irish nationalists. They were joined by a handful of radicals drawn to the district by its proximity to 'Red Blackball', the Grey Valley's own 'Little Moscow'. In 1926 the Communist Party established its national headquarters in the coaltown as part of a campaign to widen its influence among industrial workers nationally. Party members had been active in the creation of the West Coast Timber Workers' Union in 1918 and, by the time the Beardsleys arrived, its two most prominent officials, Alex Galbraith and Jack Doyle, had thrust themselves to the forefront of Grey Valley unionism.[53] For Eric's father, exposure to the radical critique of the bush ideologues proved life-changing. When the mills shuddered to a halt and the family returned to Christchurch he was an activist in the making.

Eric Beardsley's literary road to 'Blackball 1908' might thus be said to begin at Bell Hill. His understanding of those who later peopled his literary world was further sharpened by his family's experience of Depression life in the Christchurch suburb of Aranui. It was there that he discovered something of the diversity that existed within the radical working-class community. His recent memoir presents an evocative portrait of the

52 Peter McIntosh, 'The Timber Industry in Westland, 1865–1939', MA thesis, University of Canterbury, 1990, p. 175.

53 McIntosh, 'The Timber Industry in Westland', pp. 279–87; Kerry Taylor, 'Galbraith, Alexander', in *Dictionary of New Zealand Biography*, first published in 1998, *Te Ara—the Encyclopedia of New Zealand*, teara.govt.nz/en/biographies/4g2/galbraith-alexander; Alexander Galbraith, 'Reminiscences on the Early History of The Communist Party of New Zealand', ms, 1949, author's collection; O'Farrell, *Vanished Kingdoms*, pp. 263–64, 267; Richardson, 'Class, Community and Conflict', pp. 107–8.

'Radicals, Rebels and Rapscallions'[54] he knew in 1930s Aranui. At their centre was Sidney Huguenot Fournier d'Albe (1870–1960), a descendent of French Huguenots, scion of an aristocratic Alsace family and colourful activist. His life story is the stuff of socialist mythology. Educated at a German gymnasium and in England, his ideological pathway to Marx began with English Fabian Socialism in the 1890s and later embraced the revolutionary socialism that took root among the Welsh miners of the Rhondda Valley. There, during the Tonypandy Riots, he was struck heavily by a soldier's rifle and sustained a facial scar that lent a certain menace to his appearance.

Blacklisted on the coalfields, Fournier went to sea, deserted in New York and reached New Zealand as the radical phase of pre-war industrial unionism reached its peak. He found work on the Wellington wharves, joined the Socialist Party and the Red Federation of Labour and, during the 1913 General Strike, became a member of the Central Strike Committee. In 1917 he was arrested and imprisoned for his role in a Free Speech Fight on Clyde Quay organised by the Conscription Repeal League in defiance of the War Regulations. He shared the exercise yard of the Terrace Gaol with a future Labour prime minister, Peter Fraser, and other radicals who became household names in the socialist circles of the day. Denied work on the wharves after his release from prison, he moved to Christchurch and was soon on the Committee of the General Labourers' Union and conducting Marxist study groups at his home in Aranui.[55]

Beardsley's recollections provide a more intimate picture of Aranui's apostle of international socialism. He recalls a man of 'presence and passion', a 'verbose neighbour with revolutionary instincts' whose 'one empty eye socket, beaked nose, teeth like old piano keys and a voice to wake the dead marked him as a man to be reckoned with'.[56] His unmistakeable voice that boomed above the hubbub of the city's unemployed protest meetings was just as frequently heard by the young Beardsley in operatic song or reciting poetry. The general Christchurch community first became aware of Fournier in the mid-1920s when the *Lyttelton Times* ran a campaign aimed at exposing the possibility that then existed for dual membership of the New Zealand Labour Party and the New Zealand

54 Beardsley, *Sliding Down the Hypotenuse*, pp. 86–98.
55 Herbert Roth and E.G. Beardsley, 'Sidney Huguenot Fournier d'Albe', *New Zealand Monthly Review*, December 1960–January 1961, pp. 21–22; Beardsley, *Sliding Down the Hypotenuse*, pp. 86–88.
56 Beardsley, *Sliding Down the Hypotenuse*, pp. 11, 87.

Communist Party. 'Communist Creep', the paper alleged, was colouring the Labour Party deepest Red. Fournier's response was to go down on his hands and knees and creep along the footpath while asking puzzled bystanders, 'How is that for Communist creep?'[57]

Beardsley's observations about the colourful and exotic Fournier and Christchurch's radical socialist circle are the backdrop to his parents' involvement in the city's unemployed protest movement. Those who took to the streets were a fluid and ever-fluctuating group that defied the controlling instincts of civic authorities and Communist Party officials: to the former, they were an unruly menace to property and a threat to order; to the latter, they constituted a 'vast battleground of factions'[58] lacking clear ideological purpose. Connie and 'Ted' Beardsley were prominent figures in this radical community and typical of its independent character: Connie joined the Working Women's Movement founded by the Communist Party in October 1934 to establish a base among working women; Ted was even more active within the General Labourers' Union, among the jobless and within Marxist study groups. Neither escaped the conformist tendencies of the Communist Party. Connie was regarded by party officials as too individualistic and dominant a figure among the city's unemployed single women. Ted's unspecified 'deviations' brought expulsion and may be linked to an attempt by the party to distance itself from the 'reformist' Labour Party, which it denounced as a party of 'disrupters and enemies of the working class'.[59]

Blackball 08 grows from a desire to understand the experience of this diverse group of 'rebels'. The capitalist convulsion of the 1920s and 1930s had cut the working class adrift from their workplaces and, in doing so, removed the cornerstone of community and family life. Beardsley's perception of this dislocation is shaped by personal experience of the interaction between those who wanted 'to change workers' lives for the better',[60] in the here and now, and those whose revolutionary enthusiasms demanded a more radical remaking of society. At the heart of his depiction of working-class life is the relationship between a dominant, masculinist culture rooted in the physicality of work and a socialist minority that aspired to create a more egalitarian and inclusive

57 Roth and Beardsley, 'Sidney Huguenot Fournier d'Albe', pp. 21–22.

58 Maureen Birchfield, *Looking for Answers: A Life of Elsie Locke*, Christchurch, University of Canterbury Press, 2009, p. 120.

59 Birchfield, *Looking for Answers*, p. 120.

60 Beardsley, *Sliding Down the Hypotenuse*, p. 87.

society. At Bell Hill and Aranui, Beardsley observed how this territory was negotiated within his own family. For his mother, Connie, industrial and political activism took its place alongside a love of literature and music and the demands of domesticity and family. She was drawn into public protest alongside destitute single women and housewives struggling to feed and clothe their children, and threw her support behind the Communist Party publication the *Working Woman*.[61] Beardsley's reflections upon how his mother adapted to the more intense ideological fervour of his father led him to speculate about the gendered nature of early twentieth-century radicalism. Did the 'Brotherhood of Man', which his father and fellow activists hoped would be ushered in after the revolutionary overthrow of capitalism, extend to women?

In locating women's oppression in the rise of class society, Karl Marx and Friedrich Engels had provided an answer. In their view, as production moved away from the household, women had become trapped in their individual families as the reproducers of society and cut off from production. The socialists within Beardsley's acquaintance recognised the significance of the Marxist analysis, but many struggled in their own lives to align theory and practice.[62] Within the dominantly male, Communist fraternity of the 1920s and 1930s there was concern lest engagement with women's issues might expose the party to the reformist tendencies of 'bourgeois feminism' and divert attention away from the class struggle. Beardsley's firsthand observation of the progress of the 'feminist cause' within socialist circles is clearly demonstrated in *Blackball 08* when the feisty Elizabeth Rogers rebukes 'Paddy Webb' for his clumsy chauvinism: 'We don't only believe in socialism … we live it'.[63]

This awareness accurately points to a feature of radical and working-class life often submerged by the political and industrial contexts in which it is reconstructed. Beardsley rounds off *Blackball 08* by having Bob Semple reflect upon his generation's attempt to realise socialism in their time.[64] Of the Labour heroes of his day none is more associated with the masculine ethos in which the labour movement was born. He has been depicted as a revolutionary activist and rabble-rouser and as a vitriolic and vituperative orator whose physical presence intimidated opponents

61 Birchfield, *Looking for Answers*, p. 165.
62 Beardsley, *Sliding Down the Hypotenuse*, p. 59.
63 Beardsley, *Blackball 08*, p. 40.
64 Beardsley, *Blackball 08*, pp. 236–41.

and inspired followers. Neither contemporaries nor historians have found ideological consistency or coherence within his idiosyncratic version of socialism. Semple's preference for action rather than words has led a recent writer to describe his unique brand of radicalism as 'practical socialism'.[65] Firmly rooted in the rough and tumble working-class politics of pit top, street corner and protest march, Semple's socialism matched its surroundings.

Similarly, historians have had relatively little to say about the impact that radical or revolutionary activism had upon the families of individual ideologues. In his pioneering study *Labour's Path to Political Independence*, Barry Gustafson suggests that the radicals of Semple's era were 'more willing to subordinate their occupations, social life and even families to their political activities and ambitions'[66] than their rank-and-file labour contemporaries. A recent study by Carina Hickey provides a different perspective. By placing Semple's career within its domestic setting, Hickey demonstrates how the interplay between family, work and community created a distinctive working-class culture with its own style of leadership. When socialist activists like Semple moved around the country spreading the word, often spurned by timid hotel keepers, they relied upon the 'labour families' that formed the core of the organised working class.[67] Thus, when Semple, Webb or Hickey were at Puponga they were the guests of Hal and Jean Devanny.[68] Conversely, when the Devannys moved to Wellington after the closure of the Puponga mine they lived with Margaret Semple while Bob was imprisoned on Ripa (Ripapa) Island in Lyttelton Harbour. Jean Devanny subsequently recalled the experience of daily life in the Semple household: 'With motherly Mrs Semple, of typical working-class simplicity and quiet restful temperament and the whole of her unruly brood, I came to living on family terms'.[69]

65 Carina Hickey, 'From Coal Pit to Leather Pit: Life Stories of Robert Semple', PhD thesis, Massey University, 2010.

66 Barry Gustafson, *Labour's Path to Political Independence: The Origins and Establishment of the New Zealand Labour Party, 1909–19*, Auckland, Auckland University Press/Oxford University Press, 1980, p. 48.

67 Hickey, 'From Coal Pit to Leather Pit', especially pp. 14, 67–70, 89, 175; Libby Plumridge, 'The Necessary but not Sufficient Condition: Christchurch Labour and Working-Class Culture', *New Zealand Journal of History*, vol. 19, no. 2, October 1985, pp. 130–50; Nolan, *Kin: A Collective Biography of a New Zealand Working-Class Family*.

68 Ferrier, *Jean Devanny*.

69 Ferrier, *Jean Devanny*, p. 28.

As relatively new coaltowns, Runanga and Blackball in the early twentieth century lacked the deep family traditions of their old world counterparts. Their experience of family was nonetheless shaped by the chain of migration that began with the exodus of British colliers in the second half of the nineteenth century. For Bob Semple, the 'family' story was a tale that began in Scotland. His father, John, was born in Paisley in 1816, transported to Australia in 1847 and settled on the western goldfields of New South Wales, close to Bathurst. It was there, near Sofala, that Bob Semple was born in 1873, the fourth of seven surviving children, behind three older sisters and ahead of two further sisters and a brother. Carina Hickey's careful reconstruction of the Semple family suggests a strong and persistent sibling bond that was over time to shape a genuinely Australasian sense of identity. At the hub of the wider Semple family was the firstborn daughter Mary Ann. Nine years older than her brother Bob, in 1882 she married George Knight, a miner, and was to have 12 children. After the death of her mother five years later, Mary assumed a matriarchal role within the extended Semple–Knight families.[70]

Ever on the move from one mining field to another, the Semples were representative of the migrant mining families that moved about Australasian coalfields in the late nineteenth century and early twentieth century. From Sofala the family had moved to Lithgow and then to Outtrim in Gippsland, Victoria, before making their way, at the beginning of the twentieth century, to Western Australia. There they settled initially near Collie, where a new coalmine had opened in the 1890s, before moving to Kalgoorlie and Coolgardie. It was in this migratory phase that Semple's younger and only brother John had responded to the politically orchestrated, imperialistic fervour that followed the onset of the Boer War and joined the Collie unit of the 6th West Australian Mounted Infantry contingent. He sailed for Durban in late April 1901 and was killed in an exchange with Boer forces within weeks at Grobelaar Recht, near Carolina, in eastern Transvaal. His death helped Semple define his attitude to war in working-class terms: the greed of capitalists led to war and their patriotic posturing ensured workers paid the price. He subsequently interpreted the introduction of compulsory military training throughout Australasia as part of the move to shore up imperial defence in the aftermath of the Boer and the Russo-Japanese wars, and a move towards military conscription.[71]

70 Hickey, 'From Coal Pit to Leather Pit', pp. 66–69.
71 Hickey, 'From Coal Pit to Leather Pit', pp. 67–69.

Anti-militarism was part of the ideological baggage that Semple and his nephews took with them when they joined the 'Australasian invasion' that transformed the New Zealand labour movement in the first decade of the twentieth century.[72] So also was family. Two of his sister Ann's children, Hamilton (1888–1964) and George Knight, worked alongside their uncle in the pits and as his acolytes in the socialist campaign at Runanga. The 19-year-old Hamilton was elected to the executive of the Paparoa Miners' Union and became part of the socialist drive that was shaping industrial unionism. In 1914, shortly after the Red Feds were routed, their leaders blacklisted and unions driven back into the arbitration system that they had sought to destroy, he returned to the western New South Wales coalfields. Hamilton's Runanga experience was formative, launching him on a career of union and political activism that, upon his return to Australia in 1914, paralleled that of his uncle.[73]

Opposition to military training was a critical ingredient of the extended Semple household. From Runanga, as the industrial turmoil that surrounded the rise and fall of the Red Feds continued apace, he campaigned for the repeal of compulsory military training and was fined for not registering his son as required. With the outbreak of war in 1914 and the intensification of the campaign against the introduction of conscription on both sides of the Tasman, Semple and Knight were quickly in the thick of it. Frequently in Australia as agent for the New Zealand Miners' Federation, Semple played an active part in the protest that accompanied the conscription referenda of 1916 and 1917. In New Zealand, where the Military Services Bill 1915 made opposition to conscription liable to result in imprisonment, he was among a group of labour leaders imprisoned for their defiant, secular and socialist opposition to what they saw as an imperialist war.

In the years immediately after the Great War, Knight and Semple rose to prominence within their respective working-class communities in ways that propelled them to the forefront of the Australasian labour movement. As anti-conscriptionist, radical unionists, they struggled to get work on postwar coalfields. In New Zealand, Bob Semple was never to return to

72 Richardson, *Coal, Class & Community*, pp. 87–125.

73 Hickey, 'From Coal Pit to Leather Pit', pp. 67–70; Christopher Cunneen, *William John McKell: Boilermaker, Premier, Governor-General*, Sydney, University of New South Wales Press, 2000, pp. 113, 132; Michael Easson, ed., *The Achievements of Sir William McKell*, Sydney, Allen & Unwin, 1988, pp. 38, 78, 123, 135–37, 142; 'Hamilton Knight' (1888–1964), New South Wales Legislative Assembly: Former Members, www.parliament.nsw.gov.au/members/formermembers.

the coalfield that made him a household name. His subsequent career, nonetheless, set a pattern that in broad terms was replicated by his nephew in New South Wales. In 1918, after serving nine months of a three-year jail sentence for opposing conscription, Semple successfully contested the by-election occasioned by the death of the sitting Labour member A.J. Hindmarsh, a victim of the influenza epidemic, to become the Labour MP for Wellington South. The wartime protest vote that took him into parliament did not survive the peace and he lost the seat in the 1919 general election. After this false start to his parliamentary career, he organised and worked alongside his son in a cooperative party of miners to build the Orongorongo tunnel as part of a city program to augment Wellington's water supply. While engaged on this city project he entered local politics as a Labour representative on the Wellington City Council (1925–35) and became national president of the NZLP. In 1928 he re-entered parliament for Wellington East and became Minister of Public Works and Railways (1935–46) in the first Labour Government.[74]

In New South Wales, Hamilton Knight was blacklisted and resorted to adopting assumed names before being employed at the state mines in Lithgow. By the mid-1920s he was president of the Western New South Wales division of the Miners' Federation and vice-president of the national body. His subsequent political career mirrored that of his uncle. After entering local body politics in 1921, as an alderman for the Lithgow Municipal Council (1921–28), Knight was elected to the New South Wales Legislative Assembly in 1927 as the MLA for Hartley (1927–47). He was Minister for Labour and also Social Welfare in William John McKell's Labor ministries (1941–47) and retired to become a member of the Industrial Relations Commission.[75]

The similarities of these thumbnail sketches of the pathway that took two union activists into politics point to the commonalities within the Australasian coalfields experience. It is in the nature of working-class political parties that they derive their initial impetus and support from within communities of workers and their families and frequently from single industry settlements that often, as at Denniston in the 1880s, began life as little more than a campsite in isolated, remote and rugged

74 Cunneen, *William John McKell*, pp. 113, 132; Easson, *The Achievements of Sir William McKell*, pp. 38, 78, 123, 135–37, 142; 'Hamilton Knight', New South Wales Legislative Assemby: Former Members.

75 Hickey, 'From Coal Pit to Leather Pit', pp. 66–68.

settings. The union preceded community, becoming the instrument of its creation and the collective vehicle through which its collective aspirations could be achieved. Francis Bennett, Blackball's doctor during the depth of the Great Depression, makes this point with great force in a chapter of his posthumously published autobiography.[76] 'Coercion at the Coalface', he writes, by a coal company that 'paid the wages and nothing more', left Blackball miners and their families to fend for themselves.[77] Such self-help was the bedrock of coalfields life and an expression of the collective aspiration whose origins lay in the solidarity of the pits.

Family groups hastened the transformation from camp to community by adding a layer of social bonding. This combination of family and occupational cohesion that underpinned the lives of the extended Semple family can be observed in other coalfields lives. As the eldest of eight children born to Frank and Annie (Beaven) Sherman in Fernie, British Columbia, Annie Balderstone came to Blackball in the aftermath of the Great War as part of the coalfields diaspora that spread miners and their families throughout the new world. Her father had been born in Gloucestershire, England, in 1869, spent his formative years in the Rhondda Valley, moved to Canada in 1898 and settled in Crow's Nest Pass, a raw frontier region on the border of British Columbia and Alberta. The evangelical non-conformist tradition together with more secularly inspired critiques of industrial capitalism that he had imbibed in the Welsh valleys transplanted well.[78] In Canada his radicalisation was rapid. In 1903 he became foundation president of District 18 of the United Mine Workers of America and, while never entirely at ease with its doctrinaire Marxism, joined the Socialist Party of Canada. In these union-building days, before the emergence of union bureaucracies, the life of the full-time labour activist was extraordinarily arduous and drew heavily upon individuals and their families. As the eldest daughter, Annie had become absorbed into the everyday preoccupations of the peripatetic union leader, travelling to conferences and acting as her father's personal secretary.

76 Bennett, *A Canterbury Tale*; Rice, 'Bennett, Francis Oswald', in *Dictionary of New Zealand Biography*.

77 Bennett, *A Canterbury Tale*, p. 131.

78 Allen Seager, 'Sherman, Frank Henry', in *Dictionary of Canadian Biography*, vol. 13, University of Toronto/Université Laval, 2003–, first published in 1994, biographi.ca/en/bio/Sherman_frank_henry_13E.html.

In this role she met and married William Balderstone from Hull, who had joined the flow of British miners to British Columbia and was making his way within union and socialist ranks.[79]

The Canadian and family experience that Annie and Bill Balderstone brought to Blackball allowed them, in the years after the Great War, to make their mark within the Grey Valley coaltown. At Fernie they had experienced at close quarters union efforts to find a form of industrial organisation best suited to a remote mining town. Left, as were Blackball miners, to confront absentee owners with scant interest in the welfare of the community that provided their labour force, Western Canada's miners had first tried to overcome the weakness of their isolation by organising themselves as District 18 of the United Mine Workers of America. They came increasingly to the view that district or local autonomy was more appropriate to their circumstances. It was an attitude that grew naturally from an ingrained localism that had its origins in the peculiarities of the coalface and led officials to endorse a declaration of independence and campaign for the creation of a separate and progressive Canadian Federation of Labour. The lessons of this struggle were fresh in the minds of Annie and Bill Balderstone and the notion of local autonomy seemed equally appropriate in Blackball.

The Balderstones' arrival in Blackball coincided with a period of intense debate about the future shape of mining unionism. A new generation of radicals seeking to revive the traditional militant alliance with watersiders and seamen was in the process of building a new national miners' organisation, the United Mine Workers of New Zealand. For the Balderstones these were familiar coalfield debates and they were quickly immersed in them. By the early 1920s, they joined a cluster of activist couples already prominent in the community. When reviewers of Beardsley's *Blackball 08* suggest that his reconstruction of gender relations within the Rogers household is anachronistic and idealised in its feminist dimension, they fail to recognise this element of coalfields life.

79 Richardson, *Coal, Class & Community*, p. 196.

Figure 4: Ann and Bill Bromilow (seated left) with Blackball Socialists.
Source: Courtesy Bromilow family.

In Blackball, as in other coaltowns, there were few if any opportunities for women away from the home. Socialist study groups were one of few avenues in which women might participate alongside men. In part, this was because they began, as is shown in Figure 4, taken in Blackball shortly after the Tucker Time Strike, as household meetings of like-minded individuals.[80] Here we see Ann Bromilow standing in the second row, to the right of a placard proclaiming socialism as the only chance workers had of building a better world. She had come to Blackball from Wigan where she had worked as a screen-girl sorting coal. It was there she had met her husband Bill and they had migrated to Blackball a few years later as a married couple without children. Within the socialist community, Ann was an organiser, a writer and occasionally a speaker at public meetings outside the Blackball Miners' Hall. In this way, the socialist groups offered women a public presence in community life similar to that offered by the evangelical churches. Few in number and little known outside the mining townships in which they lived, the influence of these

80 Richardson, *Coal, Class & Community*, pp. 3, 5, 108–9, 131, 160.

socialist women is difficult to assess. At moments of heightened activity—during the Tucker Time Strike, in anti-conscription protest and during the bitter and divisive union struggles of the 1930s—they came briefly and conspicuously to the forefront. In giving women a place in *Blackball 08*, Eric Beardsley is not reading history backwards. He is describing a feature of the working-class socialist community that had largely escaped casual observers.

If we run forward from 1908, we can trace, through the activities of a number of Blackball socialist couples, the continuing importance of a feminist dimension to Grey Valley socialism. Not all have left a public profile but among the most conspicuous were Jack and Sophie Doyle. Unlike the Bromilows and the Balderstones, they were not part of the mining community but were a part of the cluster of timber mill settlements across the Grey River from Blackball. A New Zealander of Irish descent, Jack was radicalised during the anti-conscription campaign and in the early 1920s was a leading figure in the Communist Party's attempt to establish an industrial base among the miners at Blackball and the nearby sawmilling communities near Ngahere and Nelson Creek. From within this band of activists, it was possible for women to make their mark in more public ways. For Sophie Doyle this meant primarily a life of writing: columns for the Communist Party monthly paper, the Miners' Page in the *Grey River Argus*, and a cyclostyled newsletter for local children that set out to counteract the imperialism engendered in the classroom and the militarism imitated by a local boy scouts group.[81]

In different and complementary ways, these activist couples represent the major strands of socialism at work within the Blackball mining community. As early twentieth-century migrants from British coalfields and veterans of the Tucker Time dispute, the Bromilows were 'stayers'—a couple for whom Blackball was the final destination on the migratory chain. The passage of the Balderstones from old world to new had been less direct and, by the time they reached the Grey Valley, they had imbibed a socialism infused with an amalgam of west Canadian separatism and the more traditional radicalism rooted in the peculiarities of time and place. For their part, the Doyles' road to prominence in Grey Valley coalfield politics followed a pathway as familiar in the old world as in the new: radicalisation within the anti-conscription movement and

81 Richardson, *Coal, Class & Community*, pp. 208–12; Richardson, 'Class, Community and Conflict', pp. 106–27.

the Irish cause and subsequent commitment to the Communist Party. In the Grey Valley, the notion of an 'unholy alliance between the Reds and the Greens' was first hatched before the war in the imagination of Grey Valley Liberals fearful of being ground down between the rival forces of the Reform Party and the predecessor of the Labour Party, the Social Democrat Party. Doyle was, as we have seen, long to remain the bête noire of Grey Valley socialists, whether Green or Red, until the 1950s when Kruschev's invasion of Hungary caused him to renounce Communism.[82]

Thus, when Beardsley presents a gendered dimension of early twentieth-century Blackball radicalism, he is accurately describing an element of coalfields socialism. The notion that this is somehow reading history backwards is to misunderstand both the evolution of New Zealand feminism and the role of women in mining towns. Feminism did not stop with the achievement of the franchise and lie dormant until the arrival of what came to be called its 'second wave', nor was its influence confined to the middle-class households that were a prominent feature of early feminism everywhere. Coalfield feminists were even more invisible than their working-class sisters in the cities and towns. To airbrush them out of history would be to perpetuate the condescension displayed by the few contemporaries who bothered to take the ideological push and shove of coalfields life seriously. Within their individual coaltowns and among the wider mining community of the Grey Valley and the Buller, radical women activists were a vital part of the labour family that laid the foundation for the nation's first working-class government. Together, they represent an element of Grey Valley radicalism that deserves a greater place in the history of both region and nation. When Angus McLagan, the Blackball Scot from the Midlothian coalfields, secretary of the United Mine Workers of New Zealand and the New Zealand Communist Party, took his place in the Labour Cabinet in 1941, his wife Sophie (formerly Doyle) became the most nationally prominent of the Blackball women activists.

In many respects, *Blackball 08* stands within a coalfields literary tradition that reaches back to the old world. Its imaginative recreation of an historic event that had already become a sustaining myth came at a critical juncture as that myth was beginning to fracture. Increasingly abandoned as the talisman of working-class authenticity by Labour's political leaders, except

82 O'Farrell, *Vanished Kingdoms*, pp. 263–64.

as an occasional adornment at election time, the story of *Blackball 08* had been left to historians and a fading oral tradition. For a generation of labour supporters and union members, it stimulated a reassertion of the socialist principles upon which working-class attitudes to capitalism were grounded. It stands on the cusp of, and forms part of, the remaking of a literary relationship between people and place, first kindled in the 1960s. It marks the arrival of a second wave of historical writing grounded as much in the distinctive relationship between people and place as that which lay at the heart of its foundational generation. *Blackball 08* reaffirms the authenticity of battles long ago. In doing so, it prepares the ground for historical perspectives that, as the following chapter suggests, confront the consequences for the Coast of perhaps the most significant transformation of modern-day capitalism.

7

BEYOND THE 1960s II

The Historians

The three ingredients of West Coast history that formed the core of its written history—gold, coal and the strong Irish presence—have continued to preoccupy historians. They do so in ways that reflect the changes making themselves felt within the region as the age of industrial capitalism stuttered to its close. The continuity is marked by a greater awareness of the distinctiveness of the West Coast's exposure to the changes that were transforming the nation in the latter stages of the twentieth century. Parallel to, and at times converging with, this expanding body of regional writing, a popular narrative took root where the Coast is cast as an industrial wasteland increasingly being left behind in the new economic order. It was a process that contained the potential to obliterate the places and associated identities that had provided the fabric of regional New Zealand. The historians of the West Coast discussed here confront sometimes directly, and at other times more obliquely, this transformation and the local responses to it. Collectively, their work constitutes a distinctive regional voice that refuses to fade quietly into the past as a colourful reminder of the way things once were.

Within the second-wave of West Coast historical writing, the Irish experience has continued to occupy a prominent position. As historian Donald Akenson has pointed out, the West Coast was 'the closest thing New Zealand history has had to an Irish ghetto'.[1] Even more than in the colony at large, on the Coast Irish meant Catholic. The district has

1 Donald H. Akenson, *Half the World from Home: Perspectives on the Irish in New Zealand 1860–1950*, Wellington, Victoria University Press, 1990, p. 202.

thus provided an ideal environment for exploring what has been seen as the most distinctive feature of New Zealand Catholicism during its first 80 years—a prevailing pattern of French priests serving predominantly English and Irish congregations.[2] Neil Vaney examined this dual tradition as it developed throughout a West Coast whose parameters he defines as stretching from Karamea in the north to Jackson Bay in the south. He sees the working compromise that developed as being rooted in the need to overcome the difficulties of isolation, terrain, climate and a pressing need for religious and social cohesion. On the Coast, French cleric and Irish laity worked at the sharp end of Miles Fairburn's idealised construction of life in colonial New Zealand—an environment characterised by the transient, unattached individual, adrift in an environment that offered few communal defences. Vaney's study suggests that, within even the most inhospitable environment, the Catholic Church provided an important collective means of constructing a more congenial way of easing adjustment to colonial life. It is perhaps a measure of the importance of the French clergy in this process, as O'Farrell has argued, that when the flow of French clergy ended in the 1920s and Irish clergy came to dominate, West Coast Catholicism lost more than it gained.

This change has been reconstructed by O'Farrell in *Invisible Kingdoms* (1990) when he reflects upon the West Coast history of his family. He brilliantly describes the Greymouth Catholic quarter as it had developed on the south bank of the Grey River in an area bounded by Chapel, Tainui, Alexander and Puketahi streets. At its centre, standing slightly above the town, was St Patrick's Church. Designed by F.W. Petre, the colony's leading exponent of Catholic Church architecture, its completion in 1888 was proudly hailed as staking out Catholicism's place in the town and its determination to play a role in the district's future. Behind the church clustered the Catholic schools: a convent run by the Sisters of Mercy, a boys' school run by the Marist Brothers and a community hall that acted as a base for an increasingly active Hibernian society. These were the visible signs of a cohesiveness that flowed readily enough, as O'Farrell has shown, into politics.

The politicisation was at its most obvious where education was concerned. Since the *Bowen Act 1877*, primary education provided by the state in New Zealand was intended to be free, secular and compulsory. Outside this

2 Neil Vaney, 'The Dual Tradition. Irish Catholicism and French Priests in New Zealand: The West Coast Experience, 1865–1910', MA thesis, University of Canterbury, 1976.

there had developed a network of segregated Catholic schools—effectively a private system funded by fees and donations—that was essentially Irish and Catholic. The Irish Catholic community of the Grey Valley was in no doubt that they confronted an increasingly hostile and overwhelmingly Protestant educational system. The struggle by Greymouth Catholics to maintain their educational institutions, as elsewhere, drew more tightly the bonds of nationality, religion and, increasingly, those of class. To O'Farrell, as we have seen, the rise of the Red Feds, the new disciples of socialism, coincided with a stage in the evolution of the Grey Valley's Irish Catholic community. Ireland and Irish issues became less important in the lives of individual Catholics and Catholicism more generally. It was a shift in attitude that was hastened, O'Farrell believed, by the arrival of his parent's generation from Ireland in the early twentieth century. The product of a calmer Ireland, they brought a fresh determination to build anew.

Lyndon Fraser's compelling recent analysis of the West Coast Irish experience, *Castles of Gold: A History of New Zealand's West Coast Irish* (2007), places these developments within a broader context.[3] His richly textured monograph skilfully uses the approaches of demographer, ethnographer, family historian and biographer to produce a path-breaking study of the Irish community within a regional New Zealand framework. It follows the fortunes of the Irish from the beginning of the gold rush until the formation of the Irish Free State in 1922. His conclusions confirm and strengthen major elements of the West Coast experience proffered by May, Pearson and O'Farrell. The Irish, like the wider gold rush population May described, frequently came to the Coast from Australia and their lives continued to possess an Australasian dimension. Fraser also endorses O'Farrell's view that the attachment of Irish migrants to 'home' was seldom:

> Nationalist or ideological, or related to Ireland as a whole. It was quite a particular affection for and loyalty to, a small group of people—immediate family and close friends—and a certain limited area or specific place—in my family's case a group of villages and towns in central Tipperary: Ballinderry, Borrisokane, Nenagh, Birr. Dublin or Cork or Limerick or Belfast were irrelevant to this commitment: they were virtually foreign places, some of them totally unknown.[4]

3 Fraser, *Castles of Gold*.

4 Fraser, *Castles of Gold*, p. 156. The quotation comes from Patrick O'Farrell, 'Catholicism on the West Coast: Just How Irish Is It?', *New Zealand Tablet*, 3 May 1973, p. 54.

Something of this evolution from Irish Catholic to Greymouth Catholic was evident in political events taking place as O'Farrell, May and Pearson constructed their particular 'West Coasts'. In 1960, local Catholic activists celebrated the selection of 'Paddy' Blanchfield[5] to succeed J.B. (James) Kent as Labour candidate for the Westland electorate. Following, as he did, three Australians and a Scot, Blanchfield was the district's first New Zealand–born Labour MP. It is hard to imagine a candidate more truly representative of Greymouth Catholic Labour. The 48-year-old baker and chairman of the local branch of the Labour Party had been born in the town in 1911 as the 'unholy alliance' of the Reds and the Greens was undermining the Liberal Party's support in the district. Blanchfield had been involved in civic affairs for more than 20 years: deputy mayor of Greymouth for four years; and a member at various times of the Grey Electric Power Board, Westland Catchment Board and the local Licensing Committee. His enthusiasms were many and varied; twice West Coast steer-riding champion, he had played senior rugby league for Marist and served terms as president and secretary of both the club and the West Coast Rugby League. His voice was familiar up and down the Coast as commentator for both the racing and trotting fraternities.

In 1947, as O'Farrell has described, Greymouth's conservative Catholic Labour activists had been unable to find a candidate to succeed James O'Brien, and quietly acquiesced in the selection of James Kent. Thirteen years later, Blanchfield was publicly endorsed by the Left in terms that asserted regional independence. The suspicion that national officials of the Labour Party were about to impose their own choice on the electorate provoked a public rebuke from the Communist mayor of Brunner: such decisions, he wrote, should rest 'with the democratic mass'. Whatever else they were, the succession of Grey Valley political representatives—Webb, Holland, O'Brien, Kent and now Blanchfield—they were of the place. Greymouth was just that: Greymouth, local. A mixture of the 'Red and the Green' and the in-between.

That the historian's voice in post-1960 West Coast should find its strongest and most persistent expression in coalmining disasters should surprise no one. The litany of past tragedies was imprinted in the histories that mining communities passed down through the generations. The mass grave at Stillwater for 33 of the 65 miners who died in the Brunner disaster

5 Patrick Blanchfield (1911–1980) was MP for Westland, 1960–72; West Coast, 1972–78.

of 1896 was for many in the 1940s and 1950s a grim and decaying reminder of how great a cost mining families had borne. My paternal grandmother lived almost directly across the road from the grave and regularly took me as a youngster on her visits to the grave. Its massive size was both frightening and somehow defiant. Bob Henderson's 1956 poem, 'Stillwater',[6] powerfully captures its simple grandeur:

> No tall church spire marks these lonely grounds,
> Where virgin bush in silent peace surrounds.
> No generations past lie sleeping here
> In Land of Promise for the Pioneer.
> Seldom the name of Mother, Wife or Daughter
> Is spelt on these grey headstones at Stillwater.
>
> Here in this hallowed grounded the tombstones new;
> Each in modest form but silent view,
> Tell the brief story of a miner's death.
> In Brunner, Tyneside or in Coal-Pit Heath.
> A comrade seeks his service to relate:
> No less bare justice pleads his cruel fate.

In 1971, as I was about to follow the footsteps of Patrick O'Farrell to Canberra to begin a study of miners and steelworkers in the Wollongong area, I took a photo of the mass grave just in case, in my absence, it succumbed to the relentless growth of the West Coast bush. I scarcely needed the photo to keep the memory alive. The coalfields of the Illawarra region that were to preoccupy me for the next few years possessed their own grim monument to a disaster that took 96 lives at the Mt Kembla mine in 1902. Born of the same phase of lightly regulated industrial capitalism, the two disasters pointed to a universal reality of coalfields life. Both gave rise to studies that throw much light on the nature of mining disasters and their place in community consciousness.[7]

Such studies were part of a 'greening of the memory'[8] and owed much to the lingering death of the traditional coalfields. Decaying coaltowns, and the monuments that recorded starkly their worst fears, spoke with a dignity that demanded a continuing place in the historical landscape.

---

6 Bob Henderson, 'Stillwater', in Blackball History Group, eds, *Blackball Beckons: A Selection of Poems from Blackball, Moonlight and Surrounding Districts*, Westland, NZ, Blackball History Group, 2000.

7 Stuart Piggin and Henry Lee, *The Mt Kembla Disaster*, Sydney, Oxford University Press/Sydney University Press, 1992; Brian Wood, *Disaster at Brunner*, Greymouth, Brian Wood, 1996.

8 Piggin and Lee, *The Mt Kembla Disaster*, pp. 236–37.

They invoke overtones of utopian solidarity—a desire to perpetuate the memory or create an enduring myth that speaks to the mainsprings of humanity. They stand apart also from the sordid reality of the disasters of which they are a product as historical landmarks of occupational, community and regional identity. They possessed a largely unrealised potential to become sites of radical protest against the remorseless unfolding of capitalism's cycles of growth and contraction as expressed within the limits set by coal seam and technology. The 1896 Brunner mine disaster cast a long shadow throughout the Grey Valley coalfield, though its role in the radical upsurge that followed at Runanga and Blackball has been rarely acknowledged. Wherever Brunner miners and their families went in the aftermath of the disaster, their presence was a reminder of a brutal truth of coalfields life: death in the pits was an ever-present possibility, either as part of a single largely unremarked mishap, or by some larger conflagration from which no generation of miner was spared.[9]

By the 1960s, Brunner symbolised disaster and decay. The re-enactment of the discovery of the Brunner coal seam that marked the district's participation in the celebration of Westland's Golden Century faithfully recorded that past. It evoked eulogy and commemoration but essayed no vision of the future. Brunner had played its part in the West Coast story and the future would depend upon new vantage points. By this simple recognition of economic reality, the mayor and councillors of a soon to be legislated out of existence Brunner Borough Council effectively gifted Brunner to the historians. It is perhaps the tragedy of the demise of 'King Coal' in the Grey Valley that the decline was lingering and painful in nature. The sequence of pit closures that spelt the end of the traditional coalmining communities of the late nineteenth and early twentieth century did not signal the exhaustion of coal deposits. There was always the hope that new technologies and new markets would breathe life into the coaltowns. Coalmining did not immediately become a 'sunset industry', but increasingly exhibited the characteristics of an industry in retreat.

These uncertain times paradoxically deepened the bonds of place and identity just as they were undercut by political and ideological change. The dominance of the National Party during the postwar decades removed the political will to sustain recently nationalised mines. In the

9 John Benson, *British Coalminers in the Nineteenth Century: A Social History*, Dublin, Gill and Macmillan, 1980, pp. 28–64.

years that followed the 1951 lockout of the nation's waterside workers, Grey Valley miners accepted that industrial defeat would usher in change. They had struck in protest against the imposition of draconian emergency regulations by the Sidney Holland National Government. After the crushing of the watersiders and the subsequent return of the government in a snap election, the miners were left exposed to the retribution of a rampant Holland. In the years that followed, it became an article of faith in the coaltowns that the confrontation with the National Government marked the beginning of the end for Grey Valley mining communities.[10]

Over the next half century, economic, technological and attitudinal changes redefined the Grey Valley and its place in the West Coast identity. The most significant and obvious change was the demise of the traditional coalmining town that had grown up around the pit that gave it life. Changes in transport had, since the 1940s, been making it increasingly common for miners and their families to live in the bigger towns and travel daily to work by train or bus. The wind back of production accelerated the trend until pit closure left the once vibrant mining towns to find roles in a regional economy that was struggling to establish its place in the remaking of the national economy after Britain's decision to join the European Common Market in 1972. Unlike mining communities on the Buller coalfield, Blackball and Runanga ceased to function as traditional coaltowns, but neither imitated the demise of the goldmining towns that preceded them and quietly assumed the mantle of ghost town.

The two mining towns now sit like defiant reminders of a past that refuses to die. The untapped resources of the nearby Paparoa Range feed the hope that the right combination of new technology and rising demand for coal might encourage a new generation of capitalists to breathe new life into 'King Coal'. It is precisely this stubborn refusal to abandon a past hard won that lies at the heart of a Grey Valley identity and informs much of the region's recent historical writing. The detailed studies of the mining disasters that have punctuated the Grey Valley's history have been accompanied by community histories seeking to record a fading past. There has been a tendency to promote the Grey Valley coaltowns, and especially Blackball, as the birthplace of the New Zealand Labour Party. To a Labour Party hijacked in the 1980s by a leadership that traduced its socialist heritage, the decaying Grey Valley coaltowns offered a symbolic means of reconnecting with its past: to many, the

10 Richardson, *Coal, Class & Community*, pp. 284–303.

rediscovery of the socialist Grey Valley coaltowns was simply grist to the mill of the developing tourist industry; others found irony in the growing interest in the legacy of industrial workers whose dominance within the labour movement had vanished and whose exposure to the unfettered forces of corporate capitalism increasingly mirrored that of the late nineteenth century.

On the 19 January 1967, I was sitting in the work room of the *Greymouth Evening Star* offices working steadily through the newspaper's files. News of an explosion at the Strongman mine near Runanga brought first a stunned silence and then a rush to have something ready for the early afternoon paper. From its opening in 1939, Strongman had been the flagship of the first Labour Government's mining program and the standard-setter for the mining industry. It was, at the time of the explosion, New Zealand's largest underground mine—employing some 240 men—and its impeccable safety record was jealously guarded. The journalists, printers and compositors and general staff who gravitated to the newsroom as the tale of rescue and recovery unfolded were scarcely independent observers: they had brothers, fathers, husbands, relations and friends working at Strongman. Were they working that shift?[11]

Nineteen men lost their lives that day at the Strongman mine. It was the Grey Valley's worst mine disaster since 65 men were killed at Brunner in 1896. The explosion had sent a fireball through a section of the mine and smoke and firedamp (methane gas) made recovery of the bodies hazardous. Fifteen were recovered on the day of the explosion and it was several weeks before a further two bodies were able to be brought to the surface. It proved impossible to recover the final two bodies and the tunnel was sealed off. Within the mining fraternity, the soul-searching that began almost immediately, especially among those who worked in the pits alongside the men who had perished in the explosion, focused on the individual practices and procedures upon which they collectively relied. In the words of a truism of the pits: 'a miner's life is always in the hands of his workmates'. Nothing imperilled lives underground more than a general complacency that permitted a gradual erosion of safety standards and a casualness in following the letter of regulations. Such also was the verdict of a Commission of Enquiry set up to report on the Strongman disaster.

11 Peter Ewen, *Strongman: Three Score and More*, Greymouth, Peter Ewen, 2006.

The explosion at Strongman inevitably stirred memories of Brunner. By now the mass grave at Stillwater had become very largely separated from the emotional outpourings with their overtones of utopian community solidarity and had slipped quietly into the realm of myth and family legend. The death of Brunner as a coaltown and the distance of the grave from Runanga and Blackball diminished its historical power. By raising questions about the long-term viability of underground coalmining in the Grey Valley, the Strongman disaster brought past, present and future to the fore: would Runanga and Dunollie, Blackball, Wallsend, Dobson and Taylorville mimic Brunner and disappear as the coaltowns had done?

It is now possible to see that the demise of the older Grey Valley coaltowns had begun in the late 1940s. By the late 1960s, as the district's second century began, the Coast became increasingly at the mercy of changing economic and social goals as the nation sought to respond to Britain's decision to join the Common Market. Thereafter, the Coast was to take its place among the supplicants seeking to piece together a means of encouraging local enterprise by way of regional assistance programs, grants and subsidies. It was a dispiriting exercise. Small clothing manufacturing plants were established by Lane Walker and Rudkin in the larger centres—Hokitika, Greymouth, Reefton and Westport. In the wake of mine closure, Blackball leaders had confronted the reality of small, relatively isolated industrial communities—their populations were too small and too male. At the political level, the appetite for regional development evaporated throughout the 1970s and spectacularly so in the Grey Valley. This is clearly seen in the case of the short-lived Matai Industries. In the lead up to the 1972 general election, an understanding developed between Norman Kirk, the leader of the Opposition, and Kevin Meates, a Christchurch businessman, that a Labour Government would support the establishment of a woodware, metalware and plastics industry on the Coast. Four factories were subsequently opened in Reefton, Greymouth, Runanga and Westport, employing 347 workers. In office the Kirk Labour Government's enthusiasm for the venture waned.[12]

12 Barry Gustafson, *His Way: A Biography of Robert Muldoon*, Auckland, Auckland University Press, 2001, pp. 131–34; Margaret Hayward, *Diary of the Kirk Years*, Queen Charlotte Sound and Wellington, Cape Catley and Reed, 1981, pp. 117, 131.

The eventual collapse of Matai Industries was as sudden as it was prophetic. In early 1974 the company was placed in receivership and the protracted process of litigation that followed was a reminder that, as the Chief Justice was to put it, political promises were not binding contracts.[13] These words found fertile ground in a popular interpretation of West Coast history that adds a 'sense of betrayal' to the more familiar themes of isolation and apartness. The failure of Matai Industries to fulfil the hopes of those who put their faith in state-sponsored regional development marks the end of a generation of thinking about the Coast. The economic malaise of the early 1970s brought to an end, as Jim McAloon has written, the 'long global post war boom' and the New Zealand economy 'fell into the worst crisis since the Great Depression'.[14] On the Coast, the downturn came as a crisis within a crisis. Over the next two decades the region adjusted, as best it could, to the ideological leap back into the laissez-faire ways of the nineteenth century that put the region at the mercy of the market place.

This complex web of historical reflection, tragedy and economic downturn gave rise to new trends in historical writing about the region. The initial focus was Brunner rather than Blackball or Runanga and the impetus came from within the Grey Valley. The immediate impulses at work behind this second wave of historical writing were intertwined and complementary. They drew upon an increasing national interest in the historic place as a marker of the past and definer of local identity. Grey Valley enthusiasts successfully promoted the claims of the Brunner mine site as an industrial archaeological project for what was then the New Zealand Historic Places Trust. They were also expressed in a distinctive form of community theatre. In 1977, Susan Battye and Thelma Eakin, teachers at Greymouth High School, led their students in researching and producing *The Shadow of the Valley: A Play about the Brunner Mine Disaster, 1896*.[15] Their stated intention 'was not just to compile a factual account, but also to discover and record the people's experience of the Brunner mine disaster'.[16] The first and subsequent performances in Greymouth before audiences that 'belonged' were 'deeply moving' occasions.[17]

13 Meates v Attorney General [1979] 1 *NZLR*, p. 415; Meates v Attorney General [1983] *NZLR*, p. 308.

14 Jim McAloon, *Judgements of All Kinds: Economic Policy-Making in New Zealand, 1945–1984*, Wellington, Victoria University Press, 2013, p. 150.

15 Susan Battye and Thelma Eakin, *The Shadow of the Valley: A Play about the Brunner Mine Disaster, 1896*, Wellington, Oxford University Press, 1980.

16 Battye and Eakin, *The Shadow of the Valley*, p. 7.

17 Wood, *Disaster at Brunner*, p. 229.

In the words of Peter Hooper, Grey Valley teacher, poet and novelist, the play was: 'our own history transmitted into an art form'.[18] In sentiment and community engagement, there is a clear connection with the outpourings of Edward Hunter, the migrant Scottish coalminer who, as Billy Banjo, had chronicled West Coast coalfields life in ballad and verse when coal was king and the Red Feds were in revolutionary mood. Hunter had returned to Glasgow shortly after World War I in the wake of the death of his wife and, in the decades that followed, found his radical voice alongside the 'Clydeside Reds' and served a term as deputy mayor of Glasgow. By the 1960s he was engaging the workers of Scottish mining towns in what he called 'community dramatic musical plays' similar in spirit to that emerging in the Grey Valley.[19] And, as we have already seen, *The Shadow of the Valley* was soon to be followed by Meryvn Thompson's highly personalised rendition of West Coast mining life, *Coaltown Blues*.[20]

The Shadow of the Valley was timely. Its reception locally may be located in a mood of nostalgia that had its roots in an awareness of the passing of an age. The desire to capture the lived experience of a community before it was too late interacted with and was an expression of a 'greening of memory' and a proclamation of local identity. It thus helped shape contemporary attitudes to the past in ways that ultimately produced visible and permanent recognition of Brunner's place in the evolution of the Grey Valley. The mass grave at Stillwater was spruced and thrust back into public consciousness. The brick kilns that had been so dominant a feature of the industrial environment surrounding the Brunner mine entrance stood proudly visible once more as excavation and restoration work rescued the past from the bush that threatened to overwhelm it. The interpretative aids that signposted the plant and processes that had made Brunner the hub of the Grey Valley coal industry until the disaster of 1896, spoke of the past in ways that drew attention to present predicament.[21]

The study of the disaster as a West Coast event and a phenomenon in its own right began within this framework. *Disaster at Brunner* (1996), a commemorative history by Brian Wood, is a path-breaking and insightful account of the making of the disaster and the community responses to

18 Wood, *Disaster at Brunner*, p. 229.

19 Richardson, '"Billy Banjo"'; Pat Moloney and Kerry Taylor, *On the Left: Essays on Socialism in New Zealand*, Dunedin, University of Otago Press, 2002, p. 85.

20 Thompson, *Coaltown Blues* (1986).

21 Geoffrey G. Thornton, *New Zealand's Industrial Heritage*, Wellington, A.H. & A.W. Reed, 1982, pp. 99–103.

it. Here, and in his later *Coal Gorge and the Brunner Suspension Bridge* (2004),[22] a fascinating heritage and environment study, Wood has ensured that historians have finally done Brunner and its people justice. What defines both works is a steadfast determination to understand the relationship between people and place in its complexity. This is nowhere more clearly demonstrated than in the final section of *Disaster at Brunner*, 'Memorialising the Disaster'. Two chapters, 'Disaster Memory' and 'Disaster Commemoration', trace the ways in which Brunner's past and present have continued to march side by side.[23] The mass grave at the Stillwater cemetery was, as Bob Henderson's poem suggests, defined by its colonial and pioneering setting. Time had not yet bestowed a sense of continuity or permanence. The notion of a congregation of the Christian dead that once dominated churchyards and symbolically linked them to the congregation of the living was giving way to more secular cemeteries. As the dead increasingly came to serve the new gods of memory and history within a more secular society, gravestones and monuments regained their importance as sites of individual, family and community (both local and national) identity.

The immediate concern in the aftermath of the explosion was to answer the question—where are the dead? The desire to recover the bodies had in 1896 answered a powerful human need to keep the dead close. At Brunner, all bodies were recovered by workmates and miners from Blackball, some of whom were said to have run the 20 kilometres to relieve exhausted rescue teams drawn from a workforce whose number had been effectively halved by the explosion. It was the miners too, whether from nearby Blackball or from Brunner, whose task it was to dig 'The Big Grave'. Initially conceived as the burying place of all 65 victims, the mass grave at Stillwater ultimately became the resting place of 33 miners as family and religious preferences dictated. In its scale and form, the large concrete-stepped plinth with obelisk pointing towards the heavens, framed by an ornate wrought-iron railing, was a stark grave and a moving memorial to all the 65 miners killed in the explosion.

Erected by relatives and friends, it expressed the historical bonds of occupation that reach back to the old world and the developing ones of place that together proclaimed a singular solidarity. The list of names enshrined on the mass burial plot proclaimed community solidarity—

22 Brian Wood, *Coal Gorge and the Brunner Suspension Bridge*, Greymouth, Brian Wood, 2004.
23 Wood, *Disaster at Brunner*, pp. 217–48.

Brunner miners buried together. In the process of mourning, the grave was also a tangible way of 'recuperating the dead' or keeping them alive in the community of the living. This form of collective mourning and commemoration has, in modern times, come to invoke the dead to serve secular gods. The rituals of time and place that prevailed in Brunner in 1896 were cast in a more religious mode and sought to ease the dead out of this world and safely into the next.

Over time, the 'Big Grave' at the Stillwater cemetery became a place of commemoration. The Brunner community was never able to recapture the pre-eminent role it had proudly fashioned as a coaltown and industrial complex. The future lay with the newer Grey Valley mining communities developing at Runanga and Blackball. Brunner's population had been declining before the explosion (by nearly 600 between 1891 and 1896). Falling demand for coal led to 'short-time' in the pits and, in keeping with coalfields tradition, the young men had moved on. Brunner was in no shape to weather the impoverishment that came in the wake of the disaster. The political and legal processes that sought to explain the disaster and determine where responsibility lay brought scant improvement. A royal commission exonerated the mining company and attributed the disaster to an unknown miner who had fired a blown-out shot that backfired and ignited coal dust, setting off a series of explosions throughout the mine. A subsequent case for negligence brought against the mining company in 1898 was successful but ultimately overturned by a Court of Appeal decision in favour of the company's English debenture holders. In 1906, a decade after the disaster, the mine closed and the adjacent St Kilda pit followed in 1921, leaving small cooperative groups as the only coalmining activity at Brunner.

The legacy of the Brunner disaster was thus in the hands of an ever-shrinking community. Until the formation of the Brunner Old Boys' Association in 1930, remembrance was private rather than public. For many years local shopkeepers marked the anniversary of the disaster by closing their shops to mark 'Black Thursday'. Thereafter reunions of the association and anniversaries (of the Brunner Borough Council, European settlement of the district and of the disaster itself) became occasions of public commemoration. Such civic and public ceremonies as occurred took traditional form—the laying of wreaths, the idealisation of the mining community—and were expressed in the sentiments of secular religion. A notable feature of the commemorations was the absence of any overt attempt to link them to protest—union or otherwise. As an affirmation of an ongoing partnership of the living and the dead they stood in opposition to the logic of the marketplace that detached economics from society and reduced it to abstract calculus, assigning individuals the status of mere units of economic calculation.

There was a noticeably sharper and more political edge to the commemoration of the sixtieth anniversary of the Brunner disaster and the laying of a wreath by the mayor of Brunner at the 'Big Grave' in 1956. The ranks of the Brunner Old Boys' Association had thinned and union officials began to play a bigger role within community affairs. The new tone was in part a product of a union militancy grounded in the ideological gulf that had grown between the industrial and political arms of the labour movement in the aftermath of the 1951 lockout. It was also rooted in the frustrations that developed as the future prospects of Grey Valley coaltowns narrowed. If frequently less remarked, the Brunner disaster had also played a role in sharpening the push for safety in the mines that formed a constant element of mining unionism from the days of the Red Feds until the election of the first Labour Government in 1935. The new edge of the 1950s might also be viewed as reconnecting the commemoration of the disaster at the grave site with the community solidarity of work and place proclaimed in the commemoration of all 65 miners killed in the Brunner explosion.

Few of those gathered at Stillwater in 1956 could remember the events of 1896. Fewer still would have needed reminding of the capriciousness of the pits. Nine miners working in the nearby Dobson mine, little more than a kilometre down the Grey Valley from Brunner, had lost their lives in 1926 in an explosion reported to have been heard 10 kilometres away at Runanga. One of those killed was James Richards (47) whose father and uncle had died in the Brunner explosion 30 years earlier. If the random hand of fate captures accurately the national profile of Dobson mineworkers, the passage of time had worked little change. Five of the nine men who died as a result of the Dobson explosion had come from British coalfields and two of their number were newcomers from the depressed Scottish coalfields. Like the British colliers of the nineteenth century who preceded them, they and their families had carried with them to the Grey Valley the legacy of disasters past they had absorbed on the coalfields of the old world.

The past was ever present. Its monuments, mass grave and memorials stood nobly amid sealed mine entrances and crumbling mine buildings—the telltale signs of an industry struggling for survival and a region in search of a future. The disaster at Strongman (1967) brought past and present together once more. The mine's status as flagship of several generations of union endeavour and standard-setter for mine safety unsettled the mining community. Had laxness permeated the attitudes and practices that had served them well? This sober reflection upon the real and ever-present danger of the pits is evident in Peter Ewen's *Strongman: Three Score and More* (2006). Ewen was of the place. His coalminer father's *Far from the Sun*, published the year before the disaster, was an insightful insider's recreation of life at Runanga in the 1940s and 1950s.[24] The Ewens trace their mining pedigree back to the migrant miners who left the Yorkshire coalfields for Denniston in 1879 and despatched men to Brunner in 1896 to help in the aftermath of the disaster. To Peter Ewen, the 65 miners who perished at Brunner were 'soldiers of industry'[25] who in the Grey Valley assumed an importance akin to that bestowed upon the men of Gallipoli.

Ewen's metaphor implies the notion of the class war. Equally it embraces the idea of territory and casts the miners as the standard bearers of a local identity under siege. The disaster of 1967 stands at the heart of his history of the Strongman mine. It is tempting to see his discussion of the likely cause of the disaster, written four years before the Pike River explosion that took 29 lives on 19 November 2010, as pointing to changes in mining practices that were putting lives at risk in the mines just as pit closures eroded the ranks of experienced miners. As their number diminished, so too did the body of instinctive wariness and respect for the regulations and procedures that recognised the peculiarities of individual pits. Ewen's account provides space for viewpoints from within this working community. Nowhere more effectively than in the reflections of two of the district's most respected mining officials: Harry Bell, a former chief inspector of mines and Strongman manager (1974–77), and Tom Brazil, chief inspector of mines and manager of Strongman (1955–63). Their discussion of the difficulties maintaining safety standards within an environment that sanctioned lower levels of inspection prompts Ewen to lament the passing of an age 'when genuine Mine Inspectors carried their tools of the profession and regularly walked the beat'.[26]

24 Ewen, *Far from the Sun*.

25 Cited in Wood, *Disaster at Brunner*, pp. 245–46.

26 Ewen, *Strongman*, p. 71.

In its timing and its argument, this critique was part of an emergent regional protest. It was a protest that was both complicated and intensified by the growing national debate about the conservation of the natural environment. The continued milling of the West Coast's luxuriant native bush, the nation's last substantial remnant of unspoiled natural forest, became central to this debate.[27] The West Coast timber industry had been built by Australian capital and some two-thirds of the region's rimu-cut had previously crossed the Tasman. The introduction of export quotas for indigenous timber in the 1920s set limits on this trade, but it was the environmental impulse of the 1980s that brought the issue to the forefront of national consciousness.[28] In 1986 the David Lange Labour Government responded to concerns about the preservation of native forests by establishing a Ministry for the Environment and negotiated an 'Accord' between West Coast authorities, the sawmilling industry and conservation interests that permitted sustainable logging of native timber. An uneasy compromise that struggled to define what constituted 'sustainable', the 'Accord' was swept aside by the Helen Clark Labour Government in 1999. Thereafter all logging of native timber in state-owned forests ceased and 80 per cent of the West Coast's land area was designated Crown reserve or national park. As compensation, the region received a lump sum of $120 million for regional development to be administered by a Trust with all significant expenditure requiring the approval of government-appointed advisers. The need for this approval raised suspicion. Would the bureaucratic state once more find ways to ride roughshod over regional initiative?

The doubts were soon to be expressed in what one historian has called a 'narrative of betrayal'.[29] Its two major threads—the dismantling of the coalfields and the locking up of the forests—came, throughout the 1980s and 1990s, to colour perceptions of the Coast. This is most clearly evident in Paul Maunder's *Coal and the Coast* (2012), a highly personal response to the explosion that killed 29 men at the Pike River mine on 19 November 2010 in the Paparoa Range, near Blackball. Maunder contends that the community response to the disaster was conditioned by, and contributed to, the sense of alienation. Regulatory approval for the Pike River mine was seen by many, he argues, as 'the original carrot offered to Coasters

27 Nicky Hager and Bob Burton, *Secrets and Lies: The Anatomy of an Anti-Environmental PR Campaign*, Nelson, Craig Potton Publishing, 1999, pp. 156–78, 221–39.
28 Michael Roche, *History of Forestry*, Wellington, New Zealand Forestry Corporation/GP Books, 1990, pp. 401–32.
29 Maunder, *Coal and the Coast*, p. 66.

in return for locking up the forests into national park'.[30] The mine was situated on Crown land administered by the Department of Conservation and its proposed escape shafts were within the boundaries of the newly proclaimed national park. The tragedy at Pike River thus brought together the two threads of the developing narrative of betrayal—timber and coal.

The Pike River disaster thrust the issue of mine safety, long at the very heart of mining unionism, to the forefront of national consciousness. The efforts by coalminers to achieve greater worker control through the appointment of check-inspectors drawn from their own ranks and supported by pit committees had long expressed generic occupational concerns. The mix of mutual interdependence and self-reliance came in the Grey Valley to define a distinctive regional culture. The history of this quest for mine safety, described in my *Coal, Class & Community*, reaches back into the coalfields of the old world.[31] Here it is sufficient to remind ourselves that the coalfields of the Grey Valley and the Buller were the crucible in which mining unionism was forged in the late nineteenth and early twentieth centuries and a vital component of the rise of the working class as a political force. In 1935, the election of the nation's first Labour Government provided the means of strengthening the voices of the miners in the day-to-day working of the pits.

Never before, or since, have men who had laboured at the coalface in the Grey Valley been in a position to influence the daily experience of work in the mines. As frontrunners in the emergence of industrial unionism in the first two decades of the twentieth century, Blackball and Runanga were the launching pad for two generations of coalfield radicals. Paddy Webb and Bob Semple, who had spearheaded the rise of the Red Feds at Blackball and Runanga, were part of the influx of miners from the depressed Victorian coalfields in the first decade of the twentieth century. They were the disciples of a variety of industrial syndicalism that was American in origin and put its faith in unionism's ability to confront and conquer capitalism at the point of production. Webb had been the first to make the transition to political activism and, in 1913, was thrust to the forefront of national politics when, as a representative of the fledgling Social Democratic Party, he successfully won a by-election to wrench the seat of Grey away from the Liberals.[32]

30 Maunder, *Coal and the Coast*, p. 77.

31 Richardson, *Coal, Class & Community*, pp. 78–86, 119–25, 162–66, 260–89.

32 Richardson, *Coal, Class & Community*, pp. 142–44; Richardson, 'Politics and War: Coal Miners and Conscription, 1914–1918', pp. 129–31; Franks and McAloon, *The New Zealand Labour Party, 1916–2016*, pp. 65–66.

Semple entered parliament in 1918 as MP for Wellington South under the banner of the New Zealand Labour Party, formed in July 1916. A colourful pit-top orator who had cut his teeth on the coalfields of Victoria and Western Australia, he was in his element riding a wave of discontent and anti-conscription sentiment in a by-election campaign rooted in working-class protest. His initial experience of the parliamentary chamber was, like that of Webb, brief. In the 1914 general election, Webb retained his seat but was subsequently imprisoned for 10 years when, as an unmarried man of eligible age, he refused a conscription order. He did not re-enter parliament until 1933. Semple lost his seat in the 1919 general election and did not return to parliament until 1928. Within the first Labour Government the pair were joined by Angus McLagan, the Scot who had arrived at Blackball at the end of World War I. With thinking shaped by the second wave of syndicalism and the burst of radical expectation that flowed from the Russian Revolution, 'Gus' was to become arguably the country's most influential unionist in the 1920s and 1930s as the coal industry entered the first stages of a collapse that was to prove terminal. From Blackball, McLagan witnessed, as leader of the United Mine Workers' Union and the Communist Party of New Zealand, the first withering of coalfield communities as an international crisis in the coal industry deepened and merged with the Great Depression of the 1930s.[33]

Semple, Webb and McLagan were a powerful coalfields voice within a Labour Government (1935 and 1949) that responded to the problems of the coal industry with a program of gradual nationalisation. They brought to this process an understanding of the mentality of the coalface where public ownership was seen as a means of bringing to an end the 'tyranny of the manager' by linking nationalisation with greater worker participation in the decisions that determined safety in the mines. There can be no doubt that the trio presided over the nation's most sustained attempt to improve mine safety. Under their watch, the administration of the certification process became more responsive to local conditions and more insistent upon higher levels of competence, and the educational role of the Schools of Mines on the coalfields was enhanced. Unions that had been severely weakened during the long Depression of the 1920s and 1930s began to play a greater role in the day-to-day negotiation between management and miners that characterised work in the pits. Labour's

33 Richardson, *Coal, Class & Community*, pp. 252–60.

Industrial Conciliation and Arbitration Amendment Act 1936, by effectively making union membership a precondition of employment, strengthened the union's hand in the remaining privately owned and operated pits.

During World War II, worker involvement was formalised by the creation of pit committees charged with maintaining production and safety standards and empowered to approach Mines Department inspectors independently of mine managers. In practice, agreements reached between the Mines Department and state miners formed a basis for achieving uniform standards across the mining industry. That these agreements were achieved without recourse to the Arbitration Court reflected a higher degree of cooperation and involvement than previously experienced on the coalfields and was demonstrated in a sharp decline in the days lost due to industrial stoppages often associated with safety issues. Between 1946 and 1961, the mining industry's share of the nation's industrial stoppages fell from 40 per cent to 11.6 per cent.[34] Accidents that resulted in death still happened; most occurred in small privately owned pits standing, as it were, on the fringes of the new system.[35]

Just as it had been the crucible of radical unionism in the early twentieth century, the Grey Valley became a front runner in the remaking of democracy in the workplace. The reforms of the 1930s and 1940s had stopped short of the miners' best hopes: workers' inspectors did not possess the power to stop a place. Only a few of the more radical spirits on the coalfields persisted in the quest for the full democratisation of the pits; most miners acknowledged recent achievements and turned their attention to combating the changing economic circumstances of the postwar coalfields. Nothing divided the old Grey Valley coalfield order from the new more dramatically than the confrontation that spread from the lockout of the nation's watersiders in 1951. In its aftermath, the traditional mining community withered as pit closure became an ever more imminent reality. It was a process accompanied by fundamental changes in the methods employed in the mining and transportation of coal. Underground mining increasingly lost its dominant position to open-cast operations. Where underground operation prevailed, it became

34 Ralph Rantoul, 'The Coal Mines Council', *New Zealand Journal of Industrial Relations*, vol. 3, no. 1, May 1978, pp. 21–30.

35 W.P. Brazil, 'Legislation—Changes and Implications: A Summary of the Evolution of Coal Mining Safety Legislation Together with a Traditional Viewpoint. Presented by W.P. Brazil, Francis Mining Company, to Coal Producers Federation of New Zealand Inc., 1995 Seminar and Annual General Meeting, May 1995', ms, private collection.

more mechanised and new techniques were employed in taking coal to the surface. One of the more damaging consequences of this changing mining environment was the destruction of the communities that had nurtured and supported the disciplines and traditions that sustained mine safety.

In its smaller scale and operation, the underground coalmining landscape increasingly came to resemble that of its pioneering and most dangerous years. The explosion of gas and dust that brought 19 fatalities at the Strongman mine on 19 January 1967 was a tragic reminder of the need for ongoing vigilance in this changing environment. Yet, over the next 40 years the lessons of Strongman were forgotten and the collective 'pit-sense' that formed the basis of local practice gradually eroded. The Schools of Mines, once the principal educative organisation of the mining industry, were closed. At the same time, legislative and administrative changes stripped away foundations. The inspection processes once attached to the Mines Department were placed within the Labour Department. The positions of Chief Inspector of Mines and Check Inspector were abolished. Changes in industrial law, flowing from the *Labour Relations Act 1987*, had the effect of destroying the United Mine Workers of New Zealand (UMW)—the historic voice of coalminers nationally and the organisation that had done most to shape the safety provisions within underground mines. With fewer than the 1,000 members required to constitute a separate union, the UMW became part of a composite national body, the Engineering, Printing and Manufacturing Union.

Equally damaging to the fabric of mine safety was the *Health and Safety in Employment Act 1992*. It repealed the *Coal Mines Act 1979* and subsequent amendments through to 1988, and placed work safety within the Occupational Safety and Health (OSH) section of the Department of Labour. In the process, many coal industry–specific and long-standing protection mechanisms were removed or weakened. The regulatory looseness produced by this transfer came just as mechanisation brought new techniques into the pits. The new machines and methods opened the way for the employment of men from outside the traditional mining community with little if any knowledge of the mines they worked and largely ignorant of the legacy of disasters past.

The most incisive analysis of the decline in safety standards that accompanied these changes came in a 1995 paper by Bill Brazil—then a mine manager in the Grey Valley for the Francis Mining Company. A product of the old system working at its most robust, Brazil was a member of one of the district's most prominent coalmining families. His father Tom was manager at Strongman (1955–63) and, after a year as inspector of mines at Huntly on the Waikato coalfield, returned to the Grey Valley as assistant district manager for the West Coast and subsequently became New Zealand's Chief Inspector of Mines. Sons Kevin and Bill became managers at Grey Valley and Buller mines just as coalmining was taking on the appearance of a sunset industry. They did so in ways that reveal the different pathways that existed within the mining industry at the peak of its development: for Kevin this meant study at the School of Mines at the University of Otago; Bill, on the other hand, left Greymouth's Marist Brothers' High School in 1959 and started work at the Strongman mine managed by his father. As part of the generation that experienced the most regulated phase in the history of the nation's coalmining industry, the Brazils understood that its systems of inspection and control depended upon the interlocking involvement of unions, management and individual miners.[36]

What Bill Brazil saw before him on the coalfields of the 1990s was a safety system compromised by 'bureaucratic incompetence' and held together by a 'rubber band'. His report charted the erosion of the collective pit-sense by legislative and administrative changes that had their origin in the neoliberal infatuation with trimming the regulatory functions of the state and reducing the role of unions in the workplace. Lives, he argued, were being put at risk by changes in the nature of the mining industry and the stripping away of safety provisions driven by ideology and ignorance. It is a measure of his frustration that he reached back to the pioneering and largely unregulated coalfields of the nineteenth century and the Kaitangata disaster of 1879 as marking the extent of the decline in standards. It was a decade before a government review (2008) acknowledged shortcomings in safety provision and recommended that a 'check inspector' be made mandatory in all mines and given the authority to stop a pit. This endorsement of what had been a fundamental tenet of the traditional

36 Peter Ewen, *Pike: Death by Parliament*, Christchurch, Pit Pony Press, 2014.

view expressed by Brazil and by miners' unions for more than a century was pertinently presented as a safeguard against commercial pressures and poor decision-making in the daily operation of mines.

The disaster at the Pike River mine in 2010 revealed the full extent of the damage that had already occurred. The systems and safeguards that had been so hard won yet so quickly swept away had been the finest achievement of the collective solidarity of the mining communities. And, as Paul Maunder's evocative *Coal and the Coast* demonstrates, as pits closed and technological change reduced the predominance of the underground mine, the relationship between workplace and community loosened.[37] Amid the social dislocation that followed, the separation between making a living and making a life began to take on new and more individualised meanings. Maunder's narrative of the days immediately following the Pike River explosion in 2010 takes the form of a daily diary and records the sense of disbelief that engulfed the Blackball community as it became doubtful the bodies of entombed miners would be recovered. He describes the transformation that had been taking place since the 1960s. Blackball—once a company mining town—was now, he wrote, 'a village of 350, containing a diversity of people: some old-timers, some transients, a mix of people commuting to a variety of jobs, a few self-employed, a few beneficiaries, and a growing number of Filipino women'.[38]

The mining community that had once defined the terms of its own existence had withered. The historical rituals and traditions that once shaped community responses to tragedy had been hollowed out as the structures in which they were embedded were dismantled. Maunder suggests that a numbing social and emotional void existed in the immediate aftermath of the Pike disaster that was only too readily filled by an intrusive media. By attaching itself to 'what should have been a community ritual' the media created, he argued, an 'electronic "otherness"' that multiplied 'ad infinitum'.[39] Nothing encapsulated this more starkly for Maunder than the government-organised memorial service delivered on national television on 2 December:

37 Maunder, *Coal and the Coast*, pp. 61–93.

38 Maunder, *Coal and the Coast*, p. 11.

39 Maunder, *Coal and the Coast*, p. 29.

> On the day of the service, staged by the government's event management team at the Omoto Racecourse, most of Greymouth turned out, joined by Coasters who came home for the day from Christchurch. There was a strange configuration: the dignitaries on one side of the racetrack in a temporary grandstand, the ordinary people on the other side of the fence. The families sat in the normal grandstand, facing the dignitaries, the young women dressed in their best, faces well made up, the men looking uncomfortable in shiny suits. The union was not invited to speak.
>
> The intent, often Irish faces of the locals basked in the sun, listening but strangely detached. As the service unfolded, speakers from church, state and corporation appeared on large screens and were relayed nationally and internationally, to provide images for the networks: of the nation grieving, of the dignitaries doing their job, of Greymouth watching …[40]

Leached of its human integrity by television's insatiable quest for spectacle, the commemoration of the Pike River tragedy became an 'event'. That it was choreographed in such a manner did not so much mitigate as exacerbate the crudity with which the mining community had been exposed by the nation's politicians to the largely unfettered forces of corporate capitalism. Maunder argues it was this sense of political neglect and wilful disregard for the lessons of the past, whose consequences now became daily more starkly realised, that fed into an existing regional narrative of betrayal. 'Old Blackball' was critical to this construction of the recent past. Firmly implanted in folklore as the spiritual home of the New Zealand labour movement, by the end of the 1980s Blackball had become a metaphor for loss of community; a decaying reminder of the days when coal was king and a symbol of the economic malaise that beset the West Coast region as a whole. The tragedy at Pike River revealed the dark underbelly of the neoliberal thinking that had dominated New Zealand society since the 1980s. Men had gone to work and did not come home because ideology had triumphed over prudent stewardship.

40 Maunder, *Coal and the Coast*, p. 29.

The past was heavy in the air at the Omoto Racecourse commemoration. It was to stalk the enquiries and investigations that followed. Rebecca Macfie's *Tragedy at Pike River Mine*[41] clinically records the frustration within the Mines Rescue Service in the hours and days immediately following the explosion. Caught up in 'the lumbering processes of the police and the Department of Labour',[42] they had been prevented from taking 'the steps they believed were necessary to control the mine atmosphere'.[43] Their anger became even more palpable as there were three further explosions in the mine (on 24, 26 and 28 November). This sense of a lack of regulation and definition of duties was precisely what had motivated Bill Brazil's impassioned attempt to chronicle the dismantling of the systems that offered the best hope of making a naturally dangerous workplace less so. The anguished calls from within the mining community to reclaim the bodies of the 29 men who had perished in the explosion highlighted the void in which a corporate mining venture had operated. The Pike River mine existed as a self-regulated entity set loose among the remnants of a once vibrant and self-reliant community capable of defining the terms upon which it engaged in the coalmining industry.

Rebecca Macfie's account of the Pike tragedy presents a grim chronicle of corporate capitalism at its most brutal. Her account draws upon evidence given in the Greymouth District Court throughout the winter and spring of 2011 and the early summer of 2012 to the Royal Commission established to ascertain the cause of the explosion. Macfie presents a sequence of events that reveal an undercapitalised company unrestrained by adequate regulation, operating within an industry where the union presence was 'limp' and community understanding increasingly diminished. She catalogues a steadfast ruthlessness in the face of 'numerous warnings of catastrophe that went unheeded' as production took precedence over safety. There was no adequate monitoring system operating in a mine working a coal seam known to be high in methane. Indeed, sensors had not been working for weeks before the explosion. The company had forged ahead with the development of hydro-mining before it established a second means of egress required by law and commissioned the system without the skilled workers to maintain it despite repeated spikes in the volume of methane released into the mine atmosphere.

41 Rebecca Macfie, *Tragedy at Pike River Mine*, Wellington, Awa Press, 2013.
42 Macfie, *Tragedy at Pike*, p. 226.
43 Macfie, *Tragedy at Pike*, p. 226.

There had been, Macfie writes, '21 reports of methane levels reaching explosive volumes, and 27 reports of lesser, but potentially dangerous, volumes of gas'. The reports, which went unheeded, 'continued up to the very morning of the tragedy'.[44] The litany of breaches of law reflected a weak regulatory regime and were duly and adroitly noted by the Royal Commission in its report: 'The Department of Labour did not have the focus, capacity or strategies to ensure Pike was meeting its legal responsibilities under health and safety laws'.[45] The commission drew the obvious conclusion: 'The Department should have prohibited Pike from operating the mine until its health and safety systems were adequate'.[46] The litany of failings at the Pike River mine constitutes an indictment of a political age that blindly followed an ideological imperative even as its nostrums were discarded elsewhere. The wilful disregard for the lessons of the past exposed all who worked in the Pike mine to the naked power of international corporate capitalism. Perhaps the cruellest cut of all was that the bodies of the 29 miners were entombed in the mine and with them the forensic evidence that would have provided a clearer understanding of the proximate cause of the explosion.

This uncertainty brought frustration and added to the widespread sense of betrayal. There was little satisfaction to be gained from the political and legal consequences. The resignation of Kate Wilkinson, the Minister of Labour, was immediate and anticipated. The Pike River Company went into receivership and neither appeared nor presented evidence in mitigation when prosecutions were brought by the Labour Department. In making her judgement against the company, Judge Jane Farish pointed to 'a systematic failure of the company to implement and audit its own (inadequate) safety plans and procedures'. The 'accumulation of errors and omissions which transpired over a number of years' were 'the health and safety event of this generation' and 'a worse case [was] hard to imagine'.[47] The company was fined $760,000 and ordered to pay $3.4 million in reparation to the families of the 29 men killed and the two men who managed to get out of the mine. The receivers revealed that remaining funds would allow payments of $5,000 to each family. And still the evidence that might have enabled the police to bring a manslaughter charge remained with the bodies of the 29 miners in the bowels of the Pike mine.

44 Macfie, *Tragedy at Pike*, p. 236.

45 Macfie, *Tragedy at Pike*, p. 236.

46 *Royal Commission on the Pike River Coal Mine Tragedy*, vol. 1, Wellington, Government Printer, 2012, p. 12.

47 Macfie, *Tragedy at Pike*, pp. 238–39.

Figure 5: Protestors at Pike River in February 2017 demand that the bodies of the 29 men who died in the explosion at the Pike Mine, 19 November 2010, be recovered. Re-entry of the mine is underway.

Source: *Greymouth Star*.

A poignant memorial created out of a large boulder located near the portal of the Pike River mine and 29 smaller stones each representing a man killed in the explosion marks the beginning of the access road to the mine. Alongside the boulder a signpost points to the parts of the world from which the miners had made their way to the Pike mine. It captures the enduring internationalism of the coalmining community, and its changing hue. The old world no longer dominates: only two of the men are listed as having come from Britain, both from Scotland; three hail from Australia and one from South Africa. While nearly two-thirds of the men were drawn from the Grey Valley, only one is listed as being from nearby Blackball. The break up of the traditional mining towns that had begun to have a marked effect from the 1940s is reflected in the residences of those killed: Greymouth, nine; Runanga, five; Hokitika, two; Dunollie, Ngahere and Barrytown each contributed one; and three hailed from further afield, one from Nightcaps, a traditional Southland coaltown, and two from Christchurch. In this, as in much else, the workforce at the Pike mine was a patchwork of old patterns and improvisation born of necessity. Neither big enough nor sufficiently remote to need the working camps that made up the Australian FIFO (fly-in fly-out) mine sites, the Pike encapsulated the problems of the Grey Valley.

Viewed from a Grey Valley perspective, the Pike River mining project had seemed, at the early stage of its promotion, like an opportunity to tap into the global resources boom. That the coal being sought lay in a designated national park and was opposed by many on environmental grounds served only to galvanise support within the local community. As Macfie puts it, for 'a mere pinprick in the beautiful West Coast wilderness',[48] the Pike mine offered to open up the prospect of a new age of prosperity. There was much interest in its low-ash coal. Major Japanese steelmakers negotiated conditional long-term contracts. Two Indian companies, coke-maker Saurashtra Fuels and Gujarat NRE, a major coke-making and coalmining company, became significant shareholders. Between them they provided $64 million in loan capital and invested $84 million in shares. These international connections bred inflated expectations within a regional economy that was more familiar with 'bust' than 'boom'. The flow of work for local contractors and suppliers as development work began lifted confidence in the local economy. There was no shortage of investors keen to join in the global resources boom when Pike became the nation's sole publicly listed coal company.

The realities of geology and terrain soon imposed themselves in ways that exposed the fragility of the enterprise. At the heart of the problem was 'a 2.3 kilometre single-entry tunnel' that needed to be 'driven uphill through a major fault and into a gassy coal seam'.[49] The working assumption that tunnelling would be through hard rock that would be largely (90 per cent) self-supporting and therefore relatively inexpensive relied upon surface assessments and lacked the authentication only exploratory drill holes could provide. Bore holes meant delay and cost. Within Pike management there existed the view that conservationists would have caused more delay by opposing further intrusion upon the natural environment (though no one asked them). The cost and delay undermined confidence. What the public saw, however, was a display of optimism. In November 2008 the company announced they had reached the coal seam and were 'on track' to 'reach' the mine's 'steady-state production rate of one million tonnes per annum by mid-2009'. Greymouth's mayor, Tony Kokshoorn, welcomed the announcement as a 'major milestone for the West Coast' that 'promised enormous economic spinoffs for the region'.[50] As Macfie has observed, few saw behind the solid lump of coal proudly displayed

48 Macfie, *Tragedy at Pike*, p. 46.
49 Macfie, *Tragedy at Pike*, p. 72.
50 Macfie, *Tragedy at Pike*, p. 69.

by the company to the crumbly nature of most of the coal that had been exposed. The 2007 prospectus had predicted that by now some 250,000 tonnes of coal would have been exported.

Meanwhile, the troubles in the pit were becoming increasingly evident. In the days before the ceremony to mark the official opening of the mine, there had been numerous gas ignitions believed to be caused by a new machine designed to bore through hard rock or coal. Three months after the celebration of reaching the coal seam, the ventilation shaft collapsed and all mining ceased. It was to take several weeks and 'a thousand helicopter flights dropping cement down the hole to plug the failed section'.[51] The collapse threw into sharp relief the questionable safety provision at the mine. It lacked any emergency exit. Any blockage to the 2.3-kilometre tunnel would mean that the only available exit for men caught underground was to climb a ladder attached to the side of the 111-metre ventilation shaft. The ladder structure was capable of carrying only six men at a time and its steep, awkward climb was judged 'extremely difficult' for even the fittest men, requiring 20 minutes to negotiate. Any emergency with fire, smoke and fumes would have made a safe exit 'virtually impossible'. The pressure that these problems put on costs led to the premature introduction of hydro-mining. Unlike the more conventional continuous coal-cutting machines that could be set to operate at consistent levels, minimising the prospect of dangerous surges in methane gas levels, hydro-mining needed the support of ventilation fans to keep gas levels constant.

The Pike River tragedy invokes comparison with the calamitous Brunner disaster of 1896. Pat O'Farrell places the earlier explosion within the context of the labour–capital crisis of the late 1880s and 1890s. He suggests a tragic melodrama played out in a grim and unyielding environment with the human actors caught in the maelstrom of historical forces they dimly understood. Accepting his judgement at face value, what, if anything, we might ask, has changed a century later? The circumstances that produced the death of 29 miners at the Pike River mine do not speak of human beings as the unwitting victims of some random, haphazard event that, because its seems inexplicable, can be attributed to what a more religious age might have called a 'God of the Gaps'.[52] Nor, in our age, might we take refuge in the secular and amoral 'systemic failure'. To absolve, in this

51 Macfie, *Tragedy at Pike*, p. 81.
52 Piggin and Lee, *The Mt Kembla Disaster*, p. 5.

way, the individual human beings and the wider society that prescribed the working environment, is to deny history and the efforts of the generations who had attempted to learn from its harsh lessons. Rather, we are confronted by a needless loss of life whose causes are directly attributable to sins of commission and omission by individuals blinded by an already discredited free market ideology and the imperatives of corporate capitalism.

To the generation who remembered the genesis of the Grey Valley coaltowns and a life governed by the rhythm of the pits, the Pike River disaster seemed somehow to belittle the past that their collective efforts had helped shape. Blackball and Runanga represent complementary parts of that past. As the child of late nineteenth-century industrial capitalism, Blackball was in essence a company town whose British owners contributed little to life outside the mine. The township that emerged in the shadow of the Paparoas was the creation of the miners and their families. Their sense of community was given collective expression by the union and was grounded in the solidarity and mutual obligations of the coalface. Thus, making a life and making a living became interwoven in ways that produced a fiercely independent coal town. Runanga's tale stands at the crossroads of Grey Valley coalfield's history. Its origins lie in the cautious state experiments of the Liberal Government (1891–1912) that embraced the establishment of the nation's first state coalmine. As Brunner slipped quietly into the past, Runanga had emerged as the talisman of the future; a model mining community that pointed towards the ultimate nationalisation of the nation's coalmines. Blackball and Runanga had once stood proudly as zealous guardians of a hard-won community independence. The Pike disaster demonstrates in a tragic manner that the history and peculiarities of place cannot be dismissed as inconvenient irrelevancies.

8

CONCLUSION

Enduring Past – Elusive Future

The historians whose work stands at the centre of this book have made sense of the European experience of the Grey Valley's past in a variety of ways. Phil May's evocation of the rush of 1865 takes its stand unequivocally alongside the individual digger. His *West Coast Gold Rushes* traces the evolution of the gold rush phenomenon and the manner in which it was shaped by its peculiar West Coast setting. In the sequence of Pacific borderlands rushes that began in California in 1849 and moved to eastern Australia before washing up at Hokitika, the West Coast diggers were a comparatively experienced group. In following them along the creeks and gullies threading their way through the dense impenetrable bush, he was traversing the familiar terrain of his childhood and discovering his particular 'West Coast'. It was a Coast with which he was at ease and one that his pioneering study did a great deal to define. The celebrated final passage of *The West Coast Gold Rushes*, in which May invites the reader to motor up the Waimea Valley, speaks to an enduring past and a timeless land.

Pat O'Farrell's 'West Coast' is equally enduring, if more confronting. The combination of isolation, rugged and impenetrable bush and incessant rain created an alien environment that tested all who engaged with it. The magnates of industrial capitalism and the apostles of unionism from British coalfields struggled to impose their will upon its capricious rhythms. To O'Farrell, the struggle that took place between these two unyielding forces in the name of ideologies shaped in other environments was a tragic mismatch of time and place. The first round of industrial conflict in the Grey Valley and the Buller coalfields was, in this sense, fought out between equally uncomprehending newcomers adrift in an environment to which they were only slowly adjusting. Neither the nostrums of industrial unionism buttressed by moral argument that rested upon a sense of injustice nor the economic orthodoxies that sheltered behind the doctrine of the law of supply and demand could triumph in such an environment. O'Farrell's interest in the stalemate between these two ideas and the continued struggle between them as coal became increasingly crucial to an exporting economy forms the framework in which he reflects upon the Grey Valley environment. Whether discussing the rise of the Red Feds at Runanga and Blackball or the burgeoning Grey Valley Irish Catholic community, his 'West Coast' is shaped in the world of the mind as individuals came to build community anew. These preoccupations are later imaginatively demonstrated in his brilliant recreation of the public and private worlds of his parents as they play out their role in the Irish diaspora in the early decades of the twentieth century.

The relationship between the world of ideas and the physical environment is more directly drawn in Bill Pearson's *Coal Flat*. The people of his coalmining town exist at the fag end of unionism's attempt to build community from within a company town and with its expectations raised by a partnership with a Labour Government that had nationalised the nation's mines. Closer to O'Farrell than to May in his interpretation of the Grey Valley, Pearson shares their fascination with an enduring natural environment that demanded resilience and fortitude from those who wished to live with it and from it. Whereas May's account of the handful of years that were the West Coast's golden ones captured and revived the vibrant enthusiasm of the times, there was less optimism and precious few heroes in Pearson's coaltown. The expectations of the people of *Coal Flat* are ever diminishing; their individual lives circumscribed by both the changing economic realities of the coal industry and the limited horizons of isolated single-industry towns. The predicament of Pearson's people is, above all else, that of individuals caught in a timeless, enduring and brooding land where seasonal rhythms and landscape remain largely impervious to the passage of human beings.

Many readers have interpreted this as a pessimistic assessment of life in 1940s Grey Valley coaltowns. Whatever the validity of this reading, Pearson's treatment of the bush environment is almost reverential and may be traced to the inspirational Ted Kehoe, a teacher at Greymouth Tech and an early conservationist. His weekly radio talks on native bush, birds and Māori culture were immensely popular and have recently been the subject of a successful piece of community theatre. Written and directed by Paul Maunder, 'Ted, Poppy and World War Two'[1] weaves together excerpts of Kehoe's radio talks with a series of vignettes that explore elements of the local past through the eyes of a variety of people; most notably, Margaret Alice Joyce (1884–1964),[2] the eldest sister of Irish writer James Joyce who, as Sister Mary Gertrude, was a teaching nun in the Grey district's Sisters of Mercy community from 1910 to 1949 and a conscientious objector in a Punakaiki cave. As an attempt to draw together elements of Grey Valley experience, Maunder's conscious evocation of the recent past harks back to the balladists of the goldfields, the politically inspired coalfields verse of Billy Banjo, the song-plays of Mervyn Thompson and the more recent *The Shadow of the Valley*, the powerful stage play crafted by Susan Battye and Thelma Eakin. This impressive literary tradition acknowledges and reinforces an intense relationship between people and place.

Immanent throughout this writing was an identity that had grown alongside an, at times, aggressive exploitation of the region's natural resources. The enduring, isolated landscape that had slowly and often at great cost to individuals and communities yielded the mineral resources that supported an export economy was now, as its second century of European occupation began, called upon to serve a new ideology. Like the disciples of unionism who had sought to build the coalfields anew in the late nineteenth century, the environmentalists of the late twentieth century were cast as outsiders, people who had not earned the right to determine the future. The moral landscape of the early conservation movement and its language of extremes rubbed up uneasily against an ingrained sense of place that carried with it a sense of belonging. The wilderness aesthetic that lay at the heart of environmentalism, with its desire to maintain a pristine environment against further exploitation, was met by what amounted to a regional assertion of a custodial right to manage 'worked landscapes' rooted in the natural rhythms of growth, decay and replenishment. The contest that ensued was resolved politically. The West Coast Accord that at first sought to provide a compromise,

1 Paul Maunder, 'Ted, Poppy and World War Two', presented by Kiwi/Possum Productions, Regent Theatre Greymouth, 28–30 August 2014.

2 David G. Wright, 'Joyce and New Zealand: Biography, Censorship, and Influence', in Richard Brown, ed., *A Companion to James Joyce*, Oxford, Blackwell, 2008, p. 223; Richard Corballis, 'The Provenance of Joyce's Haka', *James Joyce Quarterly*, vol. 44, no. 1, Fall 2006, pp. 127–32.

ultimately imposed the will of the government in a manner that struck at regional autonomy and created, in the words of one recent writer, a 'narrative of betrayal'.[3]

When Philip Ross May asked, in the introduction to *The West Coast Gold Rushes*, whether it was appropriate to acknowledge a debt to a place, he was identifying with the place of his birth and childhood. He was also acknowledging a curious dichotomy that existed in the 1960s within New Zealand's attitude to its past. Attachment to a place sat uneasily alongside the canons of an embryonic historical profession. Like its British parent whose emergence had coincided with the birth of the nation state in the nineteenth century, the New Zealand academic historical community was national and imperial in its perspective.[4] In their view, the lightness of history's touch in the new society deprived it of cultural maturity, bred parochialism and led easily to antiquarianism. This attitude infused the planning for the New Zealand Centennial (1840–1940) project, but, as Kynan Gentry has pointed out, the historical enthusiasms it let loose 'strengthened the very [regional] identities they sought to diminish'.[5] The West Coast variant of this mid-century historical impulse proved to be distinctive and enduring.

Those who sought in the 1960s to interpret the West Coast's past could scarcely escape the confrontation between people and place that stood almost as starkly present as it had been a century earlier. Whatever particular preconceptions they brought to their writing, they began from a shared recognition that theirs was a pioneering endeavour, a scrap of the past that needed to be told on 'its own terms'.[6] In different and complementary ways they became involved in what a later generation would call 'a history from below'. In the specifics of time and place, and the interaction between the two, they were drawn into frameworks that made nonsense of the charge of narrow parochialism levelled from within academe and by the middle-class imperial-minded who dominated the nation's historical societies of the day. No one who follows the fortunes of Phil May's Gentleman George or Yankee Dan or Pat O'Farrell's workers or the inner workings of Bill Pearson's fictional mining community can escape the global contexts that shaped the playing out of lives on

3 Maunder, *Coal and the Coast*, p. 66.

4 Kynan Gentry, *History, Heritage and Colonialism: Historical Consciousness, Britishness, and Cultural Identity in New Zealand, 1870–1940*, Manchester, Manchester University Press, 2015, p. 3.

5 Gentry, *History, Heritage and Colonialism*, p. 234.

6 May, *West Coast Gold Rushes*, p. 14.

the Coast. Whether it was the turbulent and largely unplanned arrival of diggers drawn from the goldfields of the Pacific borderlands or the more orderly migration of miners from British and Australian coalfields as industrial capitalism spread its tentacles, those who peopled the West Coast were well aware of the impersonal forces that had propelled them there and continued to shape their lives.

Within New Zealand, the West Coast long remained an outlier, an extension of the planned settlements of Canterbury and Nelson. Not the least of its problems was where, precisely, it fitted within an evolving colonial system of governance. As André Brett has pointed out, removing 'New Zealand's wealthiest goldfield' from the provincial system and placing it under a centrally controlled experimental system of local government in 1868 recognised 'the challenges created by a sizeable transient population unsuited to bureaucracy'.[7] It was an experiment that was quickly swallowed up in the remaking of national politics that produced the briefly flowering province of Westland (1870–76) and then swept the provincial system into the dustbin of history in 1876. Hokitika's brief flowering as the goldfields capital of Westland Province was cut off before it could impose its regional leadership more securely. Before the rise of 'King Coal' made Greymouth and the Grey Valley the dominant power centre, the goldfields capital loomed large in the rise of the Kumara publican Richard John Seddon to the premiership in 1893. By the time of Seddon's death in 1906, the democratic impulses of the goldfields were being challenged by more radical demands emanating from Grey Valley coal communities.

Whatever its intent, the new radicalism grew from and expressed a new relationship between people and place. Unlike those who had rushed unknown creeks and gullies in search of alluvial gold, those who filled the coaltowns entered communities whose broad contours were familiar to them. Their interaction with the land they mined was cautious. Their work practices had been honed according to the collectivist traditions and customs of the pits they had worked. The instinct that drove the provision and consolidation of community was similarly born of familiar circumstances: remote and harsh environments, primitive housing, neglectful and absentee owners, exhausted coal seams and markets that fluctuated. Necessity bred improvisation that, over time, produced an

7 André Brett, *Acknowledge No Frontier: The Creation and Demise of New Zealand's Provinces, 1853–76*, Dunedin, Otago University Press, 2016, p. 194.

attachment to place that was at once defiant, ingrained and pragmatic. Set at some distance from the port towns of Greymouth and Westport, the coaltowns were long regarded as communities apart. Even within the Grey Valley the separate histories of individual coaltowns were well understood. Their 'foreign twangs' maintained by the continued influx of new arrivals, from Scottish and English coalfields often by way of Australia, were said by conservative critics to be matched by equally foreign ideologies. Their opposition to conscription during World War I had seen them pilloried as disloyal and cast to the very edge of an emergent national story in which loyalty to King and Country went hand in hand. With the establishment of the Communist Party headquarters at Blackball in the 1920s, the Grey Valley had its own 'Little Moscow' and a reputation as the cockpit of revolution.

These attitudes persisted in Grey Valley coaltowns throughout the next half-century. In a manner, perhaps unique within the New Zealand experience, history, people and place melded together in an enduring relationship whose influence is still apparent. The cluster of historical studies that trace the causes and consequences of the region's mining disasters—from Brunner in 1896 to Pike River in 2010—sit at the centre of a body of regional writing that possesses a rare and immediate connection with the present. In different and complementary ways, the post-1960 historical writing captured a past that was not so much retreating before the onslaught of neoliberalism as being casually cast aside. At the same time, the future of the place literally became contested terrain as environmentalists campaigned to preserve the nation's remaining native forests. The convergence of these contradictory impulses heightened political sensitivities and stimulated a local patriotism that one writer has described as a 'narrative of betrayal'. It also revealed, in miniature and in advance, the growing gulf between city and hinterland as regional economies aligned to an older economic order lost their relevance.

The last hurrah of a retreating age or part of a literature of regional resistance: how best do we characterise the second generation of Grey Valley writing? If we compare the regional/national perspectives of the two generations of writers who stand at the heart of this book there are two major contrasts. Whereas May, O'Farrell and Pearson, in different and complementary ways, asserted the regional nature of New Zealand life, they did so as part of an as yet incomplete and developing national narrative. They wrote at a formative moment that saw the emergence of two rival interpretations—the one radical, nationalist and Pacific-centred, the other suggesting more conservative and derivative foundational impulses that were British in origin. Their West Coast studies were written just as these rival streams of interpretation were beginning to influence historical thinking and writing. The generation of Grey Valley writers that followed wrote as a major philosophical shift was taking place within the historical profession. In broad terms, this change in emphasis embraced the global over the national, diversity over distinctiveness, and in doing so widened the gulf between the university and public spheres in which the historical craft was pursued.

The historical moment in which the 1960s writing of May, O'Farrell and Pearson made its appearance was at once celebratory, regional and nationalist in aspiration. It takes its place within a transitional phase of historical writing; one that witnessed a determined attempt to develop a national story in which New Zealand featured as something more than a footnote to the tale of Empire. Historians commonly date this process as having its genesis in the Centennial Project (1940) in which the nation's academic historians and middle-class-dominated historical societies predominated. Their preference, as Kynan Gentry has pointed out, was not so much regional as a national story contextualised within an imperial framework designed to avoid the parochial and the narrow.[8] The monumental regional histories of Otago and Canterbury that are its most enduring legacy reflect the depth of regional patriotism and, perhaps paradoxically, interest in the national story. The celebration of the West Coast's first century that followed took place in the shadow of this historical enterprise. It spoke of a regional experience that offered a building block for a fuller national history.

The Oxford History of New Zealand (1981 and 1992) and the plethora of subsequent general histories published over the next quarter of a century, whatever their perspectives, reflected a continuing preoccupation with the nation.[9] The standard bearer of the shifting emphasis within the universities is *The New Oxford History of New Zealand*.[10] Published in 2009, it eschewed the tale of national self-fulfilment in which European settlement of a Polynesian homeland progresses from colonial outpost

8 Gentry, *History, Heritage and Colonialism*, p. 234.

9 Belich, *Making Peoples*; James Belich, *Paradise Reforged: A History of the New Zealanders from the 1880s to the Year 2000*, Auckland, Penguin Press, 2001; Michael King, *Penguin History of New Zealand*, Auckland, Penguin, 2004; Mein Smith, *A Concise History of New Zealand*.

10 Giselle Byrnes, ed., *The New Oxford History of New Zealand*, South Melbourne, Oxford University Press, 2009.

to independent nation-state. Rather, its proclaimed objective was to move away from the quest for national distinctiveness, to draw out the similarities between the New Zealand experience and that of other settler societies and to emphasise the diversity of that experience. The use of multiple identities (culture, class, region, sexuality and gender) to refute the notion of national exceptionalism proceeds with scant attention to political context and, in the words of one Australian reviewer, presents New Zealand as 'just another ensemble of cultural forces'.[11]

Regional history sits uneasily within the cultural forces that made up the new identity History. By their very nature, the patchwork of regions that constituted the nation prized their distinctiveness. In its earliest manifestation, West Coast historical writing was, as we have seen, commemorative—a record of settlement constructed within a colonial framework. It was concerned with the national concept only to the extent that it sought to advance the colony's cause within the British Empire. The centennial generation of writers who stand at the heart of this book reached beyond imperial sentiment at the very moment that an embryonic national history was born. In different and complementary ways, May, Pearson and O'Farrell attach their particular 'West Coasts' to elements of the past that were beginning in the 1960s to define a national narrative. Through the particularities of place they were able observe how global forces made and remade life within a region destined to remain an outlier in the national story. Whether tracing the diaspora that was the nineteenth-century gold rush, or the more ordered arrival of skilled coalminers predominantly from British coalfields, or observing the inner functioning of the communities, they created in their writing a distinctive regional perspective that remains unrivalled. It provided the foundation for future writing by attaching elements of the local experience to shifts in the economic and political contexts, national and global, that reshaped lives in the late twentieth and early twenty-first centuries.

A recent writer has urged historians to 'take place seriously' and has done so in a manner that invokes Bill Oliver's earlier appeal for a new kind of history.[12] From his vantage point at the end of the 1960s, Oliver had observed a trend he called the 'nationalisation of regional life'. He believed the process had gathered pace from the 1890s and suggested

11 Stuart Macintyre, 'Review: *The New Oxford History of New Zealand*, edited by Giselle Byrnes', *Labour History*, no. 98, May 2010, p. 279.

12 Tony Ballantyne, *Webs of Empire: Locating New Zealand's Colonial Past*, Wellington, Bridget Williams Books, 2012, pp. 262–63, 274; Oliver, *Towards a New History?*

it might provide a useful framework for observing and understanding the New Zealand experience. Tony Ballantyne has observed that this prospect had instead been sunk under the weight of 'textual criticism and questions of cross cultural representation'[13] and a simultaneous tendency to privilege the global and diminish the nation-state. Set against these developments, the written West Coast/Grey Valley histories share much with the host of studies throughout the world that tell the story of regions and communities cast aside in the post-industrial age. They sought to understand the past just as the visible and tangible evidence of its shape and form slid from view.

To describe such writing as being grounded in some kind of nostalgia for an idealised past ignores the role of place in connecting past and present. Whatever their specific purpose, collectively West Coast historical writing allows us to trace out the interaction between one isolated region and the changing economic, political and social forces that reshaped it from the middle of the nineteenth century. Born in the aftermath of the last of the gold rushes of the Pacific borderlands, the Coast experience encapsulates starkly the making and remaking of modern capitalism. The Grey Valley and Buller coalfields towns were the product of industrial capitalism, at first in colonial and later in its international garb. They stood at the sharp end of the struggles between labour and capital that reshaped New Zealand politics. Until the demise of the steamship, they possessed a degree of economic power within an export economy and were able to convert this into political influence. In the 1940s they used this to achieve the nationalisation of the mines and to squeeze out more influence in the decision-making that governed work in the mines around which their communities had developed. This democratisation of work built upon the collectivist ethos that had shaped the very fabric of Grey Valley mining communities with their unions, cooperative store, swimming pool, sportsground, picture theatre and community hall. It was these constructive engagements with the circumstances of time and place that lay at the heart of the first generation of West Coast writing.

More recent Grey Valley historical writing derives its impetus rather more from the recognition that, in the last 50 years, the region has been at the sharp edge of capitalist transformation. The rolling back of the state and the concomitant deregulation of the economy and dismantling of industrial legislation amounted to the crudest political assault upon

13 Ballantyne, *Webs of Empire*, p. 274.

New Zealand's industrial hinterland in modern times. Blinded by the seductive simplicity of neoliberal doctrines, wilfully ignorant of the lessons of the region's past and disdainful of democratic engagement, the political class has left such communities to wither in capitalism's wastelands. The process of embedding neoliberalism and its corporate structures placed New Zealand among the least egalitarian of the 'developed market economies'.[14] Coincidentally, and perhaps paradoxically, the hollowing out of the region's industrial potential came in environmental garb. The proclamation of an 'Accord' between central government, local authorities and an assortment of economic and environmental interest groups defined a sizeable portion of the region as a national park. The compromise at its core that attempted to regulate the milling of native timbers was recognition that regional economic, social and political sensitivities mattered. The stealthy imposition of a total ban on milling native timber that followed indicated the limits of this dialogue and the realities of political power.

Heritage and conservationist activity within the made environment expanded in the 1970s as the decline of the region's traditional industries became evident. By putting industrial archaeology and working-class lives at the centre of their activities and by reaffirming the integrity of the past, they enhanced community understanding of the region's present circumstances. They did so as the combined forces of global and corporate capitalism continued to hollow out communities once proudly independent and defiant. They fed into and form an important element of a community response to the recasting of the regional environment that was being wrenched away from them. In different and complementary ways, they helped reinvigorate a sense of injustice first nurtured on the West Coast coalfields of the late nineteenth century. The moral component of this foundational coalfields unionism fused with a hard-nosed pragmatism that sought self-determination at the coalface and beyond to produce a community of purpose and creativity. By a combination of industrial, political and community initiative, they had used their understanding of their working and living environments to negotiate the circumstances of time and place. These achievements and the understandings upon which they rested were swept into the dustbin of history as the nation's apostles of neoliberalism legislated away the safety regulations and systems that offered the best protection against calamity.

14 Hobsbawm, *Age of Extremes*, p. 407.

The amoral adherence to an ideology that recognised neither people nor place looked backwards to the unfettered capitalism of the nineteenth century and acknowledged few constraints beyond the crude operation of the marketplace.

The attempt to ride roughshod over the past reckoned without the enduring elements of a distinctive regional culture. It was one embedded in the remnants of a once vibrant industrial community and possessed a moral authority that rested upon past achievements. The values upon which they rested reached beyond nostalgia to embrace fundamental issues of humanity. This past was hauntingly present in the effigies of protestors who blocked the road to the Pike River mine entrance in early February 2017 as part of their campaign to reclaim the bodies of the 29 dead miners entombed since 19 November 2010. Their protests reach back to invoke the spirit of countless battles past. Few of the modern-day protestors might be able to recite the once familiar coalfields litany of struggle that began with the pit-top meetings associated with the rise of industrial unionism in the late 1880s. Their protests arose directly from the pool of understanding that had supported and shaped the nature of the relationship between a community and its environment for more than a century and a half. Their actions stand in rebuke to what one historian has memorably called the 'enormous condescension of posterity'[15] and as a reminder to the ruling elites of global capitalism that the past wears a regional and a human face. To historians, the effigies of Pike conjure up W.H. Oliver's dictum: 'there is a place called New Zealand, and it is, and always has been, found where people live, and not where the evidence is easiest to assemble'.[16]

One of the reasons why West Coast writing has maintained its distinctive character may well reside in the fact that the physical determinants of life have been enduring ones. Confronting the region for the first time in the late 1990s, Pulitzer Prize–winning historian David Fischer was in no doubt about what set the West Coast apart:

> [W]e decided to visit the west coast by an old road that crossed the Alps at Arthur's Pass … we crossed the summit and suddenly found ourselves in a winter storm of extreme violence. The wind rose to a howling gale, and thick rods of rain blew horizontally in our

15 E.P. Thompson, *The Making of the English Working Class* (1963), 3rd edn, London, Gollancz, 1965, p. 12.

16 Oliver, *Towards a New History?*, p. 26.

> faces. One side of the road became a waterfall. As we crept slowly around a hairpin curve, the other side of the road had vanished in an earthquake, and nothing remained but a narrow track of mud and water on the sheer edge of the mountain. The wreckage of shattered cars lay in the depths of Otira Gorge, two thousand feet below …[17]

In Hokitika, he sensed 'a different feel from other parts of New Zealand': its 'wide streets and wooden buildings with false fronts' gave it 'the air of a frontier settlement'. Town and region looked 'west across the Tasman Sea'. In the 'manners and speech' of the inhabitants, he detected 'a strong Australian flavor'.[18]

David Fischer's fleeting encounter with the Coast and its people, and his immediate reaction to it, takes its place alongside countless incredulous initial responses to the region. The constancy of such responses over more than 150 years is unsurprising. It points to a distinctive, enduring regional identity and, perhaps unintentionally, draws our attention to the central argument of his elegant comparative study that traces the quest for fairness and freedom in New Zealand and the United States. How well have these two guiding principles fared in a region whose economy has rested very largely upon extractive industries, farming and tourism? The answer to this question has rarely been more clearly evident in fact or in its literary representation. More clearly than perhaps any other New Zealand region, the West Coast experience demonstrates how these two elements of democracy have been traduced by politicians in thrall to the market-driven, neoliberal nostrums of the late twentieth century. By rolling back the state and stripping away the regulations and customs that created the semblance of a worker democracy, they acted as agents of global capitalism. Paradoxically, as the state retreated from the workplace and from regional grants and subsidies, on the West Coast it came to be seen as the handmaiden of environmentalism. By the proclamation of a regional Accord, the political class of the day set the parameters of the region's future.

One implication that might be drawn from the evocative conclusion to Phil May's *West Coast Gold Rushes*—which invites readers to 'motor up the Waimea Valley'—is that the future might depend upon the past.[19]

17 David Hackett Fischer, *Fairness and Freedom: A History of Two Open Societies: New Zealand and the United States*, New York, Oxford University Press, 2012, p. xii.

18 Fischer, *Fairness and Freedom*, p. xiii.

19 May, *West Coast Gold Rushes*, p. 503.

The 'greening of the memory' might provide the transitional economy needed as the days of 'King Coal' recede. The centennial context in which he wrote provided an impetus to summoning up the past as a part of the wider process of shaping a future. Gold was predictably its initial focus. In November 1970, an open-air museum and historical park opened at Sovereign Hill in Ballarat, with a replica of the city's nineteenth-century goldtown providing a model that was quickly taken up. By the end of the decade, two goldfield heritage ventures had opened on the Coast: Shantytown at Rutherglen, south of Greymouth, and a historic walkway and information centre at Ross, south of Hokitika. As front runners in the field, their origins reflect community endeavour and local fulfilment. The economic use of history and heritage took longer to be appreciated.

Grey Valley coaltowns have participated variously in heritage tourism. Brunner's pre-eminent role reflects its historic status as the nation's pioneering mining and industrial site. Part of the district's importance in the renewed interest in the past lay in the excitement of rediscovering the landscape of the mining and brickworks complex that once stood boldly on the banks of the Grey River in the bleak confines of the Brunner Gorge. The combined efforts of industrial archaeologist and historian were needed to rescue the remains of a worksite largely overgrown by rampant bush. Brian Wood was at the heart of this symbiotic process. His splendidly crafted history of the Brunner mine disaster and painstaking account of the development of the suspension bridge that became the visual hub of the Brunner industrial complex represent the development in its purest form. Blackball has jealously nurtured its historic role in the emergence of radical mining unionism and embraced the title 'birthplace of the New Zealand Labour Party' increasingly bestowed upon it by those keen to retain at least the semblance of a connection with the party's socialist origins. The iconic facade of the Miners' Hall at Runanga—the final built remnant of the early twentieth-century socialist vanguard's legacy—has weathered the passage of time and now stands precariously on the edge of historical tourism. Its future prospects remain uncertain as it is shuffled through the few options open to those who strive to acknowledge the past—a potential community centre or a museum that commemorates the labour and aspirations of a pioneering mining town.

BIBLIOGRAPHY

Official Publications

Appendices to the Journals of the House of Representatives (*AJHR*, New Zealand).

New Zealand Law Reports (*NZLR*).

Royal Commission on the Pike River Coal Mine Tragedy, vol. 1, Government Printer, Wellington, 2012.

Books and Articles

Akenson, Donald H., *Half the World from Home: Perspectives on the Irish in New Zealand 1860–1950*, Wellington, Victoria University Press, 1990.

Anderson, Atholl, Judith Binney and Aroha Harris, *Tangata Whenua: A History*, Wellington, Bridget Williams Books, 2015.

Ballantyne, Tony, *Webs of Empire: Locating New Zealand's Colonial Past*, Wellington, Bridget Williams Books, 2012.

Barrowman, Rachel, *A Popular Vision: The Arts and the Left in New Zealand, 1930–1950*, Wellington, Victoria University Press, 1991.

Bassett, Michael with Michael King, *Tomorrow Comes the Song: A Life of Peter Fraser*, Auckland, Penguin Books, 2000.

Bate, Weston, *Lucky City: The First Generation at Ballarat 1851–1901*, Carlton, Melbourne, Melbourne University Press, 1978.

Battye, Susan and Thelma Eakin, *The Shadow of the Valley: A Play about the Brunner Mine Disaster, 1896*, Wellington, Oxford University Press, 1980.

Beardsley, Eric, *Blackball 08*, Auckland, William Collins Publishers, 1984.

——, *Sliding Down the Hypotenuse: A Memoir*, Christchurch, Canterbury University Press, 2011.

Belich, James, *Making Peoples: A History of New Zealanders from Polynesian Settlement to the End of the Nineteenth Century*, Auckland, Penguin Press, 1996.

——, *Paradise Reforged: A History of the New Zealanders from the 1880s to the year 2000*, Auckland, Penguin Press, 2001.

Bennett, Francis, *A Canterbury Tale: The Autobiography of Dr Francis Bennett*, Wellington, Oxford University Press, 1980.

Benson, John, *British Coalminers in the Nineteenth Century: A Social History*, Dublin, Gill and Macmillan, 1980.

Birchfield, Maureen, *Looking for Answers: A Life of Elsie Locke*, Christchurch, University of Canterbury Press, 2009.

Boston, Jonathon and Martin Holland, *The Fourth Labour Government: Radical Politics in New Zealand*, Auckland, Oxford University Press, 1987.

Bowd, Gavin, 'Comintern Cadre: The Passion of Allan Eaglesham', *Socialist History Society Occasional Paper*, no. 22, 2006.

Brasch, Charles, ed., *Landfall Country: Work from Landfall, 1947–61*, Christchurch, Caxton Press, c. 1962.

Brett, André, *Acknowledge No Frontier: The Creation and Demise of New Zealand's Provinces*, 1853–76, Dunedin, Otago University Press, 2016.

Brooking, Tom, *Richard Seddon: King of God's Own. The Life and Times of New Zealand's Longest-Serving Prime Minister*, Auckland, Penguin, 2014.

Brown, Richard, ed., *A Companion to James Joyce*, Oxford, Blackwell, 2008.

Byrnes, Giselle, ed., *The New Oxford History of New Zealand*, South Melbourne, Oxford University Press, 2009.

Calder, Alex, 'An Interview with Bill Pearson', *Landfall 150*, vol. 47, no. 1, April 1993, pp. 51–77.

Coffey, John, *Canterbury XIII: A Rugby League History*, Christchurch, John Coffey, 1987.

Coffey, John and Bernie Wood, *The Kiwis: 100 Years of International Rugby League*, Auckland, Hachette Livre, 2007.

Connolly, C. and L. Richardson, 'Kiwi and Kangaroo: Teaching Australian History to New Zealanders', *Australian Historical Association Bulletin*, no. 15, June 1978, pp. 7–10.

Conradson, Bernard, 'Politics and Penury: County and Province, 1868–1876', in Philip Ross May, ed., *Miners & Militants: Politics in Westland 1865–1918*, Christchurch, Whitcoulls for the University of Canterbury, 1975, pp. 25–47.

Corballis, Richard, 'The Provenance of Joyce's Haka', *James Joyce Quarterly*, vol. 44, no. 1, Fall 2006, pp. 127–32.

Cronin, A.J., *The Stars Look Down*, London, Gollancz, 1935.

Cunneen, Christopher, *William John McKell: Boilermaker, Premier, Governor-General*, Sydney, University of New South Wales Press, 2000.

Curnow, Allen, 'Coal Flat Revisited', in Cherry Hankin, ed., *Critical Essays on the New Zealand Novel*, Auckland, Heinemann Educational Books NZ, 1976, pp. 105–27.

Damer, Sean, *Glasgow: Going for a Song*, London, Lawrence & Wishart, 1990.

Davis, Richard P., *Irish Issues in New Zealand Politics 1868–1922*, Dunedin, University of Otago Press, 1974.

Deacon, Desley, Penny Russell and Angela Woollacott, eds, *Transnational Ties: Australian Lives in the World*, Canberra, ANU E Press, 2008, doi.org/10.22459/TT.12.2008.

Dennis, Norman, Fernando Henriques and Clifford Slaughter, *Coal Is Our Life: An Analysis of a Yorkshire Mining Community* (1956), 2nd edn, London/New York, Tavistock Publications (Social Science Paperback), 1969.

Denoon, Donald and Philippa Mein Smith, with Marivic Wyndham, *A History of Australia, New Zealand and the Pacific*, Oxford, Blackwell Publishers, 2000.

Devanny, Jean, *The Butcher Shop* (1926), edited and introduced by Heather Roberts, with notes by Bill Pearson, Auckland, Auckland University Press, 1981.

——, *Dawn Beloved*, London, Duckworth, 1928.

——, *Point of Departure: The Autobiography of Jean Devanny*, edited by Carole Ferrier, St Lucia, Queensland, Queensland University Press, 1986.

——, *Poor Swine*, London, Duckworth, 1930.

Dyer, Peter, *Coal Mines of Puponga*, Picton, River Press, 2003.

Easson, Michael, ed., *The Achievements of Sir William McKell*, Sydney, Allen & Unwin, 1988.

Evison, Harry, *The Ngai Tahu Deeds*, Christchurch, Canterbury University Press, 2006.

Ewen, J.M., *Far from the Sun*, Christchurch, Whitcombe & Tombs, 1966.

Ewen, Peter, *Pike: Death by Parliament*, Christchurch, Pit Pony Press, 2014.

——, *Strongman: Three Score and More*, Greymouth, Peter Ewen, 2006.

Ferrier, Carole, 'Jean Devanny, 1894–1962', *Kotare*, vol. 7, no. 1, 2007, pp. 99–118.

——, *Jean Devanny: Romantic Revolutionary*, Melbourne, Melbourne University Press, 1999.

Fischer, David Hackett, *Fairness and Freedom: A History of Two Open Societies: New Zealand and the United States*, New York, Oxford University Press, 2012.

Franks, Peter and Jim McAloon, *The New Zealand Labour Party, 1916–2016*, Wellington, Victoria University Press, 2016.

Fraser, Lyndon, *Castles of Gold: A History of New Zealand's West Coast Irish*, Dunedin, Otago University Press, 2007.

Gardner, W.J. (Jim), 'Grass Roots and Dredge Tailings: Reflections on Local History', *Landfall 43*, vol. 11, no. 3, September 1957, pp. 221–33. Reprinted in W.J. Gardner, *Where They Lived: Studies in Local, Regional, and Social History*, Christchurch, Regional Press, 1999, pp. 3–7.

——, *Prelude to Arbitration in 3 Movements: Ulster, South Australia, New Zealand 1890–1894*, Christchurch, W. J. Gardner, 2009.

——, 'Tradition and Conscience: Canterbury College and R. O. Page, Conscientious Objector, 1918–1919', *History Now*, vol. 9, no. 2, May 2003, pp. 6–9.

——, *Where They Lived: Studies in Local, Regional and Social History*, Christchurch, Regional Press, 1999.

Gardner, W.J., ed., *A History of Canterbury, Volume II: General History, 1854–76 and Cultural Aspects, 1850–1950*, Christchurch, Whitcombe & Tombs/ Canterbury Centennial Historical and Literary Committee, 1971.

Gentry, Kynan, *History, Heritage and Colonialism: Historical Consciousness, Britishness, and Cultural Identity in New Zealand, 1870–1940*, Manchester, Manchester University Press, 2015.

Griffiths, Tom, *The Art of Time Travel: Historians and Their Craft*, Carlton, Victoria, Black Inc., 2016.

Guareschi, Giovannino, *The Don Camillo Omnibus*, London, The Companion Book Club, 1955.

Gustafson, Barry, *His Way: A Biography of Robert Muldoon*, Auckland, Auckland University Press, 2000.

——, *Labour's Path to Political Independence: The Origins and Establishment of the New Zealand Labour Party, 1909–19*, Auckland, Auckland University Press/Oxford University Press, 1980.

Haast, Julius von, *Report of a Topographical and Geological Exploration of the Western Districts of the Nelson Province, New Zealand*, Nelson, Nelson Provincial Government, 1861.

Hagan, Jim and Andrew Wells, eds, *The Maritime Strike: A Centennial Retrospective. Essays in Honour of E. C. Fry*, Wollongong, Five Islands Press, 1992.

Hager, Nicky and Bob Burton, *Secrets and Lies: The Anatomy of an Anti-Environmental PR Campaign*, Nelson, Craig Potton Publishing, 1999.

Hancock, W.K., *Country and Calling*, London, Faber and Faber, 1954.

Harrison, Royden, *Independent Collier: The Coal Miner as Archetypal Proletarian Reconsidered*, Sussex, The Harvester Press, 1978.

Harrop, A.J., *The Romance of Westland: The Story of New Zealand's Golden Coast*, Christchurch, Whitcombe & Tombs, 1923.

Hayward, Margaret, *Diary of the Kirk Years*, Wellington, Cape Catley, Reed, 1981.

Henderson, Bob, 'Stillwater', in Blackball History Group, eds, *Blackball Beckons: A Selection of Poems from Blackball, Moonlight and Surrounding Districts*, Westland, NZ, Blackball History Group, NZ, 2000.

Hickey, P.H., *'Red' Fed. Memoirs: Being a Brief Survey of the Birth and Growth of the Federation of Labour from 1908 to 1915, and of the Days that Immediately Preceded It*, Wellington, New Zealand Worker Print, 1925; reprinted by Wellington Media Collective, Wellington, 1980.

Hight, James and C. R. Straubel, general eds, *A History of Canterbury, Vol. 1: To 1854*, Christchurch, Whitcombe & Tombs/ Canterbury Centennial Association and Literary Committee, 1957.

Hobsbawm, Eric, *Age of Extremes: The Short Twentieth Century 1914–1991*, London, Abacus, 1995.

Hoggart, Richard, *The Uses of Literacy*, London, Chatto and Windus, 1957.

Holland, Harry, *Robert Burns: Poet and Revolutionist*, edited by Dougal McNeill, Wellington, Steele Roberts Aotearoa, 2016.

Holland, H.E., R.S. Ross and 'Ballot Box' (Francis O'Flynn), *The Tragic Story of the Waihi Strike*, Wellington, The Worker Printery, 1913.

Howell, David, '"Goodbye To All That": A Review of Literature on the 1984/5 Miners' Strike', *Journal of Work, Employment & Society*, vol. 1, no. 3, September 1987, pp. 388–404.

Hunter, Edward, *Ballads of the Track*, Auckland, The Cooperative Publishing Board, 1919.

——, *The Road the Men Came Home*, London, The National Labour Press, 1920.

Irving, Helen and Stuart Macintyre, eds, *No Ordinary Act: Essays on Federation and the Constitution by J.A. La Nauze*, Carlton, Victoria, Melbourne University Press, 2001.

Johnston, Stuart, 'Review: *Coal Flat*, Bill Pearson', *Landfall 67*, vol. 17, no. 3, September 1963, pp. 298–301.

Kay, Rupert A., ed., *Westland's Golden Century 1860–1960; An Official Souvenir of Westland's Centenary*, Christchurch, Westland Centennial Council, 1959.

Kerridge, Peter, 'Obituary: Bill McLennan', *Press* (Christchurch), 18 August 2007.

King, Michael, *Penguin History of New Zealand*, Auckland, Penguin, 2004.

Koestler, Arthur, *Arrival and Departure*, London, Jonathan Cape, 1943.

——, *Darkness at Noon*, London, Macmillan, 1940.

——, *The Gladiators*, London, Jonathan Cape, 1939.

Koestler, Arthur, Ignazio Silone, Richard Wright, André Gide, E. Starkie, Louis Fischer and Stephen Spender, *The God That Failed*, edited by R. Crossman, Bantam Books, New York, 1949.

La Nauze, J.A., *Alfred Deakin*, Carlton, Victoria, Melbourne University Press, 1965.

——, *The Making of the Australian Constitution*, Carlton, Victoria, Melbourne University Press, 1972.

Laracy, Hugh, 'Kennedy, Martin', in *Dictionary of New Zealand Biography*, first published in 1996, updated 7 April 2006, *Te Ara—the Encyclopedia of New Zealand*, teara.govt.nz/en/biographies/3k9/kennedy-martin.

Lochhead, Ian J., 'Seager, Samuel Hurst', in *Dictionary of New Zealand Biography*, first published in 1996, updated May 2002. *Te Ara—the Encyclopedia of New Zealand*, teara.govt.nz/en/biographies/3s8/seager-samuel-hurst.

Locke, Elsie, *Peace People, A History of Peace Activities in New Zealand*, Christchurch, Hazard Press, 1992.

Lockwood, Janice, 'Personality and Politics: Seddon and His Electorates, 1879–90', in Philip Ross May, ed., *Miners and Militants: Politics in Westland 1865–1918*, Christchurch, Whitcoulls for the University of Canterbury, 1975, pp. 48–79.

McAloon, Jim, *Judgements of All Kinds: Economic Policy-Making in New Zealand, 1945–1984*, Wellington, Victoria University Press, 2013.

McCaskill, Murray, 'Review: *The West Coast Gold Rushes* by P.R. May', *Historical Studies: Australia and New Zealand*, vol. 11, no. 41, November 1963, p. 141, doi.org/10.1080/10314616308595270.

Macfie, Rebecca, *Tragedy at Pike River Mine*, Wellington, Awa Press, 2013.

Macintyre, Stuart, *The Reds: The Communist Party of Australia from Origins to Illegality*, Sydney, Allen & Unwin, 1989.

——, 'Review: *The New Oxford History of New Zealand*, edited by Giselle Byrnes', *Labour History*, no. 98, May 2010, pp. 278–79, doi.org/10.5263/labourhistory.98.1.278.

McLintock, A.H., *The History of Otago: The Origins and Growth of a Wakefieldian Class Settlement*, Dunedin, Otago Centennial Historical Publications, 1949.

Maloney, Pat and Kerry Taylor, eds, *On the Left: Essays on Socialism in New Zealand*, Dunedin, University of Otago Press, 2002.

Maunder, Paul, *Coal and the Coast: A Reflection on the Pike River Disaster*, Christchurch, Canterbury University Press, 2012.

May, Philip Ross, 'Gold Rushes of the Pacific Borderlands: A Comparative Survey', in Len Richardson and W. David McIntyre, eds, *Provincial Perspectives: Essays in Honour of W.J. Gardner*, Christchurch, University of Canterbury/Whitcoulls, 1980, pp. 91–105.

——, *Gold Town, Ross, Westland*, Christchurch, Pegasus, 1970.

——, *Hokitika: Goldfields Capital*, Christchurch, Pegasus/Hokitika Centennial Committee, 1964.

——, *Origins of Hydraulic Mining in California*, Oakland, California, The Holmes Book Company, 1970.

——, *The West Coast Gold Rushes*, Christchurch, Pegasus Press, 1962.

May, Philip Ross, ed., *Miners and Militants: Politics in Westland 1865–1918*, Christchurch, Whitcoulls for the University of Canterbury, 1975.

Mein Smith, Philippa, *A Concise History of New Zealand*, Cambridge, UK, Cambridge University Press, 2005.

——, *Maternity in Dispute, New Zealand 1920–1939*, Wellington, Historical Branch, Department of Internal Affairs of New Zealand, 1986.

——, *Mothers and King Baby: Infant Survival and Welfare in an Imperial World, 1880–1950*, London, Macmillan, 1997. (Revised PhD thesis.)

Mein Smith, Philippa, Peter Hempenstall, Shaun Goldfinch, with Stuart McMillan and Rosemary Baird, *Remaking the Tasman World*, Christchurch, Canterbury University Press, 2008.

Millar, Paul, *No Fretful Sleeper: A Life of Bill Pearson*, Auckland, Auckland University Press, 2010.

——, 'William Harrison Pearson: 1922–2002', *Journal of New Zealand Literature*, no. 20, 2002, pp. 164–69, www.jstor.org/stable/20112348.

Moorhouse, Geoffrey, *At the George and Other Essays on Rugby League*, London, Hodder and Stoughton, 1989.

Morgan, Patrick, 'The Irish in Australasia. Review: *Vanished Kingdoms: Irish in Australia and New Zealand: A Personal Excursion* by Patrick O'Farrell; New South Wales University Press, 1990', *Quadrant* (Sydney), vol. 35, no. 3, March 1991, pp. 72–76.

Morrell, W.P., *The Gold Rushes*, 2nd edn, London, Black, 1968.

——, 'Reviews: *The West Coast Gold Rushes*, by Philip Ross May; *A History of Goldmining in New Zealand*, by J.H. Salmon', *Landfall 67*, vol. 17, no. 3, September 1963, pp. 305–9.

Mulgan, John, *Report on Experience*, Wellington, Pen & Sword Books and Victoria University Press, 2010.

Nathan, Simon, 'Five Books about Blackball', *Scoop Review of Books*, 5 August 2008, www.scoop.co.nz/stories/HL0808/S00056.htm.

Nolan, Melanie, *Kin: A Collective Biography of a New Zealand Working-Class Family*, Christchurch, Canterbury University Press, 2005.

——, 'Personalising Class Conflict across the Tasman: The New Zealand Great Strike and Trans-Tasman Biography', *Journal of New Zealand Studies*, no. 18, December 2014, pp. 118–136, doi.org/10.26686/jnzs.v0i18.2185.

——, '"The View from Over the Hill": Developing a Balanced View of Blackball '08 from a Wider Range of Perspectives', *Journal of New Zealand Studies*, no. 8, April 2009, pp. 1–27, doi.org/10.26686/jnzs.v0i8.2.

Nolan, Melanie, ed., *War & Class: The Diary of Jack McCullough*, Wellington, Dunmore Publishing, 2009.

O'Farrell, P.J. (Patrick), *The Catholic Church and Community in Australia: A History*, revised edn, West Melbourne, Nelson (Australia), 1977.

——, *The Catholic Church in Australia: A Short History: 1788–1967*, Melbourne, Nelson (Australia), 1968.

——, 'Catholicism on the West Coast: Just How Irish Is It?', *New Zealand Tablet*, 3 May 1973, p. 54.

——, *England and Ireland since 1800*, Oxford, Oxford University Press, 1975.

——, *Harry Holland: Militant Socialist*, Canberra, Australian National University Press, 1964.

——, *The Irish Echo* (Australia), 7–20 October 1999, p. 14.

——, *The Irish Echo* (Australia), 2 October–3 November 1999, p. 12.

——, *Ireland's English Question: Anglo-Irish Relations 1534–1970*, London, Batsford, 1971.

——, 'Noble National Myths, Bitter Local Reality: 1890 in New Zealand's Grey District', in Jim Hagan and Andrew Wells, eds, *The Maritime Strike: A Centennial Retrospective, Essays in Honour of E.C. Fry*, Wollongong, Five Islands Press, 1992, pp. 31–36.

——, 'Politics and Coal: The Socialist Vanguard, 1904–8', in Philip Ross May, ed., *Miners and Militants: Politics in Westland 1865–1918*, Christchurch, Whitcoulls for the University of Canterbury, 1975, pp. 101–27.

——, 'Politics in Westland', in Rupert A. Kay, ed., *Westland's Golden Century 1860–1960; An Official Souvenir of Westland's Centenary*, Greymouth, Westland Centennial Council, 1959.

——, 'Review: P.R. May, *The West Coast Gold Rushes*. Pegasus Press, Christchurch, Second Revised Edition, 1967', *New Zealand Journal of History*, vol. 3, no. 1, April 1969, pp. 89–90.

——, *Vanished Kingdoms: Irish in Australia and New Zealand. A Personal Excursion*, Sydney, University of New South Wales Press, 1990.

O'Hagan, Sean, *The Pride of Southern Rebels: On the Occasion of the Otago Rugby Football Union Centenary, 1881–1981*, Dunedin, Pilgrims South Press, 1981.

Oliver, W.H., *Looking for the Phoenix*, Wellington, Bridget Williams Books, 2002.

——, *The Story of New Zealand*, London, Faber and Faber, 1960.

——, *Towards a New History? Hocken Lecture 1969*, Dunedin, Hocken Library, University of Otago, 1971.

Olssen, Erik, 'Lands of Sheep and Gold: The Australian Dimension to the New Zealand Past, 1840–1900', in Keith Sinclair, ed., *Tasman Relations: New Zealand and Australia, 1788–1988*, Auckland, Auckland University Press, 1987, pp. 34–51.

——, *The Red Feds: Revolutionary Industrial Unionism and the New Zealand Federation of Labour*, Auckland, Oxford University Press, 1991.

Page, Alfred William, *'He's for the Morning', Alfred William Page, His Journal; Also, Some Recollections of His Life by His Aunts, Ellen & Ann Saunders*, Christchurch, A. Wildey, 1939.

Patterson, Brad, ed., *The Irish in New Zealand: Historical Contexts and Perspectives*, Stout Research Centre for New Zealand Studies, Wellington, Victoria University of Wellington, 2002.

Pearson, Bill, 'Beginnings and Endings', *Sport* 5, Spring 1990, pp. 3–21.

——, *Coal Flat*, Auckland & Hamilton, Paul's Book Arcade, 1963.

——, 'Fretful Sleepers: A Sketch of New Zealand Behaviour and its Implications for the Artist', *Landfall 23*, vol. 6, no. 3, September 1952; reprinted with corrections in Charles Brasch, ed., *Landfall Country: Work from Landfall, 1947–61*, Christchurch, Caxton Press, 1962, pp. 201–30.

——, *Fretful Sleepers and Other Essays*, Auckland, Heinemann Educational Books, 1974.

——, *Henry Lawson Among Maoris*, Canberra, Australian National University Press, 1968.

Piggin, Stuart and Henry Lee, *The Mt Kembla Disaster*, Sydney, Oxford University Press/ Sydney University Press, 1992.

Plumridge, Libby, 'The Necessary but not Sufficient Condition: Christchurch Labour and Working-Class Culture', *New Zealand Journal of History*, vol. 19, no. 2, October 1985, pp. 130–50.

Prebble, Kenneth, 'Coal Flat', *Comment: A New Zealand Quarterly Review*, no. 18, January 1964, pp. 35–37.

Rantoul, Ralph, 'The Coal Mines Council', *New Zealand Journal of Industrial Relations,* vol. 3, no. 1, May 1978, pp. 21–30.

Rice, Geoffrey W., 'Bennett, Francis Oswald', in *Dictionary of New Zealand Biography*, first published 2000. *Te Ara—the Encyclopedia of New Zealand*, teara.govt.nz/en/biographies/5b24/bennett-francis-oswald.

Richardson, Len, '"Billy Banjo": Coalminer, Socialist, Poet and Novelist', in Pat Maloney and Kerry Taylor, eds, *On the Left: Essays on Socialism in New Zealand*, Dunedin, University of Otago Press, 2002, pp. 73–86.

——,'Class, Community and Conflict: The Blackball Miners' Union, 1920–31', in Len Richardson and W. David McIntyre, eds, *Provincial Perspectives: Essays in Honour of W.J. Gardner*, Christchurch, University of Canterbury/ Whitcoulls, 1980, pp. 106–27.

——, *Coal, Class & Community: The United Mineworkers of New Zealand, 1880–1960*, Auckland, Auckland University Press, 1995.

——, 'Politics and War: Coal Miners and Conscription, 1914–18', in Philip Ross May, ed., *Miners and Militants: Politics in Westland 1865–1918*, Christchurch, Whitcoulls for the University of Canterbury, 1975, pp. 128–55.

Roberts, Heather, 'Devanny, Jean', in *Dictionary of New Zealand Biography*, first published in 1998. *Te Ara—the Encyclopedia of New Zealand*, teara.govt.nz/en/biographies/4d13/devanny-jean.

——, 'Introduction' to Jean Devanny, *The Butcher Shop* (1926), edited by Heather Roberts, Auckland, Auckland University Press, 1981, pp. 7–26.

Roche, Michael, *History of Forestry*, Wellington, New Zealand Forestry Corporation/ GP Books, 1990.

Roth, Herbert and E.G. Beardsley, 'Sidney Huguenot Fournier d'Albe', *New Zealand Monthly Review*, December 1960–January 1961, pp. 21–22.

Salmon, J.H., *A History of Goldmining in New Zealand*, Wellington, Government Printer, 1963.

Sargeson, Frank, 'Conversation in a Train', *Landfall 21*, vol. 84, no. 4, December 1967, pp. 352–61.

Scotter, W.H., ed., *A History of Canterbury, Vol. III: 1876–1950*, Christchurch, Whitcombe & Tombs/ Canterbury Centennial History and Literary Committee, 1965.

Seager, Allen, 'Sherman, Frank Henry', in *Dictionary of Canadian Biography*, vol. 13, University of Toronto/Université Laval, 2003–, first published in 1994, biographi.ca/en/bio/Sherman_frank_henry_13E.html.

Seddon, T.E.Y., *The Seddons: An Autobiography*, Auckland, Collins, 1968.

Simpson, Peter, 'Bill Pearson's New Zealand Then and Now: Testimony of an Internal Rapporteur', *Landfall 194*, no. 3, Spring 1997, pp. 203–25.

Sinclair, Keith, *Halfway Round the Harbour: An Autobiography*, Auckland, Penguin, 1993.

——, *A History of New Zealand*, Auckland, Penguin, 1959.

Smith, Dai, 'The Longest Strike: In 1926 It Was the Employers; Now It's the State', *The Listener* (UK), 15 November 1984, pp. 11–12.

Somerset, H.C.D., *Littledene: Patterns of Change* (1938), 3rd edn, Wellington, New Zealand Council for Educational Research, 1974.

Storey, David, *This Sporting Life*, London, Longmans Green & Co., 1960.

Sturm, Terry, ed., *The Oxford History of New Zealand Literature in English*, Auckland, Oxford University Press, 1991.

Taylor, Kerry, 'Galbraith, Alexander', in *Dictionary of New Zealand Biography*, first published in 1998. *Te Ara—the Encyclopedia of New Zealand*, teara.govt.nz/en/biographies/4g2/galbraith-alexander.

Thompson, E.P., *The Making of the English Working Class* (1963), 3rd edn, London, Gollancz, 1965.

Thompson, Mervyn, *All My Lives*, Chistchurch,Whitcoulls, 1980.

——, *Coaltown Blues*, Wellington, Victoria University Press, 1986.

——, *Passing Through and Other Plays, Introduction by Howard McNaughton*, Christchurch, Hazard Press, 1992.

——, *Singing the Blues*, Christchurch, Blacktown Press, 1991.

Thornton, Geoffrey G., *New Zealand's Industrial Heritage*, Wellington, A.H. & A.W. Reed, 1982.

Wichtel, Diana, 'Commentary: Interview: Andrew Little', *Listener*, no. 3712, 2 July 2011, pp. 22–26.

Wood, Brian, *Coal Gorge and the Brunner Suspension Bridge*, Greymouth, Brian Wood, 2004.

——, *Disaster at Brunner*, Greymouth, Brian Wood, 1996.

——, *The Great '08 Blackball Coalminers' Strike*, Greymouth, Bright Print, 2008.

Wood, F.L., *New Zealand in the World*, Wellington, Department of Internal Affairs (NZ), 1940.

Wright, David G., 'Joyce and New Zealand: Biography, Censorship, and Influence', in Richard Brown, ed., *A companion to James Joyce*, Oxford, Blackwell, 2008, ch. 14.

Young, James D., *John Maclean: Clydeside Socialist*, Glasgow, Clydeside Press, 1992.

Theses and Unpublished Papers

Bishop, Catherine, 'Commerce was a Woman: Women in Colonial Sydney and Wellington', PhD thesis, ANU, 2012.

Blackball Miners' Union, 'Blackball Miners' Union Hall and Welfare Society Minute Book, 1946', ms, private collection.

Brazil, W.P., 'Legislation—Changes and Implications: A Summary of the Evolution of Coal Mining Safety Legislation Together with a Traditional Viewpoint. Presented by W.P. Brazil, Francis Mining Company to Coal Producers Federation of New Zealand Inc., 1995 Seminar and Annual General Meeting, May 1995', ms, author's collection.

Dawber, Carol, 'Voices of the West Coast: An Investigation into the Development of a Distinctive West Coast Character in New Zealand Fiction', PhD thesis, University of Canterbury, 2012.

Eldred-Grigg, Stevan, 'The Pastoral Families of the Hunter Valley, 1880–1914', PhD thesis, ANU, 1978.

Fox, Karen, 'Representing Difference: Celebrated Maori and Aboriginal Women and the Print Media, 1950–2000', PhD thesis, ANU, 2009.

Francis, Nicola, '"My Own Sort of Heaven", Rosalie Gascoigne's Stellar Rise to Artistic Acclaim', PhD thesis, ANU, 2015.

Galbraith, Alexander, 'Reminiscences on the Early History of The Communist Party of New Zealand', ms, 1949, author's collection.

Hickey, Carina, 'From Coal Pit to Leather Pit: Life Stories of Robert Semple', PhD thesis, Massey University, 2010.

McIntosh, Peter, 'The Timber Industry in Westland, 1865–1939', MA thesis, University of Canterbury, 1990.

May, Philip Ross, 'The West Canterbury Gold Rush to 1865: The Analysis of a Gold Rush of the Mid-Nineteenth Century', MA thesis, Canterbury University College/ University of Canterbury, 1953.

Mein Smith, Philippa, 'Reformers, Mothers and Babies; Aspects of Infant Survival: Australia 1890- 1945', PhD thesis, ANU, 1990. (Revised and published as *Mothers and King Baby: Infant Survival and Welfare in an Imperial World, 1880–1950*, London, Macmillan, 1997.)

Nolan, Melanie, 'Uniformity and Diversity: A Case Study of Female Shop and Office Workers in Victoria, 1880 to 1939', PhD thesis, ANU, 1989.

O'Farrell, P.J., 'H. E. Holland and the Labour Movement in Australia and New Zealand; With Special Emphasis on the Activity of Militant Socialists', PhD thesis, ANU, 1960.

——, 'The Workers and Grey District Politics 1865–1913', MA thesis, Canterbury University College/University of Canterbury, 1955.

Plumridge, Elizabeth, 'The Negotiation of Circumstance: New Zealand Women Artists, c.1890–1914', PhD thesis, ANU, 1985.

Richardson, Len, 'The Labour Movement in Wollongong, New South Wales, 1928–39', PhD thesis, ANU, 1974.

——, 'The Workers and Grey District Politics During Wartime, 1914–1918, MA thesis, University of Canterbury, 1968.

Richardson, Peter, 'An Architecture of Empire: The Government Buildings of John Campbell in New Zealand', MA thesis, University of Canterbury, 1988.

Richardson, Shelley, 'Family Experiments: Professional Middle-Class Families in Australia and New Zealand c. 1880–1920', PhD thesis, ANU, 2013. (Revised and published under the same title by ANU Press, Canberra, 2016, doi.org/10.22459/FE.11.2016.)

Vaney, Neil, 'The Dual Tradition: Irish Catholics and French Priests in New Zealand: The West Coast Experience, 1865–1910', MA thesis, University of Canterbury, 1976.

www.ingramcontent.com/pod-product-compliance
Lightning Source LLC
Chambersburg PA
CBHW041752010726
47507CB00009B/362